DEAR READER

Joey Adams is known best to millions of Americans as a television comic, as one of the best funnymen in show business.

But, there is a serious side to Joey Adams. "On the Road for Uncle Sam," is his eighth book. It is based on his tours for the U. S. State Department.

We in organized labor are accused of being interested only in that next nickle or dime we hope to squeeze out of our employers. Joey Adams' tour in the key area of Southeast Asia dispels the lie that organized labor is interested only in its own selfish little world.

Here, the president of the 20,000 member American Guild of Variety speaks out labor unions' concern for a better American image abroad and tells what one group of unionists did about it.

We think you will find the message in "On the Road for Uncle Sam" very worthwhile. It is made available to you with the compliments of the **INTERNATIONAL BROTHERHOOD OF TEAMSTERS, CHAUFFEURS, WAREHOUSEMEN AND HELPERS OF AMERICA.**

James R. Hoffa

General President

John F. English

General Secretary-Treasurer

ON THE ROAD
FOR UNCLE SAM

Other Books by Joey Adams

FROM GAGS TO RICHES

THE CURTAIN NEVER FALLS

THE JOEY ADAMS JOKE BOOK

CINDY AND I

STRICTLY FOR LAUGHS

IT TAKES ONE TO KNOW ONE

JOEY ADAMS JOKE DICTIONARY

On
the
Road
for
Uncle Sam

BY JOEY ADAMS

PUBLISHED BY
BERNARD GEIS ASSOCIATES
DISTRIBUTED BY RANDOM HOUSE

To the United States Information Service,
the Peace Corps, the Foreign Service,
our Cultural Exchange emissaries,
and to all of the other traveling salesmen
who are on the road for Uncle Sam

Contents

CHAPTER 1

Have Jokes . . .
Will Travel

It ALL STARTED when I got a letter from the United States Government. I couldn't understand what they wanted. I knew I was too old to be drafted and too young for social security. The letter from the State Department asked me to head a troupe to the troubled areas of the world on behalf of President Kennedy's Cultural Exchange Program. They said we opened on August 23rd, 1961, in Kabul, Afghanistan. Then a split week in Katmandu, Nepal and Phnom Penh, Cambodia. Followed by one-night stands in Thailand in places like Chiengmai, Udorn, Hua Hin, Lopburi, Korat and some of the smaller towns. I've heard of playing the sticks but this was off-Broadway even to the Asians.

Being as how I've got the type of manager who books me in Miami during the summer, Boston during Holy Week and Vegas during the atom bomb tests, it seemed only natural I should play Southeast Asia during the Communist uprisings. I'm used to hecklers anyway and I figured this way: the worst that could happen to me is Nikita & Co. won't like my act. And I got news for him. I ain't too crazy about his performance, either!

I was all for the idea of taking a troupe of minstrels to the troubled areas of the world on a good will tour. I figured if we could make them laugh, how could they hate us? And if they applaud, how could they turn us away? I knew if they enjoyed our music, we must find harmony some place. I knew we couldn't lose if we pitted our jazz musicians against the martial music of Khrushchev and his band.

This is no new gimmick to show people. Ever since young David played on his harp to soothe King Saul, through the era of the court jesters to the age of the wandering minstrels and on to the era of two-a-day at the Palace, variety entertainers have been called upon to ease the tensions of a troubled world. Actors are always front and center to help every cause. It is not uncommon to find these soldiers in greasepaint in the front-line trenches entertaining our boys in wartime. It is not unusual to find a Negro dancer, an Italian singer and a Jewish comedian on one stage, with arms entwined, helping to lift the mortgage on a Catholic Church. We've worked for every charity . . . from the Heart Fund, Cancer Fund, March of Dimes, to raising money for research for the cure and prevention of athlete's foot. Once I even gathered together a few bucks for a pool table for a group of needy murderers in Brooklyn.

When I said we would be proud to be the first variety troupe ever sent out by the State Department, I was speaking for twenty thousand members of the American Guild of Variety Artists, of which I am President. AGVA is the largest entertainment union in the world. Our members encompass everybody from Bob Hope to the aerialists in the circus, from Sinatra to the chorines at the Copacabana. From burlesque performers to opera stars, from outdoor carnivals to indoor theaters, from rodeos to night clubs, they're all AGVA. I'd seen our talented army in action on the home front. Platoons of jugglers, singers, dancers and magicians have gone forth to battle juvenile delinquency on behalf of the AGVA Youth Fund.

We go into the classrooms and the recreation centers, the correction institutions as well as the hospitals, and work with these youngsters to bring them a little entertainment, a little instruction and a lot of love and friendship. We were able to advance on the evil that is juvenile delinquency by invading the sickest areas of New York with a troupe of specialists whose only vaccine against the ills of JD was laughter and entertainment. This program worked so well that Mayor Robert F. Wagner appointed me Commissioner of Youth in New York City. Governor Rockefeller also encouraged me to spread my program throughout the entire state. Eventually, our program moved westward to California.

Having pitched in on the home front, how could we refuse to advance the cause of democracy abroad? And so, when I answered the Government's letter, what I said, in effect, was, "Dear Mr. President: Have jokes. Will travel."

I rushed home to tell my wife, Cindy, the great news that we were pushing off for Afghanistan, Nepal, Thailand, then on to Cambodia, Laos, Indonesia, Singapore, Hong Kong, Vietnam, all through India in cities like Bangalore, Madras, Bombay, Calcutta, Chembur and New Delhi; Teheran, Iran, and points east on behalf of the President's personal program for Cultural Exchange.

"Seems strange," Cindy cracked, "that the best way you can serve your country is by leaving it."

"I told you, didn't I, that if you stick with me you'll be playing the Big Leagues?"

"Big Leagues? Big Leagues! All I know is that where we'll be playing the press notices will trickle back via tom-tom."

Of course you've got to dig Cindy's sense of humor. And I do. But then I dig everything about her. We've been very close since the day I said, "I do," and she said, "I guess so," on Valentine's Day 1952. Perhaps it's because we have so much in common. And we each have the same sense of humor.

Cindy and I thrive on punch lines. We feed on laughter. Even when everything seems to be stacked against us, somehow we can always manage to kid about it. Somewhere in this big, fat, beautiful world we really found each other.

My wife, who used to be an entertainer before she became a newspaperwoman, was all excited. "I can't believe I'm really going," she said. "I'll do anything I can to help. I'll dust off my old act, I'll start rehearsing immediately and I'll . . ."

"Just a minute, let's get this straight. You're not going to do any act. We want to win new friends not lose the ones we've got."

"I imagine, in some quarters, people would consider that a quite humorous remark."

"When I married you nine years ago and took you out of show business, it was not only because of my great love for you —it was also because of my great love for show business."

"Let us hope and pray that the Indonesians find you so funny."

"Come to think of it, your old act might fit into some of these areas, because I can't recall ever having seen anything as underdeveloped in my life."

"Save your jokes for the King of Thailand. He hasn't heard you before."

"I'll tell you something, honey," I said, "and this time I'm serious—I've got your job all planned."

It had always been my thought that if we ever made a good will trip, we should try to learn a little of the language of each country. What better way to prove that you're interested? What better way to show that you care? Mrs. Kennedy was a big hit in Canada and again in France when she addressed the people in French. They loved her in South America and Mexico when she made her little speech in Spanish. When the Robert F. Kennedys were in Tokyo, everybody was so pleased that they'd made the effort to speak Japanese. Even if it was just a few words. This had always been my feeling. People the world over are flattered when you take the time to understand them. To reach them. To show them that they mean something to you.

Cindy is a linguist. She can get around in a couple of languages, and she's able to pick up others very quickly. It was my plan for her to learn enough of the language in every country so that she could make the opening speech and explain the reason for our visit. But not enough for her to make with the back talk to me. I can just barely handle her in English.

In Washington, the State Department officially informed me we were blazing a new trail. They told us how important this all was to the United States. Uncle Sam was picking up the tab for this package and the commercial was: Let's be friends.

This was to be democracy in action. In choosing our show we selected entertainers with character and talent and not because of the church in which they worshipped or the color of their skin. Our program had Jew and Gentile, Negro and white—all working together in harmony on one stage, and incidentally proving to the world that America is not Little Rock nor the bombing of a house of worship in Atlanta, nor a Nazi called Rockwell.

For years, American vaudevillians have circled the globe bringing a bit of U.S. show business to foreign audiences. But this was really the big time. Now the payoff was to be a better understanding of the democracy that is America. It was my thought that maybe we could bring a little joy to a troubled world.

I had no great daydreams of stopping wars or halting aggression. Don't misunderstand. I never for one moment believed that a magician and a balloon act would make Khrushchev be a good boy. It never occurred to me that a trio of singers from Idaho would make Mao Tse-tung play nice.

But I found out a long time ago that if you stick out your

hand in friendship, the good people of the world will take it and shake it. I only know that if you want your children to live in harmony with the neighbor's children, you let them play together. Many of these people had never even seen Americans, still less played with them, talked with them or laughed with them. The idea was to show that we were nice people like they are. To show them that the laugh and the tear are the same all over the world. That we were neighbors who wanted to be friendly. We were being sent as a living, breathing, three-dimensional valentine.

I knew this wasn't going to be an easy trip. We were going on the road—but the Burma Road. We'd be playing forest clearings and jungle caves. Inner Congo and outer Russia. South Vietnam and downtown Rangoon. But this was a command performance no actor could refuse. It was the role of a lifetime—a comedian in striped pants.

Cindy was fully aware that this was not going to be a pleasure cruise. She knew she'd be playing cities where water and electricity are turned on only a few hours a day. It didn't frighten her a bit that she'd be working in 110-degree temperature, where fans and plumbing are nonexistent and they never heard of air conditioning.

I explained, "In some areas where the housing is poor, we'll be billeted in the King's palace. In other areas where the King himself is poor, we'll be billeted in private homes."

"So what?" Cindy cracked. "I'm used to roughing it. Didn't I struggle along one week last summer with a busted air conditioner?"

We hadn't left on our trip, we hadn't even started to pack when the toughest part came up. I had to break the news to the commander-in-chief of our family: my mother-in-law. Cindy hasn't been separated from her mother since the day she was born. I'm still convinced my mother-in-law resented our honeymoon. She considered it an intrusion on their privacy.

They see each other every day. They talk on the phone

several times a day. They even call each other to say they can't talk now but that they'll call each other later. And those calls to say they can't talk to each other now could last a half an hour. I'm thinking seriously of asking my mother-in-law to move in with us because then, at least, I'd be able to talk to my wife once in a while.

As per usual, my mother-in-law walked into our house with her own key and found us sitting on the floor surrounded by maps. "We're going to Afghanistan," I said, standing at attention.

"Afghanistan!" she growled. "That's overseas, isn't it?"

"Yes," I said, saluting. "We've been called to serve our country."

"If you're such a red-hot patriot and you want to serve your country, do jury duty."

"Jessie, dear, you don't understand. This is a very big honor for me to have been chosen to represent our country."

"I understand. What I don't understand is if you're so valuable to the national effort, how come we were able to win the last war without you?"

"But, Mother," Cindy interjected.

"And, anyway," Jessie continued, "where's Afghanistan?"

"Whaddya mean, 'where's Afghanistan?' " I said. "Everybody knows where Afghanistan is."

"Okay," she said, "so I'll bite. Where is it?"

"Simple. When you get to Beirut you make a left."

CHAPTER 2

Getting the Show
on the Road

I KNEW I needed a show that would transcend all language and social barriers. We had to reach the royal families of Asia who had been educated abroad, yet we had to appeal to the lowliest farmer in the field. We were playing to the prince and the pauper. The educated and the illiterate. We had to find a common denominator that would reach the Hindu, the Buddhist, the Christian and the Moslem.

The star of the Latin Quarter in New York could fall on her face in Katmandu. The top banana on TV could go into the ground in the up-country jungles of Hua Hin. We needed something as basic as Mickey Mouse, as typically Yankee as baseball, as clean as a church choir, as fast-moving as "Friendship 7" and as entertaining as an All-Star Ed Sullivan lineup.

The acts had to be visual. Therefore, the basic comedy had to be pantomime. One of the great sight comics of all time is a funny little fellow called Chaz Chase who was the first to pack his props and scrapbooks and hit the road for Uncle Sam.

I picked Chaz Chase, not only because he's acclaimed as one of the greatest clowns in the world, but also because he's been a seasoned trouper since the Stone Age. Chaz is on the road fifty-two weeks a year. His home is in his trunk. One week he's in Kansas City and the next he's in Tokyo. I needed a veteran traveler as well as a veteran performer. Chaz was my A-Number-One choice. I finally found him in a *boîte* in Paris, so I plucked him out of his bookings in Europe to bring him back to the States to take him to Asia.

From a farm in Idaho, by way of the Ken Murray Show, came my singing trio, the Sylte Sisters. Three typically American girls who, only a year before, were pushing tractors and milking cows on their parents' farm. Now the farmer's daughters were going to be traveling salesmen for the USA.

I was looking for a group of pretty people whose specialty was harmony. I figured if the pop tunes didn't get them, the pretty girls would. And I wanted this bouquet of American beauties to be as typically USA as apple pie. After months of searching, I was led to the Riverside Hotel in Reno, Nevada. There I found the Syltes, the twins Deanna and Deanda— aged 18—and big sister, Joan—aged 22—working with my old vaudeville pal, Ken Murray. I fell in love with them. They were scrubbed and beautiful and talented and they were the kind of kids who read the Bible every day of their lives. Now how are you going to beat that kind of combination?

The girls were desperate to go, but there were a few problems. I had to get them out of a contract with Ken, and I hadn't yet talked to their manager. When I left the club that evening, the most I could say to them was, "I'll let you know."

"You have nothing to say about it," one of the twins said softly. "The Lord sent you to us and He'll arrange everything." They were so right. How could they fail with such a booking agent?

There was never any question in my mind as to my dance act. From the very first I knew I wanted the Step Brothers, the four greatest show-stopping tap dancers in the business. France is loaded with ballet dancers; in Russia they've got kazotzky dancers they haven't even used yet; they'll sell you acrobatic dancers by the yard all through Europe; but good, solid, lay-'em-in-the-aisle hoofers grow only in the United States. And the cream of the crop are the Steps.

These four great Negro stars are Rufus "Flash" McDonald, the baby of the group; Prince Spencer, the dude of the group; Maceo Anderson, the daddy of the group; and Al Williams, the businessman who, along with Prince Spencer, also owns a dancing school in Chicago. Flash, Prince, Maceo and Al eagerly cancelled several weeks of lucrative bookings to dance their hearts out with us in Loew's Bangkok and RKO Djakarta.

I've worked with these boys ever since we were kids in show business. They have show-stopped with Dean Martin and Jerry Lewis, Frank Sinatra and Kay Starr. In fact, they taught Dean and Jerry their first dance steps. They've appeared in movies and on almost every top television show in the country. They've headlined theaters and clubs all over the world. Me, I think they're the greatest, not only personally and professionally, but also because theirs is the kind of patriotism that comes in handy when you're 12,000 miles from home—as I was to find out when the chips were down.

John and Bonnie Shirley, who make animals out of balloons and who'd accompanied Ed Sullivan on his sleeper jump to Russia the year before, were the next to join up. I wanted a novelty act. An act that could work to children or grown-ups, indoors or out, that would be just as amusing in an arena as in a hospital ward. A balloon act encompasses every facet of entertainment for an international variety show. It's gay, it's colorful, it's fun, it has a sort of holiday spirit about it and every performance is like New Year's Eve.

John Shirley is the Picasso of balloon sculpture. By his own count he can make 176 kinds of animals, from a swan to a giraffe. John and his wife, Bonnie, who assists him, left their son and their home in Milwaukee, packed their rubber menagerie-to-be of 40,000 balloons and joined up for eighteen weeks.

You just can't have a variety show without a magician. Oh, I don't mean it's against the law or anything. It's just that it wouldn't be right. It's just not complete. It's like a sundae without whipped cream. Magicians have always fascinated me. Even when I was a kid in vaudeville, I used to stand in the wings during every show watching the local Mandrake bewitch, bother and befuddle his audience. Maybe I'm just a sucker for these acts. Maybe it's because I can't even figure out how the ordinary doorbell works. I only know if I'm going to head a variety show I'm going to have a magician.

Since I was going to India where they breed men of magic, I had to bring them something they didn't have. So I did. I brought them a lady of magic—Celeste Evans. Celeste differs from most magicians in three respects. First, she's one of the few women prestidigitators we have in the world. Second, she certainly is the most glamorous. And third, she's the only man, woman or sorcerer who uses live doves as part of her act. Celeste needed only a few minutes' notice to join our caravan. She already had had her shots since she'd only just returned from the Congo, the Gaza Strip and some other suburbs in that neighborhood. When I reached her in Dallas she grabbed her visas and her doves and the first plane out.

In Birdland, "The Jazz Corner of the World," on 52nd Street and Broadway, New York City, I found my band. Buddy Rich and his combo. The sextet included Mike Manieri, vibraharp; Rolf Erickson on trumpet; Sam Most who plays flute, saxophone and clarinet; Dave Lucas the bongo player; Wyatt Ruther, bass; and John Morris, piano and accordion.

For the past twenty years, Buddy Rich has been considered one of the top jazz drummers in the business. He started at the age of five when his parents, vaudeville performers, included him in their act. At eleven he was leading his own band. In '38 he began his jazz career with some of the world's famous, including Dorsey, Artie Shaw and Harry James. His records have sold in the millions.

Jazz, which has become a universal language, was born in the United States. I knew if I wanted to show off America's genius for jazz, it had to be the best. Buddy Rich is one of the best. I warned him that this was going to be a tough trip. "You kiddin'?" flipped Buddy. "Have you ever played one-nighters through Texas on a bus?"

Famous last words.

My last recruits were Jed Horner and Jerry Bell. Jed Horner is a fine young stage director whom I met when he directed me in *Guys and Dolls* in the summer of 1960. So eager was he to be part of our safari that he signed on as company manager. Jerry Bell, who'd worked at Radio City Music Hall and toured several seasons with Frank Sinatra, is an expert on lighting and sound. Since we wanted to be seen and heard, we needed Jerry Bell for our stage manager.

We were booked on the biggest circuit of them all. Our minstrels gathered together from the four corners of the earth. From New York, New Haven and Hartford to Atchison, Topeka and Santa Anita. They dusted off their passports, flexed their best smiles and were ready to roll for Uncle Sam.

Of all the hardships everybody anticipated, the biggest pain in the arm were the shots. We were inoculated against smallpox, typhoid, paratyphoid, cholera, tetanus, typhus, yellow fever and a couple of things they don't even have diseases for.

After the third set of shots, there was no room left on our arms so the doctor started looking for greener pastures. Propriety and the mid-Victorian upbringing I acquired whilst growing up in Brooklyn preclude my mentioning the section of my anatomy where that worthy practitioner rammed his damn needles. Suffice to say that when the State Department called us together for a briefing just prior to our departure, most of us stood up throughout the entire speech . . . and they weren't even playing the Star-Spangled Banner.

I'd always heard the cheapest commodity in Asia was human life. However, when trouping for our country's Cultural Exchange Program, you soon discover that even more plentiful than rice bowls are your lists of Do's and Don'ts issued by the State Department.

For females, high on the list are low necklines. They're verboten, forbidden and you positively dassn't feature them in Moslem countries. And you *DON'T* wear slacks or shorts. And, for men, you *DON'T* trot about with sport shirts, no jackets and 5 o'clock shadow.

The biggest *DON'T* is *DON'T* discuss politics. Second, *DON'T* boast how wonderful our wonderful U.S.A. is. Third biggest *DON'T* is *DON'T* call the locals "Natives." *Do* call them "Nationals." (Anybody ever hear that oldie, "The nationals are restless tonight"?)

In Afghanistan, if we were to buy hats, turbans, their embroidered national dress or other indigenous garb, *DON'T* wear it locally. It's felt you're trying too hard. In Hindu India, *DON'T* whack anybody on the back in palsy-walsy Yankee style. And, so's we don't look too openhanded, *DON'T* over-tip; *DON'T* feed the beggars. In Buddhist Nepal, *DON'T* call the Nepalis "Indians." *DON'T* dare touch or even graze a lady. *DON'T* shake hands unless she offers first. It's an unpardonable offense, punishable by the unwritten law, the written law and any other laws the menfolks got laying around. And *DON'T* step on orange or yellow rocks—they're considered gods.

But, like the gentleman says, "You ain't heard nothin' yet" until they brief you on Bangkok. Here, they have two number one *DON'T*s. First number one *DON'T* concerns *The King and I*. Just *DON'T* mention it. They're sensitive about this. They deem it fiction, not truth, and consider that it demeaned a great ruler who was Thailand's Father of Education and that it reduced His Majesty to the role of one of us ordinary mortals rather than a Supreme Being.

Second number one *DON'T* regards the worst word in the

Thai language, which is the bottom of your foot. To Thais, the bottom of one's foot is even worse than where we got rammed with those damn needles. Because of this, even shoe-shine parlors are taboo hereabouts. So, *DON'T* expose the soles of your shoes. And *DON'T* point your feet at anyone.

Comes next the bunch of *MAKE SURES*. *MAKE SURE* you don't mention President Kennedy more than once in your official speeches. Sounds as if we're pressing. *MAKE SURE* you throw in a kind word for our ambassador, but *MAKE SURE* you don't lay it on too thick. Sounds like log-rolling.

Then there's the second-string *DON'T*s: *DON'T* touch a Thai on the head or shoulders. That's the sacred part of their being. *DON'T* point or shake your finger. In Thailand it's a gesture of accusation. *DON'T* stand over a seated Thai when conversing. Nobody knows why, unless maybe that it's just plain rude. For females, *DON'T* touch orange-robed monks. For everybody, *DON'T* raise your voice even to shout at anyone. *ALWAYS* keep smiling. In a haggle with a taxi driver, you can be as insulting as you like but *ALWAYS* in a low voice and *ALWAYS* keep smiling. And *DON'T* kiss or display affection publicly.

"Get a load of all this," Cindy whispered to me. "And this is only our very first briefing."

"Yeah," I said, "and we haven't even left the country yet."

"Wow," she replied, "we got so many *DON'T*s to do, who's got time to do the *DO*'s?"

CHAPTER 3

Curtain Up
in Afghanistan

As THOSE theatrical folk say, "We opened in Afghanistan . . ." Well, I mean, doesn't everybody?

Afghanistan is 12,000 miles away from the U.S. It's 250 miles away from Khrushchev's boarding-house reach. It's smack up against 400 miles of Siberian border. It's ten days away from anything by airmail, and if Rand McNally himself quizzed me, I still don't know where we were. I only know we had breakfast in New York, lunch in London, a snack in Paris, tea in Geneva and heartburn in Cairo before changing planes in Bombay and again in New Delhi, India, where we inherited a barefoot pilot.

Nice and early August 18, 1961, twenty-five strong, we grabbed ourselves a jet at Idlewild airport, and nice and late Monday, four days later, we landed in the capital city of Kabul. So, if your travel agent claims it's a keen place for a week end—forget it!

A desert plateau 6,000 feet high, surrounded by mountains, Kabul is hot and dry in the daytime and cool and dusty come night. It's the home of the karakul, or what we call Persian lamb. It's where you order postage stamps in advance because they're printed as needed. It's where the Army is trained by Soviets and outfitted by Germans. It's where main boulevards, mostly unpaved, are shared by sheep, oxen, horse-driven carts, camels, and brand new Ford station wagons. And it's where you have to guzzle bottled water even to brush your teeth.

"You're not here by chance," explained our Ambassador, Henry A. Byroade, dramatically, when he greeted us at The Residence. "You're here because I went to Washington and asked for you. In fact, I begged for you. The day immediately following President Kennedy's inauguration I made a special trip to Washington about your show. Your coming here saved the day for me."

He went on to explain that Afghanistan had been petitioning our country for millions to help their Five-Year Plan. They had been turned away, while at the same time aid and arms went to Pakistan, their next-door neighbor and archenemy. This created a barrier in Afghanistan-American relations. The Afghans figured the Americans didn't care about them any more. This placed our country and our Ambassador in an untenable position.

"I needed a big-time show at the Jeshyn Fair to prove to the people that we do care," explained Byroade.

"What's the Jeshyn Fair?" I asked.

"It is the annual Independence Week of this Moslem country, which actually falls in May but gets celebrated in August because the weather is better. It's held outdoors with booths and pavilions."

"I get it," said Cindy. "It's like the World's Fair, only turban style."

"Right," he smiled. "Traditionally, every year all the major powers send exhibits and shows which they present in specially constructed pavilions. I wanted this to be the biggest and the best and the most fun-packed show. Especially this year when our friendship seems to be in jeopardy."

"Don't worry about a thing, Mr. Ambassador," I said. "The Joey Adams Show is here."

"That's what he's worried about," my loving wife said.

I knew this had to be a great show. There was more than ego riding on our performance. Because besides all the other trouble the Ambassador had outlined, immediately following our arrival the Pak-Afghan border shut. And this corner of our planet seemed tapped to join Laos and Korea as another household word fresh from the morning headlines.

We'd barely arrived when the temperamental Pakistan Government shut their consulates in Afghanistan, bounced Afghan consulates from Pakistan and tightened the border. The Royal Afghan Government threatened to sever relations entirely. Things were really up for grabs.

When the border finally closed down altogether, we asked the Ambassador, "What does this mean to the United States?"

"Our efforts here are hitting a dead end," he said sadly. "We're left alone with Russia who is inching toward Pakistan. And Afghanistan's 400 miles of Russian border could pass from neutralism to virtual satellite status."

It was explained to us that, with Afghanistan's only port being Karachi in Pakistan, and that now being in enemy territory, their lifeline to the West was blocked. As he did once before, Khrushchev might again tempt this hungry country with delicacies, such as tasty bites of aid and trade possibilities. And Russian penetration here, in proportion to size and population, is greater than anywhere in the world.

What worried everybody was the fact that, if we left Afghanistan to the Soviets, the future of Afghanistan's next-door neighbor to the West, Iran, America's friend, would be shaky. That could paralyze our efforts in South Vietnam, Thailand, Laos and India. Trouble here could set off a far-reaching chain reaction.

"I have 1200 Americans here," explained our Ambassador, "who are tense and nervous. They don't know what's going to happen. They don't know how supplies are going to come in. And they don't know when the shooting's going to start. That's why I'm so glad you're here. I want this to be the gayest, happiest show you've ever done in your lives. Our people need it just as much as the Afghans."

"Don't worry, Ambassador Byroade, we'll murder 'em, we'll kill 'em, we'll fracture 'em," I said, putting on a bravado I didn't feel.

It was our opening night in Afghanistan. From a peephole backstage, I looked out at my audience. There were 10,000 Afghans sitting cross-legged on the ground. Thousands and thousands more stood outside the row of American flags which marked the entrance to the American pavilion.

I had a sinking feeling in the pit of my stomach. How do you work to 20,000 turban-tops? How do you establish a rapport with an army of people who are barefoot? How do you win those bearded faces who have stepped out of the pages of an ancient civilization? How do you reach women in chadari? Women who are veiled from head to foot. Women whose faces you can't see.

The crowd was getting unruly. They'd been massing since early morning for our show, which was scheduled to go at 7:30 P.M. They were restless and they were overcrowded. They were crushed together. They were on top of each other. They were spilling over. And they were growing impatient. And to top it all off, a dust storm began to whip things up around our outdoor arena.

As little eruptions broke out here and there among the spectators, police shouldered their way into the mob with their belt buckles ready. When the overflow crowd surged toward the stage and knocked over our spotlights, the police closed in swinging their belt buckles in every direction. One little boy, about eight years old, his face cut badly, was brought into the fenced-in area which served as backstage. He was bleeding profusely and needed first aid. We already had a doctor in attendance ministering to Deanda Sylte, one of our singing stars, who was heaving and burning up with fever.

Jerry Bell, our stage manager, was in a frenzy because the dust had choked up his microphones. Buddy Rich was upset because the dust had settled in his band instruments and clogged the keys. Chaz Chase, our pantomimist, Celeste Evans, our magician, and John Shirley, our balloon artist, were worried that several of their show-stopping tricks would have to be cut because of the increasing winds. And between the dust and the 6,000-foot altitude, our four dancers, the Step Brothers, were having difficulty breathing. Over the entire witches' brew hovered the head of the United States Information Service in Kabul, Joe Kitchen, who tried valiantly not to show his tension.

Out front, our Ambassador, Henry A. Byroade, sat quietly chatting with the Royal Family and the leaders of the Royal Afghan Government. On the surface he appeared calm and nonchalant. But, beneath that polished exterior he too was tied up in knots. There was a lot riding on this show. He was depending on us. For the first time in years I had stage fright. I was petrified. I knew how much this show meant—far beyond its mere entertainment value.

The trumpets blared. The drums rolled. And I walked out on our home-made wooden platform, holding my jaunty straw hat with one hand and my pretty wife with the other.

"Salaam aleicham," I shouted in greeting. *"Durstan baradaran."* A roar went up from the crowd. I had said, "Welcome, my friends and brothers," and the reaction was explosive. Then I introduced Cindy, *"Khanumha khod ra moarrifi me konam."* They screamed. I was home.

Cindy stepped front and center, made a deep curtsy and delivered her opening speech in Parsi, the language of the country. She'd been learning it phonetically for two days from a responsible teacher provided by the American Embassy. As a matter of fact, it was from a Princess of the Royal Family. The teacher had to be reliable because Cindy didn't know what she was learning. For all she knew she could have been spouting, "Let's bomb Washington."

"Khanumha va agayanay mohtaram," she began. They cheered. I was flabbergasted. In all my thirty-five years in show business, this is the first time I ever heard of anyone saying, "Good evening, ladies and gentlemen" and stopping a show cold.

"Jahyay mohsarahtast kay nemoonaye az naymoyay shahtay mukhtalifay tafrihiay Emrikara beyhozooray shoma takdeem meedoram," Cindy continued. Which means, "On behalf of the American people and with great love and friendship between our two countries, may I present the best in our American variety entertainment." At the end of her speech, she said, *"Aknoon sitara nomamayish-e ma*—Joey Adams." I always knew my cue because there's no Parsi word for Joey Adams.

We opened with a big, brassy, flashy production number that had no language barrier. It was razz-a-ma-tazz all the way. I'm sure even the Russians heard us 400 miles away. The cymbals banged. The horns blared. The Syltes sang, the Steps danced, Chaz ran on and off with assorted masks, and for a big finish, Flash McDonald, Prince Spencer, Buddy Rich and I—with our canes and straw hats—strutted around the stage à la George M. Cohan to the tune of "Yankee Doodle Dandy."

Celeste Evans came on with a full-length, form-fitting gown replete with feathers, sequins, beads and enough neon to light Times Square. Even with her magical charms camouflaged, she was a knockout. In line with the *DON'T* wear decolletage, *DON'T* show bare shoulders, she'd bandaged herself from neck to ribcage with a couple of yards of tulle. She opened with a few sleight-of-hand tricks, confused them with her rope trick, dazzled them with her disappearing water trick and threw them for a loop when, from a bunch of handkerchiefs which she juggled, she produced about eight real live, gaily colored doves.

When Celeste finished her act, I bragged to the audience, *"Man maolem hastam."* ("I am the teacher.") They snickered unbelievingly. It sounded a little like a Bronx cheer—a noise with which I regret to say I have had some experience. *"Man maolem hastam. Man maolem hastam,"* I insisted, flourishing a colored silk handkerchief from which I elaborately produced a long black cane. This was followed by my big trick. Accompanied by much fanfare and much abra-cadabra-ing, I dove into the depths of my straw hat and produced a tired, wizened-looking, busted-up old rubber chicken. It was a howl. The $14.25 I blew at that Magic Store on 53rd Street and Broadway was the best investment I ever made.

When Deanna, Deanda and Joan Sylte came out next in matching red dresses, they looked like long-stemmed American beauties. They did only up-tempo songs. No slow ballads. Nobody was going to sleep while our show was on. As the program explained, their last number was a series of imitations of America's most famous singing trios, like the Andrews Sisters, the McGuire Sisters and the Lennon Sisters. This was followed by a flash finish where Deanna plays the French horn, Deanda plays the trumpet and Joan tootles the clarinet. And there's nothing that can follow this short of a real-live *Playboy* calendar.

After their encore, in which Maceo Anderson, Al Williams and I joined the Syltes in a big song-and-dance number, our beaming Ambassador came backstage. I was in a panic. They weren't applauding out front. There was no hand at all. Not for anybody. For us to have traveled 12,000 miles to go over with a big, fat hush was just too much for me.

"You're a big smash!" Ambassador Byroade said, pumping my clammy hand and slapping me on the back.

"Wow! If this is what it's like to be a big smash here, I can just imagine what happens if you lay a bomb."

"But they're loving you," he exclaimed. "Can't you hear them? They're laughing and hollering and yelling."

"Yeah, but they're not applauding," I said. "They're not applauding."

"The Afghans never applaud. They don't know what it is. Applause is strictly a Western custom. They've just never done it here before. The Afghan people are unused to applause."

"So is Joey," teased the dear wife, who was unfortunately beginning to regain her sense of humor now that the strain was over.

"They're absolutely crazy about you out there," the Ambassador laughed, "but it's just not their custom to applaud."

"Well, far be it from me to interfere with their local traditions, but with your permission this is one custom we've just got to break. I can't stand it. A week of successful shows like this and I'll kill myself. I've just got to show them how to bang their hands together. I must teach them how to applaud."

"Yeah, but then you'll get used to it and what'll you do when you get back to the States?" Cindy ribbed.

"Never mind," the Ambassador said happily. "Did you notice that the women even removed their chadari to see the show better?"

"Yeah, but when Joey came out they put it back on," Cindy giggled.

I did what any other self-respecting husband would do under the circumstances. I bit my leash.

I walked out into the audience just as the Step Brothers were finishing their big acrobatic trick. This is the bit that killed the people all over the world. Prince Spencer brings on a portable stage the size of a drum. On it he does slides, knee-drops and splits. The four boys then tap themselves into a frenzy as they leap-frog over one another and hurl themselves from the stage onto the ground, landing in a perfect split.

The whole audience sucked in their breath. They oohed, they aahed and they gasped. It's just that nobody applauded but me. I walked into the audience and started banging my hands together. I beckoned them to do the same. From the stage the Steps smiled gleefully and started to bang their hands together with me. The Afghans began to realize that this was some sort of gesture of joy so they laughed and banged their hands together, too. Before you could say, *"Man maolem hastam,"* Afghanistan had taken its first lesson in applause.

Now it was time for me to run onstage and do my bit with the Steps. The Steps were standing there panting, dripping with perspiration and mopping their faces. They had just finished killing, murdering and ruining the audience with their talent. *"Man maolem hastam,"* I said cockily. "I am the teacher of these boys." This time they didn't snicker. They shook with laughter. Especially when Maceo started to clobber me with his straw hat.

"O diwana hastam," I hollered to the audience. "He's crazy." I nonchalantly glanced at the lining of my straw hat where I had my punch lines written in Parsi. I picked up another cue. *"Man diwana hastam.* I am crazy," I said. When they all laughed, I threw an eye at the lining again, then *"Ma diwana hastam.* We're all crazy," I hollered.

At this point I did a well-rehearsed bit of trick dancing with the boys, which was theoretically supposed to prove that *Man maolem hastam.* It was about a ten-minute routine. At the end, the four Steps and the one mis-Step went into a challenge dance which features each of us doing a specialty solo. Mine was a deep knee bend dance where I fall flat on my pratt for a finish, and the four boys physically drag me offstage.

The audience started to applaud spontaneously and furiously. We never did find out whether it was because they enjoyed our dance or if they were glad that I was being dragged offstage or because they just liked to clap now, but in any case we never took any chances. We always did the bit exactly the same way for the next four and a half months.

I looked into my hat to introduce John and Bonnie Shirley, Afghan-style. On this show, if anybody accused me of talking through my hat, I couldn't argue with them. John and Bonnie do fantastic things with ordinary balloons. They make them bounce on the ground like a basketball, they make them whistle through the air like a comet, they make them circle overhead like a satellite. They fashion swans that lay eggs and poodles that wag their tails and animals that leap in the air. After all the creations were given out to the children in the audience, we did our big William Tell finish.

John fashioned an apple out of a red balloon and balanced it on my head. From several long balloons knotted together he made a bow and arrow. The drums rolled. I braced. John aimed. And the audience cheered as he shot the apple off my head.

Everybody loved the little man in the baggy pants, ill-fitting frock coat and top hat. During his twelve-minute routine, Chaz Chase ate cigars, burning cigarettes and boxes of lit matches. He topped off this tasty soufflé by munching the fresh-picked flower in his buttonhole—stem and all. For dessert he greedily relished his starched shirt front, all the while walking a tight rope with both feet firmly planted on the ground. He dances, he pantomimes, he does impressions that have filled theaters from Iceland to Beirut with laughter.

When I came out to start the applause for him, he grabbed the handkerchief out of my tuxedo pocket and chewed it up— initials and all. The audience loved it, but I didn't because after a few shows I had no more hankies. So we substituted Kleenex. Some countries, where we couldn't lay our hands on fresh Kleenex, we'd have to scrounge some crumpled ones from somebody's purse. And now it can be told. In these instances we actually had to iron these beat-up, crummy old pieces of tissue which were so precious to us.

The biggest laugh of the show came when Chaz snatched my straw hat off my head and opened his mouth wide preparatory to taking a big bite out of the brim. Just as I rescued my pretty skimmer from the jaws of death, Chaz produced an enormous salt shaker from his vest pocket and liberally salted me from head to foot. If ever there was an exit cue, that was it. I ran screaming offstage with cannibal Chase close on my heels.

The closing act was Buddy Rich and his sextet. One hunk of our Western culture that's trickled through all the way from Basin Street to the Volga is jazz. Over the past few years, certain parts of Asia have been treated to such giants of jazz as Benny Goodman, Louis Armstrong and Red Nichols. And like, man, them Moslems, Hindus and Buddhists dig it the most. Our group opened with a swing version of "Lulu's Back in Town," featuring Sam Most on clarinet, a man tagged by *Downbeat* as one of the greats. This was followed by "Misty," with a solo by the award-winning 21-year-old Mike Manieri on vibes. The band concluded their medley of hit records with "Caravan," at which point they wound up the wild man of the drums, Buddy Rich, and let him go. And boy did he go! It was Go all the way.

Buddy did a frenetic, frantic, hysterical ten-minute spot in which he massacred everything from the drums to the cymbals to the stage, the microphone, the piano and anything standing in his way. There was nothing that could follow this—unless we blew up the stage altogether.

After this peak of frenzy, we crashed into our grand finale. To the blaring of "When the Saints Go Marchin' In," the whole company marched onstage, down the steps, into the audience, around the park and back onstage. Chaz was doing a comedy dance, while Celeste was juggling doves and the Steps were somersaulting over each other and the Syltes were singing and I was doing a crazy Lindy with Buddy Rich. This was a perfectly timed, well-rehearsed, elaborately staged piece of organized confusion.

From the midst of this five-ring circus sprang John and Bonnie with their crates of 400 red, white and blue balloons. Each one of the cast took his position on the firing line, grabbed the three-foot-long balloons and—with a trick John taught us—pressed his forefinger into the top as far as possible, twisted it to give it English, aimed it at the corner of the audience assigned to him and then let go.

The show closed with 400 red, white and blue missiles being

shot into the crowd, as women in chadari, bearded turban-tops and barefoot children jumped high in the air to retrieve them. When the chaos subsided to a college yell, I stepped forward with the whole company behind me and delivered the commercial.

"I hope," I said in broken Parsi, "that the fun and friendship that is present tonight will always be there between all of Afghanistan and all of America."

Then I bowed low and pronounced the Afghan blessing, *"Khoda hafiz,"* I said. "God go with you."

CHAPTER 4

Learning the Ropes in Kabul

It DIDN'T take us long to encounter our first piece of sabotage. It happened at the Command Performance for the King and Queen of Afghanistan. Our show in the American pavilion was in direct competition to the German, Indian, and Russian troupes. We appeared nightly in our outdoor pavilion, which squatted 20,000 per show. The Russians, meanwhile, were kazotzkying in their indoor theater into which they crammed—tops 500. This 40 to 1 seemed a fair split to everybody except the Russians, who insisted we come indoors three of the seven nights. They not only insisted. They cried, they carried on and they ran tattling to the Afghan Government. They did all but write their Congressmen. They complained bitterly that favoritism was being shown to the Americans.

Finally, after many meetings, they dried their tears when it was agreed we would perform indoors three of the seven nights to appease the Afghan Government. Our Ambassador said there was no other way. But, much to the delight of our

27

Ambassador, we found a way. Like good kiddies we obeyed mommy and daddy and went indoors three of the seven nights. However, like the smart grownups that we are, we figured out a way to tell them what they could do with their hammer and sickle. We arranged to double. Instead of the one show those three nights, we did two shows. After we'd play to the 500 indoors, we'd run like hell to set up shop and play to our 20,000 outdoors. We all felt that we wanted to get to as many Afghans as possible.

We'd have done twelve shows a day if necessary. The Afghans wait all year for their big annual festival, the Jeshyn Fair. And they wait several years for an International Jeshyn such as this one.

People come from all over the countryside during Jeshyn week and camp right on the fair grounds. The admission is roughly two Afghans or, when you smooth it out, it's about a hot nickel. For these two afs you can see fireworks, the national exhibits from every major country all over the world and wrestling, football, hockey and acrobatic exhibitions. You're even entitled to sleep-out privileges. All you do is grab yourself a handful of ground and lie down on it for the night. For this same hot nickel, you're also entitled to see our show. This was another reason the comrades sulked. To see them in their little theater, you had to pay an extra admission. To see us it didn't cost an extra bean.

The Command Performance at the indoor theater followed our opening night show. The Command Performance for the King and Queen and the heads of all the governments was to be like the Olympics of show business. The Indians were scheduled to open the show pushing their music and dances. Next came the Germans who were selling their high wire artistes and acrobats. They were followed by the Russians who paraded their booted dancers, balalaikas and ochichornya singers. We were slotted to close the show.

Every nation had been officially warned that Their Majesties, King Mohammad Zahir and Queen Humaira, had to leave at 9:55 P.M. exactly. Therefore, each nation was allotted twenty-five minutes in which to take their best shot. It wasn't easy to cut our hour and a half show down to twenty-five minutes. First of all, each of our acts was a showstopper and we didn't know what to cut out. Secondly, our whole show was routined like a revue, each act segueing into the next and building up to a crescendo. In order to consolidate this, it meant extra hours of rehearsal for us. In keeping with good sportsmanship and fair play we finally shaved it down to twenty-five minutes on the nose.

Not so the Russians.

We finished our outdoor show at exactly 9:00 P.M. We were scheduled to go on at the Command Performance at precisely 9:30. Trucks and jeeps and eager hands were standing by to strike our props, instruments and costumes and speed us across the fair grounds to the theater. We made it with ten minutes to spare.

The Russians, however, were in no hurry. They'd condensed their twenty-five minute show to forty-five minutes. I won't say they purposely did it, you understand. You can beat me, hang me, stab me or deport me and I wouldn't accuse them of doing this deliberately. I can only tell you that I was introduced just three minutes this side of when the King and Queen were scheduled to leave.

My crew and I went into a huddle P.D.Q. and we changed our signals. We opened with the finale. I figured if I'm going to have a short show, I'm going to have a blockbuster. This way, if Their Majesties had to leave, at least they'd have something to remember us by. But they didn't leave. They even waited to meet us and extend their congratulations after the performance.

According to Ambassador Byroade's report to the State Department, if this Olympics of show business was rated on the basis of 100 per cent: "Our show would get 70 per cent,

Khrushchev's company 20 per cent and the Indians and Germans 5 per cent apiece."

"Would I lie to ya?" I crowed to my wife. "I agree with our Ambassador."

"I'd be very much interested," she trilled, "to see what the Russian Ambassador sends back."

This little brush with the Soviets on opening night was only an appetizer. Whenever we had to work the Russian-manned theater, we found a cold war going on backstage. The Russians were running the equipment and they deliberately knew from no English. They even seemed to have forgotten sign language.

In order to get a light cue, it went through a chain of command. It was like a Tinkers to Evers to Whatshisname. Our stage manager threw the cue to an Afghan who passed it to a German helper, who then wigwagged to the Russian—who didn't do it. Many a time we worked to a dead mike, a dark house and a fouled-up stage. Once we punched a certain button ourselves and nearly provoked a theatrical world war.

One day our electrician, Jerry Bell, set up at three in the afternoon. Come showtime, 8:00 P.M., everything was torn down. And nobody knew from borscht. Another time we almost had an international incident. Jerry couldn't find the key to the switchboard. When he threatened in five languages to kick the board down, somebody found the key. I wouldn't say it was sabotage, but it seems only honest reporting to mention that whenever the Russians were performing everything worked perfectly.

And y'know something, it's a funny thing, but suddenly on the last day everybody—Russians included—blossomed forth with real, high-class, grade-A, United States dialogue. And we discovered, as we were leaving, that they all spoke a lot more better English than what we did.

As is quite understandable, the United States Information Service was hard pressed to find places to house us and places to feed us when they learned that a large troupe of twenty-five was about to descend on them. Room and board is at a premium in Kabul. In fact, they ain't got it. Some of our troupe were billeted at the best and only hotel, the Kabul Hotel. Others divided up in private homes. Cindy and I were guests of Ambassador Byroade at the Embassy. And what a thrill it was to come home every night and see that big beautiful bald eagle on the door. And what a comfort to get up every morning and see the American flag flying overhead.

"As you know," Byroade said to us, "appearances of American entertainers are few and far between in Afghanistan. Kabul is a long way from the Orpheum-Pantages circuit and only a few Afghans have had any opportunity to see our really good American artists perform. There are troupes that come to this part of the world, but they only stop in the more convenient spots. None of them come to Afghanistan. That's why your show means much more than we can ever tell you."

USIS and the Embassy did everything they could to make us comfortable. Since restaurants are at a premium in Kabul —in fact they ain't got it—the Ambassador had arranged for a different American family—there are 1,200 Americans stationed there—to wine and stuff our troupe every night after the show. These were all chip-in meals. We were all taxed two dollars per person per dinner. Lunch was one dollar per person at the officials' club.

When I tucked my crew in at the Kabul Hotel, I reminded them to drink only bottled or boiled water so that they wouldn't get what's known in this part of the world as "The Dysentery Blues." I was remembering what Merriman Smith of U.P.I. told me at the Plaza Hotel the night before we left when we gave our preview performance before the U.S. press. Merriman, who is the Big Daddy of the White House correspondents, had accompanied Eisenhower when he stopped off in Kabul on his trip around the world. At the Plaza that night he recited a poem to me that I never forgot:

I felt good,
I felt swell—
Till I brushed my teeth with water
From the Kabul Hotel.

Moslem Afghanistan has segued from the thirteenth century to the twentieth overnight. In a jet-propelled hurry, the Afghan ladies are going instant Western!

Going, going and soon to be gone is the centuries-old "purdah," which means "curtain," and the "chadari"—the opaque hood that covers a woman from head to foot. Following their progressive theories, the Royal Afghan Government two years before decided that the veil must go. Well, sir, before you could say, "Allah be praised," the old chadari was out, the New Look was in and the emancipation was on.

The first women to go Westward Ho! were heavily guarded by secret police lest fanatics toss stones and/or names. Everyone recalled the ex-king who passed a similar edict thirty years ago. He never did succeed in carrying out his orders but the revolutionists did succeed in carrying out His Majesty.

This time it wasn't mandatory. To maintain some Islamic uniformity and to teach ladies proper garb, initial suggestions were long skirts, long sleeves, high-necked blouses, heavy cotton hosiery, head scarves, loose-fitting duster coats and no make-up. Bare arms are forbidden. Even today, if you're naked from the wrist to the shoulder, you get dirty looks.

Inch by inch the hemlines are getting shorter, females are getting bolder, dresses tighter, necklines lower and, today, the more daring are even beginning to wear bathing suits—in private. Lifting the veil also banished other restrictions for some Moslem females. The modern woman doesn't want to be an inferior, second-class citizen any more. Most women are still only allowed out in the company of their menfolk. They still walk, talk, stand and yawn solely at the bidding of their lord and master. And their mommies and daddies still arrange their marriages.

But the emancipation is growing daily. Suddenly, there are women working in public places. Occasionally, Mrs. Afghanistan has actually begun answering Mr. Afghanistan back. The more bold are daring to smoke in public and, shades of Carry Nation in reverse, there are a few who are even beginning to take a nip in public.

The largest proportion still haven't unveiled. Either they're forbidden by their men, who reserve the right to force them back into chadari, or it makes them feel more secure and sheltered, or they're zealots who believe this style was decreed by the Koran.

Afghanistan is a fricassee of old and new, featuring women in ankle-length veils alongside women in knee-length sheaths. So, maybe East is East and West is West, but when Kipling figured the twain wouldn't connect, he hadn't figured on Afghanistan.

I had read that this was a feudal country still dominated by tribal laws. I had heard that the Afghans were a proud and haughty people. I only know they were kind and friendly and warm wherever we went. They were patient with us when we couldn't make ourselves understood in the bazaars. They were eager to smile and wave whenever they saw us on the street. Wherever we walked in the town they swarmed around us by the hundreds, pointing, giggling, chattering. But always friendly. Sometimes even a little too friendly. I happen to have it on very reliable authority that, in at least one crowd, my dear wife was the recipient of an extremely friendly pinch.

Everybody knew us because every single person in the town had been to Jeshyn at least once. When we were in the bazaars shopping for their famous suede leather jackets with the sheep fur lining or the Afghan rugs or the gold embroidered skullcaps which are worn under the turbans or the Persian lamb coats and hats, the shopkeepers greeted us affectionately with the key phrases they remembered from our show. *"Man maolem hastam,"* they shouted as we passed their little booths. "I am the teacher."

"O diwana hastam," they pointed to me and giggled. "He's crazy!"

We did have a little excitement because of Cindy's Parsi. She spoke it so well onstage that wherever she went offstage the locals tried to get her into conversation. This was a little embarrassing for my poor wife because she'd only learned that one speech about the American Government and the American entertainment and the love between our countries. And how often can you shove that into conversation? I mean, those sentences are all very well and good but if someone asks you would you like to taste some of their rice pilau, or have you seen The King's Gardens, or would you like to buy an Afghan carpet bag cheap, you can't just answer, "On behalf of the American Government . . ."

After a while, whenever someone tore off some rapid Parsi in Cindy's direction, she'd just smile so wide it looked as if her throat had been cut and she'd mutter, *"tashakor"* which means "thank you" and takes care of everything. She figured, quit while you're ahead.

American movies are very big here. They change them daily. Even though they run in English, you need a scorecard to follow the plot. Kissing is cut out, sex is taboo, clinches they censor and dialogue often gets scrambled. It's not uncommon to see a hot love scene switch to a battleground. In this early Audie Murphy job that we saw, Our Hero was just zeroing in for a clinch with the heroine when the scene changed to an animated struggle with 30,000 Injuns. What makes it more ridiculous is, this wasn't even a Cowboy-'n'-Injun picture.

The main object when traveling as a good will ambassador is to integrate with the customs of the country. I, who am known as the Barney Oldfield of the AAA, could have integrated with one custom very quickly. In fact, this is one custom I'd like to bring back to America. It's the custom of no traffic tickets. Kabul *polizei* don't give out tickets. They don't give out any because they ain't got any. And even if they had any, they don't have any courts.

Because they have no courts, you can literally get away
with murder here. All you have to do is hide behind the walls
of a nearby town from which there is no extradition. When it
comes to traffic, cops take care of all violators with one
whanggg of their belt buckle. The drivers in Kabul may not
be the greatest in the world, but they sure are the lumpiest.
Of course, it is a little tough for any newcomer to learn their
traffic laws. How are you supposed to know that on a main
highway an ox has the right of way?

Our troupe had been briefed that in Moslem, Buddhist and
Hindu countries, we shouldn't whack anyone on the back. As
it turned out, we remembered the briefing just a couple of
physical contacts too late.

Now, take for instance the Crown Prince of Afghanistan.
He loved us. He came back four times to see the show. He and
his younger brother are jazz buffs. His brother plays the saxophone and he plunks the guitar. His Highness was very eager
to meet everyone in the cast, especially Buddy Rich and the
musicians.

On his fourth trip around, I introduced His Royal Highness
to Al Williams. Our exuberant dancer gushed, "I sure am delighted to meet you, sir, and I sure hope I can play your
country some time." I jumped in quickly. "But this is his country." Al threw his arms around The Royal One and apologized, "Gee, I'm sorry, Prince-y, you don't look like a local!"

You can't really blame our gang. In some of these tiny
kingdoms, where they have more royalty than roads, you can't
tell the princes without a program. Anybody can goof, and our
way through Southeast Asia was paved with a few bloopers
as well as good intentions.

You don't have to travel to Afghanistan to wind up with
egg on your face. Once we were in Honolulu when former
President Eisenhower made his swing through Asia. He was
en route home by way of Hawaii, and Governor Quinn decided to throw a party for Ike to show him the people of the

new fiftieth state were behind him all the way. Cindy and I were invited.

We arrived promptly, and MP's and Secret Service guys checked, rechecked and fluoroscoped us when we showed up. The hors d'oeuvres tables were heaped high with assorted tasties arranged in the form of Marine Corps and White House emblems in honor of the President. It all looked good enough to eat. Since I just happened to be starving, I immediately commenced vacuuming up foodstuffs before I noticed that nobody else was even nibbling. "Maybe they ain't hungry," I said to Cindy, already elbow-deep in the White House that was made of chicken.

"Guess not," agreed Cindy, who'd already gnawed halfway through the Marine Corps hat made of shrimp.

I ignored the stares. I just figured the other guests had recognized me and couldn't tear their eyes away from me. I was just in the process of busting up my fourth flag when I noticed Merriman Smith, the U.P.I. man, gesticulating to me wildly.

"Not now," I shook my head. "Can't you see I'm eating?"

"I know," he growled. "That's what I want to see you about. Don't you know it's not protocol to touch any food until the President has at least seen it?"

I wiped the cocktail sauce from my ruby lips and went to work. I must say it was very embarrassing trying to form Marine Corps hats, anchors and flags out of olive pits, shrimp shells and missing hors d'oeuvres.

Later, while I talked with the President, Cindy was in a corner chatting happily away with a very nice lady named Barbara. She never did catch the last name because Barbara had said she read Cindy's columns and loved them and, naturally, my hammy wife had blocked out everything except that. It was strictly on a first-name basis all the way. It was Cindy and Barbara. Barbara and Cindy.

Merriman and I inched over just as Barbara asked, "Where did you get your gorgeous gown, Cindy?" Said Cindy, strutting like a peacock, "It's an original. It's a Scaasi."

"Oh, I know all about Scaasi," said Barbara. "My mother-in-law has several."

"Oh, yeah?" gushed Cindy. "Well, Scaasi charges a fortune. Your mother-in-law must be loaded, honey. What does she do?"

At which point Merriman and I announced that it was time to leave and waltzed Cindy across the room without her feet touching the ground. "Barbara," her very dear friend, was of course Barbara Eisenhower, Mamie's daughter-in-law.

Meanwhile, back at the ranch in Afghanistan, there was the night that Flash McDonald was holding court at one of our after-show suppers. He was telling a joke and didn't get any response from a handsome gentleman at his table. Undaunted, our boy smashed him across the shoulders with a "Doncha get it, Mac?"

"Mac" turned out to be His Royal Highness, the King's brother. Fortunately, nobody ever took offense at any of our goofs. In fact, if anything, they seemed to like us more for being all too human.

We liked them for their goofs, too. Like the beaut they pulled on our boys for our opening night reception. The Steps, Jerry and Jed were staying at a private house. There was nobody in the house but them, and their entire staff consisted of a gardener. He became their chief cook and pants-presser. He could make a geranium grow like mad. It wasn't his fault he'd never pressed pants before. Four days in the suitcase, however, and the boys' tuxedo trousers looked like they belonged on Emmett Kelly.

They showed the gardener how to fold them and press them. Al then pressed one of the legs as a guide. The gardener couldn't have been more obliging. He followed Al's sample exactly. When the boys put on their pants that night, each one had only the left leg pressed, but the right leg was still crumpled up like a paper bag. All night—at the reception—the rest of us took turns standing in front of their right legs.

Goofs notwithstanding, the American pavilion was an overwhelming success. The only thing that never got off the ground was the TV exhibit. The Afghan has never seen television, so for Jeshyn our Embassy had ordered the country's first sending and receiving set. It came with a complete do-it-yourself kit. Thirty of us tried to put it together. But either one of the parts was missing or that Russian stagehand was in again. So, when we left Kabul, the country was still in the era of live entertainment. Vaudeville isn't dead—it just moved to Afghanistan.

While living the life of a vaudeville trouper, taking care of the language onstage and taking care of me offstage, my darling Cindy was also keeping her drip-drys washed, staying one jump ahead of dysentery, going sightseeing, presiding over the official receptions and writing letters home to her mother. In between the letters to her mother, she was sending material home for her syndicated column and was filing stories for the wire service for which she works, NANA (the North American Newspaper Alliance).

Ambassador Byroade, who is now with the United States Arms Control and Disarmament Agency in Washington, cautioned Cindy about the kind of copy she should or should not file. We were in the back of the busy Ambassador's official limousine as, with flags flying, he whisked us to the airport.

He explained to Cindy that most reporters figure nobody else knows anything more about these out-of-the-way places than they do anyhow. But what's out of the way today isn't out of the way tomorrow. As witness Korea, Laos, the Congo and other spots Americans knew previously only through fiction. One top magazine sexed up Afghanistan to create the impression that the King had a harem. "Wasn't true but it was more interesting," the Ambassador commented dryly.

"The government was very much upset and protested officially to Washington at this vile treatment of their country. That particular magazine was barred here, which in turn hampers our effort to spread democracy through the printed word. Another wrote that the Pathans, the warring tribe of nomads on both sides of the Pak-Afghan border, quote—

'Love to fight even more than they love to lust.' Just so happens lusting is not an outstanding occupation among these people. But what'd he care? It's a catchy phrase. Any news about the Khyber Pass is exciting. So what if he doesn't know the people? So what if he's never seen any of them? This is a little-known part of the world anyway."

The chauffeur, at that point, swerved to avoid an unescorted sheep that was sauntering down the dirt road, which is to Kabul what the Champs Élysées is to gay Paree. Without dropping a comma, the Right Honorable "Hank" Byroade continued. "These people begin to doubt us. They feel such irresponsibility, such misinformation, sways public opinion in our country where public opinion determines the government. We cannot afford the luxury of misinformation just to sell newspapers." Cindy was careful to follow this expert advice on all the pieces she filed from Southeast Asia. But she figured that since I was not an Asiatic, she could still say anything that came into her head about me. And she did. And does.

We were departing from Afghanistan just as the Khyber Pass of fiction was becoming a real plot. "I'm sorry to be leaving in the midst of all this tension," I told the Ambassador.

"And I don't care what anybody says," Cindy cracked, "Joey didn't cause it."

As a gesture of friendship between our countries, the King had presented us with a priceless, hand-loomed Afghan rug.

"It is the custom," Byroade explained, "to give visiting VIP's the prize possessions of the country they visit. This might occur wherever you go."

"Oh, great," said my wife. "We're on our way to Nepal and do you mind telling me what we're gonna do with an elephant in our five-room apartment?"

CHAPTER 5

Nepal – Getting There Is Half the Battle

NEPAL is rushing into the sixteenth century. Katmandu, the capital city, is the furthest you can be from central USA. From here on in, wherever you wander, it's nearer home. Here I was further away from America than I ever thought I'd be and closer to Red China than I ever want to be. Here in Katmandu, ringed by the Himalayan Mountains, we were eighty miles away from the Red border of Tibet. We were— one might say—within spitting distance.

Nepal is considered to be among the most underdeveloped countries on this planet. The tiny picturesque kingdom, with its beautiful lakes, richly cultivated valleys, and snow-covered peaks which include Mt. Everest and Kanchenjunga, is far removed from America figuratively as well as geographically.

It has zillions of gilt-encrusted Hindu and Buddhist temples, but no sanitation. Also no lack of hospitality. Should a stranger knock on a door, he's automatically welcomed to share whatever food, lodging and comforts there are within. The country of nine million people has but eighty miles of railroad. In this area of 54,000 square miles there are but 300 miles of navigable dirt road. Navigable meaning just barely "jeepable." Except for occasional bicycles, jeeps are the mode of transport for foreign dignitaries. Locals make it on foot.

The poorer Nepalese, the majority of the populace, go to bed by candlelight. They have no electricity or oil. The average housewife rises about 5:00 A.M., brushes her teeth by chewing a twig from the neame tree, which has medicinal properties, then hauls her morning water from public taps or community wells.

She has no wagon, no cart. In the whole kingdom there's practically no sign of that recent invention called the wheel. Brick and wood are toted on one's back with straps around the forehead. There is not even a revolving wheel in the wells. The women lower their buckets by hand and carry the water in pails hung from a pole across their shoulders. Or you see them with their swaying walk, balancing big metal containers on one hip.

The Nepalese homes feature a puja, or corner, where stand their gods. Each morning the woman of the house lays flowers and food at the feet of her favorite god. Holy water especially for washing the icons is hauled at certain intervals by the barefoot housewife who vocally heralds her coming so that she's accorded the right of way. If she is accidentally brushed by some passer-by while carrying this holy water, the whole process must be repeated, for she and her burden will have been contaminated.

Unlike many American husbands, the Nepali menfolk are never left to shift for themselves when it comes to breakfast. By the time they rise, around 6:00 A.M., a yummy spread of tea, rice and vegetables awaits them. The routine seldom varies. Food is cooked on a tiny, built-in mud hearth, or on a clay pot over a wood fire; the pots and pans are scrubbed with the ashes which contain lye.

If her husband is a farmer, the wife then helps in the field by harvesting or plowing side by side with the oxen. If he's a woodcutter, she chops wood or hauls it. A young mother carries her infant papoose-style while doing the chores. There are no baby carriages, no babysitters. Each child has the responsibility of the one immediately beneath him. Children five years old carry children two years old on their hips. This newly developing nation's literacy rate is still low, and few children attend school.

Come washday, if there's no river nearby, the housewife squats on her doorstep, using a rock as a washboard, a pail of water instead of the river and animal fat for soap. She presses her saris and cholis (blouses) with an iron heated over charcoal. Washdays are not all drudgery, however. They take the place of our bridge games, club meetings or afternoon teas, since the average Nepali woman has no social occasions whatsoever, goes nowhere outside her house, has no girl friends over and isn't even allowed to be present when the master of the household entertains. She serves, she hovers in the background to be on call if needed, but never partakes of the pleasantries, never participates in the proceedings, never mingles with the male company. It is on the doorstep that the women congregate to exchange local chit-chat and gossip about the other women.

If served at all, lunch is tea and bread. Again at 5:00 P.M. a meal of rice and home-grown vegetables, probably potatoes, okra or beans, is eaten. There ain't any such thing as refrigerators. There also ain't any such thing as leftovers.

The evening's festivities consist of conversation within the family. Television, movies, radio and night clubs are nonexistent. The same thing applies to books and periodicals, since most of the people neither read nor write. Although Nepali children play Yankee games like hopscotch, until recently the country has been almost wholly untouched by the Western influence. Until ten years ago, foreigners were barred, except for occasional mountain-climbing expeditions. Today there are a few sportsmen on elephant and tiger hunts, but otherwise tourism is still low. There are not even many missionaries, since proselytizing is forbidden.

Among the 108,000 inhabitants of Katmandu there are no savings institutions. Dry ears of corn hanging outside one's door denote wealth. The more corn a man has, the more cash he has. If he's very rich he puts his wealth into gold and silver ornaments and parades the bankroll by hanging it on his wife. (This is one custom we have in America, too.) The color of mourning is white. The day that's commemorated is the anniversary of a loved one's death. When a brother or father passes on, the men shave their heads. The bereavement is further marked by wearing no leather and refusing to bathe or trim hair or fingernails for approximately ten days to two weeks.

When it comes to marriage, all negotiations are begun by the parents and then finished up by an astrologer. If the stars are not right, the union is off. And Nepali daughters obey Nepali mamas. (Which is one custom we do not have in America.) If the marriage is astrologically proper, the wedding must take place on a holy day suitable to each family's gods. The precise day's precise hour is determined by lunar calendar. The engagement is sealed by a gift of betel nuts sent to the bride's relatives. The girl's kin then give a dowry of furniture, animals and food. On the seventh day of the wedding ceremony, the bride, whose father probably betrothed her at the age of eight, meets the bridegroom's family gods. She then moves into his family's home.

Fixed price for a divorce is 250 rupees, or roughly about thirty dollars. The female seldom instigates proceedings, because unmarried women are liabilities in Nepal's social system and if you're husbandless you immediately lose all standing in the community. Should this rarity occur, the husband gets the news by those same betel nuts which are shipped back to him and placed beneath his pillow. If the male wants out (which is also infrequent, since he's permitted several wives, all of whom with their children usually dwell together in harmony), he simply banishes the rejected spouse to her parents' home. It is an unwritten law that she may never darken his door again until he sends for her.

I dug this cozy custom and I lost no time in mentioning it to my Cindy when we arrived. Poor Cindy, who was standing on her lower lid, was almost too tired even to wisecrack. With a song in our hearts and a pain in our passports, we'd arrived after a roller-coaster flight from New Delhi, India, the over-night stopover between Kabul and Katmandu. "Will you please tell me," she yawned, "why we had to be up at five in the morning to make an 8:00 A.M. flight which naturally didn't budge until twelve noon? Will you please tell me why we had to be up at five o'clock in the morning?"

"Because," I explained, "the plane was scheduled to leave at 8:00 A.M."

"Well, how could it be scheduled to leave at 8:00 A.M., when I happen personally to know that the pilot didn't even get waked up until half-past eleven?"

"I only know that's the way it was booked."

"Well, who's your travel agent, Khrushchev?"

Never let it be said that I'm the type husband what takes needling from a wife. I really let her have it. "Oh yeah?" I said. "Would you like to ship me back my betel nuts?"

"I don't get it," my doll continued, "but seems to me that wherever you're going—if it's Scranton, Wiesbaden or my mother's house—whatever thing it is you're traveling on, it always leaves around six in the morning. What is it with you?"

"Maybe it's a Communist plot," I said.

Of course, one of the main problems was that we didn't exactly have a wide menu of appetizing flights to choose from. Our contract stipulated that we fly either Air India or Indian Air Lines. It sounds good, doesn't it? But when you realize that Indian Air Lines is a subsidiary of Air India and vice versa, you don't need a swami to tell you that you don't exactly have a choice. Air India is the international carrier. Indian Air Lines is the intercontinental carrier. Both of them are owned by the Indian Government. So, when we were on the continent of Asia, it was either Indian Air Lines or a slow boat to China.

Suppose, for the sake of argument, Pan American had a big, beautiful, empty plane. And suppose it was going in our direction. And suppose it was a nonstop, three-hour, door-to-door job, leaving at noon. That's nice, huh? But do you think we could take it? No! Certainly not. If there was one Indian Air Lines flight out that day and it was only headed in our general direction, and it left at five in the morning, and it had three stops with an eight-hour layover in Tibet where we'd pick up a connecting mule to our destination—*that's* the flight we'd be on.

Don't misunderstand, it wasn't the fault of Indian Air Lines. That was the only service they had that day. And they were very nice to us all the way down the line. The stewardesses in their saris on Air India were beautiful. The food was delicious. The officials were most courteous. Their safety record is second to none. The same with Indian Air Lines. It's just that there were a couple of times you got the feeling that maybe the plane had made a sudden transformation into a flying carpet. You don't exactly get a feeling of security when you're thousands of feet up in the air and the pilot saunters down the aisle resplendent in his peak cap, gold braid uniform and bare feet.

The reason we were contracted with Air India and Indian Air Lines exclusively was the fact that Uncle Sam was our travel agent. We couldn't go on a MATS (Military Air Transport Service), since the Administration had instituted a new ruling that you have to pay for a seat on a MATS just as you would on a commercial liner. So, since we weren't saving any money and the Military and Defense had priorities anyway, we were booked on commercial liners.

The first rule is to favor domestic carriers like TWA or

Pan Am, since the President has said he wants American money to stay in American hands. However, the United States Government has frozen assets in India and Air India made a deal whereby we could pay them off in rupees. This proved just as beneficial to our country because we used up some of our frozen assets and kept our dollars here. Now, this is all very good for Uncle Sam, but for his twenty-five nephews and nieces it was a big pain in their itinerary.

On this trip to "The Land of Temples," we were ticketed as usual on Indian Air Lines. But even if we were flying Royal Nepal Airlines, it's still not that easy to get in and out of Katmandu Valley. You gotta go when they want to take you and not when you want to go. It's like with the cabdrivers in New York.

This was the tail end of their monsoon season, when Katmandu is steamy afternoons and rainy come night. There's only one road, and come monsoon season that's washed out, so the only exit and entrance is by air. And in bad weather the DC-3—the only aircraft that can set down here—can't land, thereby virtually isolating Nepal. There are very few phones. There is only one cable office, and that is in the Indian Embassy. Airmail is on a par with the Pony Express, because in this out-of-the-way spot planes do not arrive or leave more than a few times a week. The only thing you are sure of in this part of the world is the hot breath of Red China.

In Katmandu we worked in what once was a cement water tank which somehow got filled in and converted into the Phora Durbar Theater. In every country we were sponsored by a local organization. All the money we raised from our appearances remained in that community for their charities. In Nepal we were sponsored by the American Women's Organization of Nepal, or "AWON" as it is affectionately called. Started in 1953 by the wife of the first Director of the United States Operations Mission in Nepal, AWON boasts a membership of seventy today. Its funds aid the sick and needy

Nepalese, stimulate interest in Nepalese culture and promote friendship between the women of our two countries. So, every rupee that was cast upon the box office to see our show came back buttered.

When arrangements were made for the Joey Adams Variety Show to appear in Katmandu, the original plan was to parcel us all out to private homes à la Kabul. It was a great idea. But just as the landladies were making ready their guest rooms, some boy genius realized it wouldn't work. For one thing there are no cars. There are only a few jeeps that service the whole Embassy and USIS and whatever dignitaries are coming in and out. If the twenty-five of us were burrowed into twenty-five different nests, it would require a fleet to gather us together for our various appearances.

Another thing. Each of us wanted to bring his bag of tricks to hospitals and schools and whatever other performances they could load on to the schedule. This meant that two dozen people had last minute arrangements every five minutes. And since there are no phones in any of the homes and none of us can read smoke signals, they decided to put us in the Royal Hotel. This at least would serve as a control center. The transportation problem was immediately solved in the form of one jeep out front. The communications problem was instantly solved in the form of the one phone in the lobby.

Opening night, Cindy and I also used our hotel as a dressing room, since backstage facilities at the Phora Durbar Theater were not. I put on my beautiful mohair tuxedo with the satin bow tie under the collar and my patent leather pumps with the tassels. I must admit I looked like a doll. Cindy threw on her Scaasi—the same number that had gassed Barbara Eisenhower three years before. I must admit she looked fair. Like two fugitives from an opening night at the Met, Cinderella and her Prince Charming swept out of their room and paraded majestically down the circular staircase through the lobby, out the door, down the steps and into their waiting coach—a mudspattered, olive drab Willys Overland jeep.

AWON and USIS had arranged a series of receptions for us following opening night. A big fringe benefit of Cultural Exchange is to encourage offstage mingling. I like people, so for me being pleasant isn't difficult. On the other hand, remembering names is a little tougher. Even if I'm in home territory—say, like in Iowa—names don't stay with me. But at least in the States if you get in trouble you can always cover up by calling someone "Mac" or "Pal." But you just can't do this on the striped-pants circuit. It ain't nice you should call a cabinet minister "Buddy" or an ambassador "Kiddo." Consequently, I'd try to crib the guest list in advance so my crew and I could bone up on the Who's Who and the What's What of every town we were in.

But no matter what you called them it was not too easy to make conversation with Asian women. They are brought up in the centuries-old tradition where women are shy, demure and modest. Unlike the grand and glorious emancipated USA, in Asia the man wears the pants in his family. And that's not because the Asian woman doesn't look good in slacks. It's simply because in Asia the man's always been the boss. As a result, the women on this continent are retiring and they let the man of the house do the talking. And we're trying to Westernize them? Better they should Easternize us. I'd like to leave my wife there a few months and maybe it'll be catching.

The receptions in Nepal were held in the homes of the officials of the Embassy and USIS. In order to enable the maximum number of Nepalis to meet the new Americans, they divided our troupe into a half dozen groups. At the party to which we were assigned, there were some twenty-five townspeople plus their Royal Highnesses, Prince and Princess Himalaya Beer Bikram Shah, and His Excellency, Viswa Bandhu Thapa, the Minister of Education. The Minister and the Prince speak excellent English. Over the hot soup, they said how pleased they were with our success but since all our performances were already sold out, they regretted that thousands of their countrymen were going to be deprived of seeing us.

During the rice course I talked it over with Henry Stebbins, our Ambassador, and it was decided we'd throw in an extra matinée at the Phora Durbar Theater. This theater, however, only seats about 700. So, in addition, we scheduled two outdoor performances that would have an unlimited capacity and be free to everybody.

By one in the morning I was having difficulty holding up my head, let alone my end of the conversation. We'd been up since five o'clock in the morning, but, natch, us commoners couldn't amscray before Their Highnesses, and they were having a ball, so by the time we got to bed we'd been up some twenty-one and a half hours, nonstop. If we'd come there to climb Mt. Everest we couldn't have been more exhausted, and our two shows the next day loomed higher than that mountain.

CHAPTER 6

Katmandu Valley:
Way Off-Broadway

OUR FREE OUTDOOR SHOW was held in a huge swampy area which somehow got filled in and converted into a stadium. Only it never really got filled in and it never really got converted. It wound up just what it was originally: a big, mushy open lot. We needed the wide open spaces to accommodate the thousands who couldn't get to see us indoors and who couldn't afford it even if they could.

We weren't able to hold the show in the evening because we had our scheduled performances at the Phora Durbar Theater then. We couldn't hold it at high noon because it was much too hot. Therefore, it was suggested that the show begin at 4:30 because that was sundown. But this presented another problem: lights. It's a little tough to plug a socket into a clump of grass. And Jerry Bell figured that by the time the show was three-fourths over, it would be pretty dark out. So he hollered for help. It was the United States Information Service to the rescue. They commandeered their motor pool and presented their jeeps ready for action. Our fleet of two khaki green limousines was backed up, jacked up, ignitions were switched on, headlights were focussed and *voilà!* Instant spotlights!

Our dressing rooms were Army tents, only the GI's from whom we borrowed them were those famous Nepali Gurkhas. This country is actually called "The Land of the Gallant Gurkha." These are the same Gurkhas who were the world-remembered guerrilla fighters of World War II. Our boys who fought with them acclaim them as the roughest, toughest, bravest, most fearless commando force of all time.

Our room clerk at the hotel best described the guts of the Gurkha with this story:

One division, who had just joined the paratroopers, was instructed to jump when they reached 5,000 feet in the air. The hardiest of the Gurkhas refused saying, "We don't mind jumping 500 feet, but 5,000 is too much even for us." "But," said the Captain, "if you jump 500 feet you won't have enough time to open the parachute." "Oh," grinned the Gurkha leader, "if we have a parachute we don't mind jumping 5,000 feet!"

Their headquarters were just down the road a piece from our stadium. So, instead of dashing over neighborly-like and borrowing a cup of sugar and some eggs, we dashed over friendly-like and borrowed a couple of pup tents and some Gurkhas. There wasn't a damn thing to guard us against, but I'll tell you we all felt safe at the sight of those two uniformed soldiers with the snappy hats who stood watch in front of our dressing room flaps.

Everybody cooperated. They couldn't have been nicer. Our Ambassador even sent over thermoses of cold boiled water and buckets of boiled ice cubes. Our platform was constructed from bamboo flooring which was hacked from the countryside in the morning. Plywood, suitable for our dancers and SOS'd from our New Delhi Embassy in the afternoon, was laid over the bamboo. It had rained in the morning so the ground was flooded. Over this swamp was erected our home-made showcase. The only trouble was that as the afternoon progressed and the audience settled down, so did our stage. Near the end of the show we were halfway into the ground. If I hadn't hustled the finale on in a hurry, we'd have been buried altogether. I can just see the tombstone: Joey Adams & Company Died Here!

Our lend-love program also reached into the public square of Patan. Patan is the second city of the valley and is two miles southeast of Katmandu. It is an ancient center of Buddhist culture. It was near Nepal about 2,600 years ago that Buddha himself was born, so naturally the country reveres him.

We set up shop on a tiered terrace of a temple in Durbar Square which is the ancient Royal Palace area surrounded by dozens of gilt-encrusted temples, shrines and sculptured monuments. This constitutes the Fifth Avenue of the town. Framing our band of minstrels was the Hiranya Varna Mahavihar Golden Temple of Lord Buddha, whose walls are decorated with scenes from his life; the Mahaboudh Temple, a masterpiece of Buddhist architecture and Nepalese terracotta on which every brick is engraved with the image of Buddha; the Hindu temple of the god Machindra (Red Face) built in 1408 A.D., and the Krishna Mandir Temple with scenes from the Maha-Bharat and Ramayana Hindu epics engraved on its walls.

On this main drag we packed thousands of Nepali children. They came out of everywhere to follow our pied pipers. They were suspended from the ledges of the temples, they hung from the branches of the trees, they stood on the shoulders of their parents and they were perched on the rooftops. Behind every curved moulding, in back of each cupola and from every window ledge we could see the faces of laughing children. Some even joined our show onstage. The joy and laughter we brought to remote Nepal was heard round the world. *The New York Times* even carried a rave review.

As usual, our shows were completely clean. Which is more than I can say for the famous erotic etchings in and on some of the Hindu temples. These colorful carvings leave nothing to the imagination. Here, it is part of a religion. Like one of the musicians in the troupe said, "Man, them cats must have had an eleventh commandment some place!" Tourists come from thousands of miles to see this art. All I know is, my principal used to smack me for scratching a lot less on the bathroom walls. I was so repelled by what these carved cats were up to, that I could force myself to make the tour only three times.

Although our show was clean, it was a major achievement for the members of our troupe to stay ditto. I mean, when you're traveling it ain't easy to stay glamorous and chic at best, but on this tour it was murder. Dry cleaning, like TNT, is at your own risk. In fact, it's an explosive issue.

I had a stunning three-button herringbone tweed suit that had one large spot on it. I gave it to my wife to have it cleaned. This was my second mistake. The first was leaking the gravy on my stunning three-button herringbone tweed. At home my wife is a clod in the housekeeping department. When it comes to housekeeping, not only can't my wife do anything but she can never seem to find the right people who can.

My stunning three-button herringbone tweed with the one large spot came back with the one large spot broken into five smaller ones. "Look, will you please look at what they did to my herringbone?" I sobbed to Cindy.

"Whassa matter," she asked sweetly, "didn't they remove the spot?"

"They didn't exactly remove the spot," I pointed out. "They just redistributed it."

"I can't understand it. I gave it to the best cleaner in town. In fact, I think he's the only cleaner in town. I mean, recommended by the Diners' Club he isn't."

"And another thing, my herringbone now stinks like a herring."

"What do you want from me? Gasoline is the cleansing element around here. I sent a dress to the same cleaner. It was returned spotless. It's pungent but it's spotless. And how about my velvet coat?"

"What's with your velvet coat?" I asked, tenderly stroking my bruised three-button herringbone.

"Well, they ironed it on the right side. The velvet now resembles sealskin. On a clear night it shines for miles."

"Why didn't you give it to the dhobi?"

"I gave it to the dhobi."

"You did? What's a dhobi?"

"A dhobi, you dopey, is a washerman. He suggested I sponge it with warm vinegar to restore the nap."

"So?"

"So, I did. Now it looks like sealskin, but it smells like vinegar."

Our boardinghouse was named the Royal Hotel because it once was one. Once upon a time it was the Rana Palace, traditional home of the ruling family. Up until 1950, when came the revolution, the prime ministers and their kinfolk parked their crowns there. Since 1950, the closest it has come to housing royalty was putting up our Prince Spencer, who shared a double room on the second floor with Al Williams.

The owner-manager of the Royal is Boris Lisonovitch, a White Russian, who emigrated to Katmandu by way of Calcutta because he found favor with the royal family a couple of kings ago. Seems Boris was a cabaret performer. And seems Calcutta is where the Nepalese go to enjoy. And seems the father of the present King, Mahendra, and Boris became quite chummy. As a result, Boris packed his balalaika and his Danish wife, Inga, and set out to acquire fame, fortune and a hotel in the valley of Katmandu.

By Moscow, Calcutta, Katmandu or even Broadway standards, good old Boris is a swinger from way back. He really goes. According to those of my cast who stayed up with him, at Boris' open-house parties the vodka really flows like boiled water. Boris is a great host and it's for sure that he's the brightest light in his establishment. Everything around him is dim by comparison. And I do mean dim.

The electricity is so poor that fireflies give more light. Theoretically, the voltage in the hotel and in the rest of the country is 220. Come eventide when everyone flicks on the lights, the current dips. The only time it hits 220 is when the authors of those guidebooks pass through. Just when our girls had to apply make-up for the show, the voltage invariably shriveled to around 40 and—give or take a few volts— hovered there until dawn. They had to resort to candles. Their poor faces were stuck so close to the mirror they kept bashing their heads against it.

The last vestige of the ex-palace's once regal splendor is the Rama Room, a long, narrow ballroom which serves as a royal rogues' gallery. Lining the walls are almost life-size, gold-framed oil portraits of the Who's Who and the Who Was of Nepal. Now it's used as an alley. We had to cut through it to get to our room, which was off an outside porch on the second floor. Or to get from our room to the dining hall.

Late at night the great Rama Room became a rumpus room. It was the only spot in the whole hotel—or even in the whole town—where you could scratch together enough light to read or write. That's because of the once splendiferous crystal chandelier, which still hangs majestically by a tarnished gold chain in the center of the room. No longer does it shed its glorious light on kings and queens who are wining and dining. While we were there it flickered half-heartedly down on a troupe of vaudevillians who were painting their toenails, writing letters home, eating crackers and peanut butter that they'd bought in the Kabul commissary or playing a hot hand of gin rummy to while away the hours. Maybe the chandelier had seen better days, but never more gratitude. Like moths around a flame, we gratefully clustered night after night around this one bright spot in Boris' famous rooming house.

Water at the hotel ran during certain hours only. This we discovered the hard way. Like between 11:00 A.M. and 5:00

P.M., it's shut off. One morning I soaped up, turned the tap—
and nothing! As I slowly stiffened away to the consistency of
plaster of Paris, some cold water issued forth in a torrential
trickle. Cindy finally had enough bottled water heated for me
to demarbleize myself.

Hairdressing becomes unimportant in this part of the world
when even hair washing becomes unbelievable. My wife's hairdresser in Afghanistan had two living-room chairs back to
back. Across the tops she had bolted a large tin baking dish,
scooped on one end for a neck rest. The other end was con-
nected to a pipe that emptied into a bucket. From a pail, fresh
water was sloshed onto the customer. It ran down into the
baking dish, through the pipe and into the bucket which was
periodically emptied. After this primitive hair wash, Cindy
still had to use her head for figuring the tab. The German
beautician, married to an Afghan, figured her bill in marks,
translated it to afs, whereupon Cindy broke it into dollars.

And when it comes to hair dryers, nobody guarantees results. Midway, the current often conks out, and either the
women exit with wet snails on their heads or sit for hours until
power is restored. One American stationed here brought her
own dryer. Her husband attached a generator to the refriger-
ator to maintain constant voltage. So, whenever this woman
needs to dry her ringlets for a special Embassy function, she
plugs herself into the icebox.

When touring hereabouts, beauty care should be slashed to
a minimum. Long hair and nails should be cut. Our girls stuck
mainly to drip-dry fabrics. They all took plenty of facial tissues
and packed special soap for use with hard water. They did
their best to stay glamorous, although glamour is not what you
would call "big business" here.

The average Nepalese are light years removed from what's
going on at Hollywood and Vine. The poor people of Nepal
are very poor. This fact came home to me strongly when one
of my troupe asked someone for a cleaning rag. Answered our
English-speaking helper, "We don't have any rags. Here we
wear them."

The Joey Adams Yankee Doodle Dandies, ready to take off on their good-will tour for Uncle Sam. Left to right: Joan Chase, Maceo Anderson, Buddy Rich, Deanda Sylte, Cindy, Deanna Sylte, Joan Sylte, Jackie Green, Al Williams, Chaz Chase, Celeste Evans, Joey, Bonnie Shirley, John Shirley, Flash McDonald, Wyatt Ruther—(up the stairs) Rolf Erickson, Jed Horner, Sam Most, Prince Spencer, John Morris, Dave Lucas, Jerry Bell, and Mike Manieri.

Left above: Ambassador Henry Byroade and Cindy, in a sea of turban tops, watch the show at Jeshyn Fair in Afghanistan.

Left below: Buddy Rich on the Afghan drums collects a crowd on a Kabul street corner, while a local dancer and I strut our stuff.

I'm teaching this crowd of Afghan youngsters how to applaud. Until they learned, the silence was deafening.

Left: Chaz Chase clowns for the kids in Nepal.

Our troupe gets a lesson in showmanship from a small Nepalese musician. This is true Cultural Exchange.

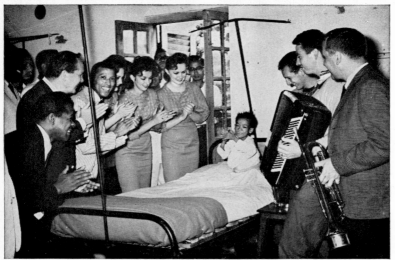

We bring our funniest bedside manner to the children in the hospital at Katmandu.

The Queen of Cambodia has a little trouble pinning a medal on Cindy's ruffled Scaasi gown.

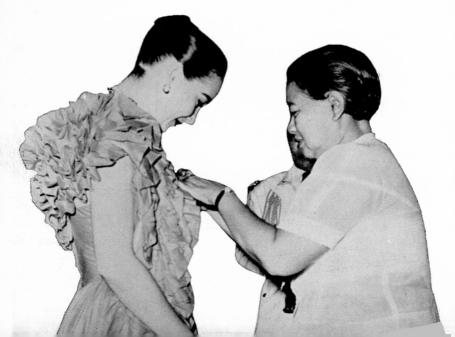

Even Prince Boun Oum of Laos wants a souvenir balloon.

John and Bonnie Shirley fill outstretched hands with their balloon creations—souvenirs of American friendship.

Left above: The King and Us. (Cindy and I thank His Majesty, Phumiphon Aduldet of Thailand, for the gifts he presented to us and the troupe.)

Left below: Chairman of Entertainment and Special Events for the Boy Scouts of New York, I manage to do a performance for the Scouts of Vientiane.

Mrs. Adams making like a schoolmarm in Laos. To her, "closet" is a must in any language.

The troupe is welcomed in Saigon by Vietnamese stars Tran Van Trach, singer with the "lion head mane," and Miss Thanh Nga.

Right above: As a striped-pants emissary, I am introduced to President and Mrs. Sukarno of Indonesia by Ambassador and Mrs. Howard P. Jones.

Right below: As a comic, I read jokes in the local language right out of my hat. Cindy and I do a bit with Tran Van Trach.

Vietnamese orphans: I'd fly a million miles for one of their smiles!

Left above: The Sylte Sisters, Step Brothers and I go into our song and dance at a Veterans' Hospital in Vietnam.

Left below: President Sukarno gets into the act at the Command Performance in Bogor Palace.

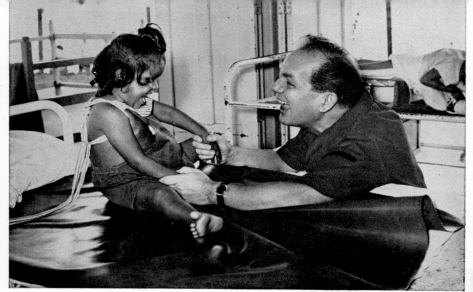

Laughing Lalida, age 4, stole my heart at St. Andrew's Hospital in Singapore.

The Step Brothers and I entertaining the lepers in the Beggars' Home in Chembur, India.

The Voice of America in Bombay, where we get in some plugs for Uncle Sam.

Prime Minister Nehru receives us in his office and receives a copy of my book in return. We look more thrilled than he does.

Ambassador Julius C. Holmes presents me to the Empress of Iran. I wonder if Her Majesty found me as funny on-stage.

H — O — M — E !

Nepal's progressive young monarch, King Mahendra, is unceasing in his efforts to raise the social, economic and educational standards of his country. He is working with our State Department's Agency for International Development (AID), which started to help Nepal develop a public school system eight years ago.

His Majesty has decreed that vocational training must begin in the first grade. The new technical school will have courses in internal-combustion engines, general mechanics, metal work, foundry work, electrical wiring, welding, general science, mechanical drawing and commercial work. A completely mechanized farm, with a four-year course in farm management, is planned as part of the school. Nepal's new school system already is exerting considerable influence in the former hermit kingdom of the Himalayas. Illiteracy has been reduced from more than 98 per cent in 1954 to less than 85 per cent today.

Of course, the steps that have been taken to help the social and economic level of the country are important to the Westernization of Nepal. But when you see the people's receptivity to joy, their acceptance of friendship and their open-faced and open-hearted simplicity, you begin to wonder just a little bit if it's so important to have mascara or washing machines or frozen TV dinners.

Maybe it's more important to have peace of mind, to have close-knit families, to have contentment. Maybe they're better off if they don't have to keep up with the Joneses. Maybe it's wrong to attempt Westernization, because Westernization could only bring them a whole new set of problems. Sure, their standard of living isn't as high as ours, but then neither are their prices. For instance, at a jewelry bazaar on Indra Chowk I bought Cindy a long rope of carnelian, amber, agate and other semi-precious beads. It was three dollars even. Several months later in New York I saw a similar string on sale at a Madison Avenue antique shop. The price tag said: $150 plus tax.

I loved the character of these people. I loved the simplicity of these people. I loved the serenity of their countryside. I loved the price of their beads. I even loved their cleaners. I regret that I had but one suit to give to this country. And I was sorry when we had to pull out.

Well, like the MC says, "A funny thing happened to us on the way to Bangkok." Nobody got sick. We were all getting our land legs back. From Kabul to Katmandu, our company had been dropping like flies. It looked as if ours was the only peacetime battalion that was going to need a built-in medic. We had a little trouble adjusting to everything all at once. The altitude in Kabul was so high and the air so rarefied that we were sent there two days in advance of our first show in order to get acclimated. And with all the tension and excitement and rugged schedule and constant traveling, almost everyone in the cast took their turn in sick bay.

But little by little, we were beginning to build up an immunity. Between the injections we took before we left and the ailments we developed after we arrived, there was very little left that could affect our stalwart little company—unless, maybe, a stagecoach ran over us in Bangkok.

The day before we left, The New Light Circle, the variety performers of Katmandu, prepared a little entertainment in our honor. In turn, I made them honorary lifetime members of the American Guild of Variety Artists. And with their songs and their dances and their good wishes ringing in our memory, we left Katmandu for Bangkok.

Once aboard, I discovered my next-seat passenger on the Indian Air Lines kite we were flying was the Red Chinese Ambassador. I wished him a safe journey. I had no choice. After all, we were on the same plane.

CHAPTER 7

Adams and the King of Siam

ALL MY LIFE I've wanted to play the Palace. I finally got my chance. Only this wasn't the RKO Palace on 47th and Broadway. This was the Chitralada Palace in Bangkok, Thailand. Here the booker was the King of Siam. This was a Command Performance for Their Majesties, King Phumiphon Aduldet and Queen Sirikit, and the royal family and the royal hangers-on.

Our room at the Erewan Hotel the afternoon of the Command Performance was like a Mack Sennett comedy. We only had an hour to get ready. We had waited out at the airfield for a bus which was supposed to meet our plane and whisk us to the hotel. It didn't. About forty minutes after we cooled our heels in the hot sun, it chugged up slowly. That particular day they had picked to repair the main highway—the only highway—leading from the airport to Bangkok. Instead of the usual two congested lanes, we had only one bumper-to-bumper lane. Traffic was backed up clear to Rangoon.

When we finally crept into the Erewan, we hurled our hot, sticky bodies into the air-conditioned room and began to unpack like maniacs. We were racing against time. It was like playing that game, "Beat the Clock."

Cindy and I were hollering orders to each other. "Get out my blue mohair suit," I yelled as I dashed into the shower. "And call the valet and have him come immediately to press it and tell him I need it in ten minutes. Tell him it's a Command Performance. Tell him it's life and death. Tell him anything."

"Hey, where'd you pack my iron?" Cindy screamed, banging on the bathroom door.

"How do I know? What am I, the iron keeper? That's all I got on my mind now is an iron? What do you need an iron for?" I sputtered above the noise of the shower.

"What did you say?" Cindy asked. "I can't hear you. Will you stop with that shower already and tell me where you put my iron?"

I turned off the shower. "What do you need an iron for?" I asked, irately.

"What do you mean what do I need an iron for? I've got to iron my dress. That's what I need an iron for. What did you think I wanted with it? You think I want to play badminton with it?" she snapped. "My red linen sheath is wrinkled."

"So take another dress," I said, turning on the shower. "You got nothin' but dresses. They can't all be wrinkled."

"What?" she hollered. "I can't hear you! What are you muttering about? All I want to know is where is my iron?"

I turned off the shower again. "I said," I said through my teeth, "that you should wear another dress. This is no time to tell me you've got nothing to wear. You've got nothing but dresses. Pick another dress. Forget about that one cockomaimie red linen sheath."

"Don't you understand? I've got to wear it," Cindy hollered through the door. "It's the only dress I have with a hat."

"So what?" I said. "What do you need a hat for?"

"Because Ambassador Young's wife told Chaz Chase's wife, Joan, and me that it's considered proper for us to wear hats in front of the King and Queen. The girls who are in stage costume are excused, of course, but since Joan and I are in regular dress, she said we should wear hats. So the only hat I've got with me goes with the red linen sheath. And the red linen sheath is wrinkled. So get your fat, pudgy body out of that shower and find me my bloody iron before I kill one of us."

I don't know if it was the hot air or what, but something snafued the prevailing atmospheric conditions. I only know that suddenly our air conditioner went on the fritz altogether. After that, the whole thing was a blur. The engineer came up to fix the air conditioner. He came up with an assistant and a ladder. Both were in the center of the room. Unmindful of the pandemonium that was going on around him, he was cheerfully banging away on the pipes.

The valet joined our gay foursome to find out just what it was I wanted done with my suit and to tell me he couldn't do it anyway because it was getting near closing and besides the steam was shut off and would tomorrow morning at ten o'clock be all right?

Buddy Rich was screaming from his room next door that his damn laundry was missing and that somebody better find his damn laundry in a hurry because all he knows is when he checked in he had that damn laundry and now that damn laundry is gone and if he doesn't get that damn laundry right away he won't be able to do any performance let alone a Command Performance.

While Buddy was screaming and clopping the wall, I got on the phone to find out about the laundry. My wife, who'd found the iron, was busy pressing the red linen sheath on top of my suitcase. All through this the air conditioner man and his aide-de-camp were in business for themselves in the center of my room.

Our room was the size of a walk-in closet. It had twin beds, one chair and a luggage rack. "If anybody else walks in they're going to have to lie down," Cindy muttered, laying out the red linen sheath on the bed. Right on cue, Donald Neuchterlein entered. Don is the tall, handsome, crew-cut Cultural Attaché of the United States Information Service in Bangkok. It was his job to worry. Naturally there's no percentage in worrying alone so he came over to worry with us. He chose well.

There wasn't any room for him to pace up and down. "Listen," he said nervously as he sat down on the bed—on top of Cindy's red linen sheath. "It's getting late. Willya be ready in time?"

"I'd have been ready long ago if this weren't an alley," Cindy answered as she pulled her red linen sheath out from under him.

"Okay," he said. "I'll meet you in the lobby in ten minutes. Now don't forget what the protocol man said. Don't forget you all have to line up in a semicircle before the show to be presented to Their Majesties when they arrive. And don't forget that after the show you'll walk out single file. Now remember, it's first Joey, then Cindy, then Buddy Rich. After that, all the girls followed by all the boys. And when you meet the King and Queen the girls curtsy and the men bow. And Cindy, don't forget to wear your hat."

Cindy was doing a waltz with the air conditioner man, trying to get past him so that she could weave her way into the bathroom to finish dressing. "Don't you worry," Cindy said as she disappeared out of sight. "I'm worried enough for both of us."

"And don't forget to do the new speech like we rehearsed it. Not the old one," hollered Don to her as he, the air conditioner man, the air conditioner man's helper and the ladder all made their exit together.

"Tell Buddy," I yelled to his back, "that his laundry is on the way up."

When Cindy stepped out of the bathroom all dressed in her

red linen sheath, matching hat and little white wristie gloves, she looked as if she really belonged at the Palace. "How do I look?" she said.

"Like a queen. How do I look?"

"Like a slob. Take off your pants, I'll iron them."

As the world's best-dressed valet was pressing my pants, I asked, "Are you nervous?"

"Yeah. Are you?"

"A little. Let's face it, girl, I and you are peasants. Before this trip, where did we ever see a king or a queen, except, maybe in a card game?"

" 'Twas rumored," she needled, "that you are an anti-royalist. True or false, sir?"

"Rot says I," I said. "Besides, I don't know what it means. I hear that Their Majesties are very gracious people. Remember two years ago when we were at the Royal Hawaiian Hotel in Honolulu at the same time they were?"

"Remember? How could I forget? We were on the same floor. Like neighbors we were. We were so close that I could have rushed over and borrowed a cup of emeralds."

"Everybody there loved them. Everybody all over America loved them when they made their State Visit," I said, as I put on my hot pants.

"I hope everything comes off all right," Cindy sighed. "The only tough part about this whole thing is that it's on-the-job training for us. After all, where does an American go to school to take a course in kings and queens?"

"You're so right," I agreed as I handed her my jacket to press. "Where would we know from royalty? Did we have a Changing of the Guard in front of my father's shul in the East Harlem section of New York? Did we curtsy and bow over an egg cream at the candy store on the corner of Pitkin and Saratoga in the Brownsville section of Brooklyn? And how about you? You had protocol in that three-room apartment in the Bronx?"

"Protocol? We didn't even had steam heat! If you really

want to know something, my grandmother would have thought I was coming up in the world if I just met an assistant manager from somewhere."

On our way downstairs in the elevator, Cindy said, "You know, even famous people who've had years of training can make a goof with royalty."

"I don't think we have anything to worry about," I said. "We had all our goofs in Afghanistan. We should be goofed out by now." That's what we thought! Maybe this was the end of our goofs but it was the beginning of our problems. It was here that a little irritation we had in our troupe for some time blossomed into a full-scale infection. It was here that we discovered that we had a Bad Boy amongst us. Traveling and working under these difficult conditions, we all blew our top occasionally. But this time, unfortunately, it was in public.

This fellow had been a minority of one in many instances, frequently pulling in the opposite direction. If everybody agreed that reveille was to be at 8:00 A.M., the Bad Boy insisted on sleeping till ten. He didn't like traveling with the rest of us, so he often made his own plane connections, missing the official reception and showing up just in time for his own performance.

Now, on our way to the Command Performance, he again demonstrated his unerring flair for doing the wrong thing at the right time. In the bus going to the palace, with everyone dressed in their Sunday-go-to-meetin' clothes, and wearing their best party manners, the Bad Boy decided to haul off and try to punch one of our guys in the mouth. When the smoke cleared, we continued on our way to the palace, outwardly calm, but inwardly shook up. All of us sensed somehow that this was probably only a warm-up for the main event.

The King has his own private theater on the grounds of his all-white Chitralada Palace in Bangkok. This is the same fabulous royal residence depicted in *The King and I*. When our Jed Horner and Jerry were setting up hours before, the

King's Royal Lighting Men pronounced our lights too un-attractive for Their Majesties. So our boys hustled out and borrowed jazzier ones from a movie company that was in town filming *The Ugly American* with Marlon Brando.

The private theater seats about 300. All I can tell you is, we packed 'em in! There was kneeling room only. They cheered us. They hollered "Bravo" . . . "Encore" . . . "More" . . . Of course, the fact that His Majesty sat in with our band had nothing to do with it. The King, a jazz buff, who's jammed with that other king, Benny Goodman, really knows his way around a clarinet. He not only talked jazz with us, he brought his own private band onstage for a giant jazz session with Buddy and the boys. His Majesty tootled a couple of solos and even played some of his own compositions. So hipped is he on jazz that his son, the Crown Prince, besides learning reading, writing and royalty, is also taking clarinet lessons.

Cindy and I had picked up some Thai lingo which we'd been throwing around pretty good onstage, but we were told to ixnay it at the Palace. Seems in the presence of Their Majesties there's a whole different type of Thai that's spoken. It's not the common, everyday, garden-variety type Thai. It's more what you might call a high Thai. Furthermore, the King, born in Boston, loves to talk English.

After our performance, His Majesty was very complimen-tary. He was very grateful to our President for "sending the type of entertainment that was good for youngsters as well as grownups." Like any other parent who has tickets to a free show, he brought his children. And his youngsters brought other youngsters. The theater was equally divided between the children's section and the adults. We worked to both.

Came the finale, we shot out our 400 red, white and blue balloons as usual. It may not be subtle but it sure is a smash finish. The children scrambled out after them, the princes and princesses leaped for them. Even Their Majesties reached out for them.

After the show, we lined up backstage, as we'd been briefed

earlier, and marched out to be received by Their Majesties. A red carpet had been rolled out in front of the divan on which they'd been sitting. As we filed past, they stood upon the carpet and shook hands with everyone. They presented our girls with sterling silver compacts and the men with similar cigarette cases. All with the gold crest of the King. Later a souvenir hunter offered to buy it from me. "Guess what," I broke the news to Cindy, "some clown wanted to buy my cigarette case."

"What nerve," she said. "I never heard of such a thing. A gift from the King and Queen and he would think you would sell it. How much did he offer you?"

"A hundred and fifty bucks."

"American money?"

"Yeah. Isn't that ridiculous. As though I would part with this beautiful gift from His Majesty, King Phumiphon Aduldet for any amount of money. As though I could bring myself to give this up for a lousy $150."

"Absolutely," Cindy giggled. "Hold out for $500."

Their Majesties had arranged a tea in our honor after the show. It was served in the outdoor gardens which adjoined the theater. Surrounded by Court Ministers, Ladies-in-Waiting and royal policemen who were trying to preserve the peace as much as possible, the King and Queen remained the only island of calm amidst the waves of noise, chatter, clinking teacups and organized confusion.

Across the gardens from the buffet tables stands the all-white three-story palace. Mother, father, princes and princesses live on the third floor. The second floor is for servants. The ground floor for receptions.

Each one of the 300 or so invited guests—including the ninth King of the House of Chakri and his Queen—made the rounds of the buffet and brought his platter back to one of the many tea tables decorating the lawn. The woman sitting opposite Cindy was beautiful enough to be a fairy princess.

Only she wasn't. She was much better. She was a real 14-karat queen—Queen Sirikit of Thailand.

At the other end of the table I was breaking cake with the Monarch, whose revered title is King Rama the Ninth. I still don't know whether my sprightly conversation couldn't hold him or the lure of the clarinet was too strong. I only know that after a few minutes of my sparkling dialogue, he suggested that we apply ourselves to what was uppermost in his mind—jazz. "Let's sneak backstage," he whispered to Buddy and me.

We left Cindy and Her Majesty discussing what any two females—queen or commoner—discuss when they get together: fashions, make-up, men and other women.

Even among royalty, it is the Asian custom to be soft-spoken and modest. Sirikit smiled about her occasionally hesitant but always delightful English. "I learn most of it from studying your American magazines of fashion. If it were not for them I would never know what to wear. I read them aloud to practice."

When my wife complimented her on her excellent English, she looked down and said softly, "It is better when I am practicing alone. But when I am with people who speak English, then it is not so good, I think."

The daughter of His Royal Highness, Prince Chandaburi Suranath, Sirikit has, for the past several years, been high on the list of the Ten Best Dressed Women of the World. Now a permanent member of The Fashion Hall of Fame, she modestly told Cindy, "No, I don't dress to please the King. He never notices my clothes. It is not that he is not interested, I am sure. It is simply that he always seems to notice what all the other women have on, but not his wife. It is probably the same with most husbands, I think, no?"

Considered the world's most beautiful Queen, Sirikit blazed with more jewels than Cartier's. Around her neck hung a four-strand pearl necklace with a diamond clasp, that matched her platinum and diamond earrings. Both wrists glittered with yellow gold bangle bracelets studded with sapphires, rubies and a stray emerald or two. Third finger left hand bore a diamond circlet and a pearl solitaire the size of a soup bone. It was worth a queen's ransom. It, too, was drowned in baguettes. This jewel of the Orient was simply dazzling. She looked—pardon the pun—like a queen.

Daintily stretching her figure-hugging white embroidered Balmain linen over her knees, she continued, "I think Balmain is too expensive, don't you? Even for a queen."

She was reported to have carried 200 outfits in the $40,000 wardrobe she brought to the States on their State Visit two years before. Cindy asked if it was true that she traveled with a retinue of fifty-eight servants, of which three were Ladies-in-Waiting whose sole duty was to care for her gowns, since she never wore the same one twice.

Her Majesty laughed merrily, "I am well known to wear the same dress several times. I have to. I couldn't afford it otherwise. Besides, this is also good for Thailand husbands. This way they say to their wives, 'If the Queen can wear a dress more than once so can you.' When I am here quietly all alone in the afternoons, I wear the *pa yoke,* our native Siamese sarong and sandals. In official photographs, I wear the traditional one-shouldered gown of our country. But when I appear publicly where I will be seen by many Western women, I wear outfits made for me by Balmain. This way I'm sure I look right.

"Shut up as I am here in the palace," she continued, smoothing the tight sheath over her knees, "I don't know how Western women dress. Nobody has gloves, sweaters or furs here. Is too hot. Not only can't you wear furs, you can't even keep them in this climate—their hairs fall out. We don't even wear closed shoes or stockings. Balmain even teach me how to put together . . . how you say . . . how to accessorize. I didn't even know about gloves. So Balmain say, 'Always wear white gloves. Is best.' So I do. Whenever I carry gloves, I take white ones."

Cindy asked her what does royalty do with a used wardrobe. She found out that, like us ordinary peasants, the Queen tries passing it on to her poor relations. "But my sister is not my size, so I give to the Red Cross of which I am President," she said.

They took another turn at the sweet tables, where the Queen picked half-heartedly at fruit and snubbed the gorgeous pastries. Mother of four, Sirikit, a once-upon-a-19-inch waistline, now measures 23. She watches carefully that it never makes 24 by playing badminton, taking ballet lessons twice a month, swimming daily, drinking Ovaltine and taking Swedish gymnastics from an American teacher every other day.

There was a time Siamese commoners hid their faces and were forced to bolt their doors so as not to behold their monarch when he passed through the streets. There was a time Thai custom forbade touching royalty. The rule was so strong that many years ago a group of able-bodied swimmers stood around and watched their queen drown rather than touch her.

Phumiphon and Sirikit are very progressive. The Queen, who is never tired and loves dancing, remarked shyly, "Many of my people cannot get used to the new ways. They seem uneasy and awkward when dancing with me."

A passionate believer in Westernization, she explained how she installed a school of forty-six children in the palace so Their Royal Highnesses would avoid the private isolated tutoring to which their station usually subjects them. Nonetheless, the King and Queen, both of whom are almost painfully unprepossessing, are forced into certain ancient Oriental customs. For one, she walks behind him. And, for two, the children must do them reverence.

Each of the princes and princesses has his own nurse. Each nurse is under a head nurse. But no matter how heavy her official schedule, Sirikit, who exudes love and affection, supervises their meals and plays with them for a certain time every day.

As Cindy and Her Majesty sat there chatting, the second

child, nine-year-old Prince Vajiralongkorn, came within about six feet of their table, then fell to his knees and crawled the rest of the way. When he reached the Queen's Balmain shoes, he performed his obeisance. He lay prostrate until his forehead touched the ground. Then, and not until, did Her Majesty deign to become his mama. She nuzzled him and off he skipped.

In their mind's eye, people have conjured up a vision of this woman who is one of the most famous beauties of the world and whose any whim could conceivably cause a country of 25 million to shake, rattle and roll. Reading about her over his morning instant coffee, the average citizen would imagine she's a rather haughty, regal individual who takes herself very seriously and spends afternoons clapping her hands and imperiously summoning one or the other of her subjects. He would be fully unprepared for a delightful, easygoing conversationalist who amiably and, in fact, eagerly answers every question. He isn't ready for someone who seems just as pleased to share a confidence as your girl friend next door. He doesn't figure that she'll suddenly lean over and confide—without anyone even daring to ask—"I have been married eleven years. I am twenty-nine." And then, "But I don't look my age due to the moisture in the air here. This keeps our skin from drying out. My mother is fifty but she only looks forty. It is the same with all Thai women."

Meanwhile, back at the stage, the King was in his third hour of the jazz marathon. At that moment he was personally banging out a whale of a good, old-fashioned jam session. The very Americanized, Massachusetts-born King loves jazz. Said Benny Goodman about the King: "He's a good musician —for a king!" His Majesty maintains his own thirteen-piece jazz band which plays concerts over Thai radio. This particular afternoon he and his aggregation had been ricky-ticking and razz-a-ma-tazz-ing with our boys straight through from 3:00 P.M. to 6:00 without stop. And they were going right on.

Like any other devoted wife, the Queen cast him an admiring glance while he beat out his solo. She, too, is a music lover. She, too, plays an instrument. But hers is piano, and it's of the symphony variety. She gave him her undivided attention for about 90 seconds then, opening her purse—which matched the white kid shoes—she applied perfume from "Queen Fabiola's Spanish dressmaker" (she meant Balenciaga) and whispered to Cindy that she uses Charles of the Ritz cosmetics and that she has a hairdresser, who lives in the palace, coif her upsweep daily.

On a cool day Bangkok hits 100 degrees. Everybody around her, drenched with perspiration, was reapplying powder with the zeal of an engineer filling in a sinking beach. Not Sirikit. Not once in the whole afternoon did she dive for mirror or puff.

Said our Ambassador's wife, Mrs. Kenneth Young, who joined them at the table, "The Queen once said she made up her mind she won't perspire and she doesn't."

As usual the gracious Queen smiled. From the moment Their Majesties stepped from their chauffeur-driven silver Mercedes, she had been smiling. It is rumored that when the King was once asked why he usually looks so solemn, he replied, "I do not have to smile. She does enough for both of us." He refers to her as "My Smile."

While His Majesty was giving out some hot licks on his clarinet, the Queen broke into heavy questioning about Jackie Kennedy—what she wears and how she wears it. Cindy and she were knee-deep in Caroline, Macaroni and Oleg Cassini when her audience with the Queen of Thailand, and everybody's audience for the King of Thailand, was over. Sirikit of Thailand can best be summed up by the comment of one of the musicians later that evening. Said he, "Man, that's sure a tasty dish to set before a king!"

CHAPTER 8

Deep in the Heart
of Thailand

WE DID our public performances—starting September 11th—at the Thammasart University Auditorium in Bangkok. All of our matinee and evening performances were sponsored by the Thai Government's Department of Fine Arts.

In Thailand I took out one little piece of business that we'd been doing straight along. It was never a show-stopping bit but the audiences loved it. It came after Cindy did her big opening speech, which always started the show off with a bang. Just as she was taking her bow, I would pretend to be very proud that she had gotten the words right. I would puff up my chest and strut around the stage like a peacock shouting, in the local language, "That's my wife!" Then I'd put my arm around her and kiss her on the cheek before I escorted her off the stage. Everybody enjoyed it.

In Thailand, however, we were briefed that you *DON'T* kiss publicly; *DON'T* display affection publicly. So we *DIDN'T*

72

kiss publicly; *DIDN'T* display affection publicly. We did without that whole routine altogether. In fact, we didn't even do it privately. They weren't going to catch me making any more goofs!

Anybody who thinks the State Department books a tour through Afghanistan, Nepal, Thailand, Cambodia and those other Asiatic whistle stops on a willy-nilly basis, thinks wrong. Thailand, for instance, has crises to the right and left of her. On one side is Burma, whose political color might be termed a little cerise. Her other border, 100 mountainous miles, is shared by Laos, of which you might have read. Between both, sits Thailand. Not only is she the most pro-Western but the most pro-United States country in the whole of Southeast Asia. Her friendship is important to us.

I have played one-night stands in my time, but I can only tell you that Scranton, Bridgeport and Gloversville are the big leagues compared to the Thai circuit, which is Lopburi, Hua Hin, Korat, Udorn and Chiengmai. In these remote outposts there were thousands of Thai soldiers, Thai Air Force and U.S. Marines. In fact, they had more troops based up there than they had civilians. Every one of them is trained and ready to go at the drop of a Communist. We were sent to boost morale.

We never questioned our Uncle Sam as to where he sent us. I knew there must be a reason for Chiengmai, Udorn, Korat, Hua Hin, Lopburi. These towns are so small they scarcely even show up on a map, so I wondered why we were being sent there. I found out. Take Chiengmai, for instance. Despite Laos, Berlin, Canaveral and its other hungry dependents, Uncle Sam still allocated a few shekels of foreign aid to a people so primitive that they even question whether the earth is round. Airplanes prompt them to run for the witch doctor, because "The Spirits keep great silver bird in air."

These are the tribes to whom home-sweet-home is in the hills of North Thailand's Chiengmai-Laotian border. Theoret-

ically, they're Thais. Actually they're loyal to nobody. War-
riors, like our injuns of the good old days, with their own
language and customs, they lived unnoticed, undisturbed and
unclaimed until recently. With crises all around, Thailand
suddenly proclaimed them VIP's for several reasons:

1. They're ripe for subversion.
2. Whoever wooed and won 'em first would have a powerful fighting force on his side.
3. These hills, called the "watershed of Thailand," are the
   water sources supplying all Bangkok.
4. The time had come to annihilate an ally of Red China:
   opium. And these tribes were among its largest pro-
   ducers.

Immediately following the government's commandment:
"Thou shalt not grow opium" came a great hullabaloo. Opium,
never outlawed before and now all of a sudden illegal, con-
stituted the hill tribes' prime revenue. Thailand SOS'd its
good friend, the United States, who shipped experts. They
found that the poppy fields could be sprayed from the air
and collectively destroyed. But this would turn 220,000 angry
hillsmen into looting, killing outlaws. They would become
anti-government, anti-Thai and, for sure, anti-American.

America brought coffee, lacquer and fruit trees to supplant
the poppies. Slowly the hill tribes realized that, while their
annual opium take had been $200 per family, coffee now
earned them $700. Now, instead of importing its coffee, Thai-
land was buying it from the hill tribes. Both sides benefitted.
However, it takes three or four years for new trees to bloom
and the hill tribes weren't fixing to wait.

Came next operation livestock. Rhode Island chickens were
imported. Pure-bred Western hogs were also imported. Until
the tribesmen learned better, the hogs ate and slept with them
and lived the life of Li'l Abner's Salome. When a hog sneezed,
a hillman trudged four days to town for medicine, something

he had never done for his wife. All machinery sent here bore America's emblem of hands clasped in friendship. To the hill people, the U.S. was a great powerful land 'way over the horizon, "beyond where the heavens meet the edge of the world." To them, Americans are all good, loving farmers who teach people how to make more money. To them, Americans are missionaries who teach about soap and sanitation. It was a good investment.

This was what was going on with the hill tribes of Chiengmai. This was what was going on along the North Thailand–Laotian border. These were the first seedlings of Westernization. We were glad to accelerate their growth.

Chiengmai, in the northern tip of the country, is the center of Thailand's teak industry. In the nearby jungles, elephants haul the teakwood to the river for shipment down to Bangkok. When we played there at the Suriwong Theater, the river was flooded and all proceeds of our show went to assist the victims of this disaster area.

Our home for the three days was the only hotel in town, the Railway Hotel. It was more like a bungalow colony. There was a main building where we took our meals. Number One in the house rules was "Don't forget to slam the screen door as soon as you come into the dining room." That is, unless you were the type who couldn't eat alone and required the company of a few thousand insects.

The rest of the hotel, set into a thick bushy area, was a series of small wooden cabins painted slate gray and set up high on stilts. Cindy and I bunked in a two-room cabin which we shared with Buddy Rich.

Our room had just enough space for two beds, one dresser and some wall pegs for our clothes. The beds were completely encased in mosquito netting. They were bandaged in gauze from pillar to post. It was a scary sight. It looked as if you were going into an oxygen tent. But this thin strainer, this few yards of filmy material, became a symbol. To us it represented more protection than a fox-hole, more security than an army tank. We couldn't wait to creep into our bed at night.

As soon as we got to the room, we'd quick jump under the netting. Once inside our tents, we'd get undressed and wriggle our hands out from underneath the netting to toss our clothes onto the wooden chair. Then we'd tuck ourselves in for the night. It was our only veil of safety from the omnipresent army of insects. We'd take care never to leave our shoes on the floor, for you'd never know what would be in them in the morning.

We'd go to bed without even washing our faces or brushing our teeth. My fastidious Cindy used to go to sleep every night with her make-up on. First of all, the sink was outside. And outside was a jungle of ants and bugs and lizards and snakes and mosquitoes ready to attack at the first light.

We always came home in darkness to a pitch black room. We were warned and rewarned never to leave our lights on when we went to work at night or we'd never be able to fight our way into the room. Even if we were brave enough or desperate enough to venture out in the dark to wash, how would we see? And to put on a light was worth your life. The toilet was also outside. In a little shed. It crawled with millions of red ants.

The nights we were there we had to make up and dress by candlelight because they had one of their "infrequent" power failures. The heat was unbearable. The only air conditioning —a busted fan. We were hot. We were sticky. But we couldn't bathe because the facilities was a pipe shower attached to the inside wall of that same shed which housed the toilet. Instead of soaping up we just heaped on more layers of insect repellent. After a few days we not only repelled the insects but one another.

At the Suriwong Theater, Bonnie Shirley and Celeste ran into added difficulties. The dressing room had a little open window leading to an alley. There were police on guard at all times. But at that one split second when even the cops were watching the show, some stray sneak thief made off with their handbags. Celeste was relieved of her passport, traveler's checks and wallet, which contained Thai bahts and American dollars.

Poor Bonnie was upset because the wrist watch her husband had given her as a wedding present was gone. The whole town was up in arms for us. The police went into action immediately. They organized searching parties and turned the town inside out. They eventually apprehended the thief, but we had pulled out by that time. Eight countries later, Bonnie's wrist watch caught up with her, as did most of Celeste's effects. We still don't know what happened to the poor light-fingered soul who made off with the goods. We only know that if the townspeople had their way, he'd have been boiled in oil.

After several such forays into the jungles, it was back to home plate: Bangkok. We'd sleep overnight and the next morning—out again. The itinerary presented to us on one such morning said simply, "Fly Udorn." It sounded so easy. It was only two little words: "Fly Udorn."

To accomplish these two words, it meant getting up very, very early in the morning. We'd have to pack, pay our bills, grab some sort of breakfast and board the bus and cars for the airport. And it wasn't that easy. Each night we'd be briefed for our schedule the next morning, but not everybody boarded the bus and cars for the airport at the precise hour they were told to board the bus and cars for the airport. We were a very large family. We were a very hot family. We were a very tired family. Somebody always forgot his shoes. Another had to borrow money for his bill. A third didn't want to rush his coffee. None of us could leave without the other. We were always waiting in some stifling vehicle until everybody gathered.

Then there was the sitting on the broiling airfield while they loaded the luggage and equipment. Then there was the sitting in the sweltering Royal Thai Air Force plane until we arrived in Udorn. Then there was the sitting on the broiling airfield while they unloaded the luggage and equipment. Then there was the sitting in another sweltering bus or car or truck while we chugged into town. This kind of routine was guaranteed to fray the most even tempers, and we were not immune. No wonder there were occasional blowups!

The hotel in Udorn was on the main drag. We had our rooms in a walk-up on the second floor. Beside the standard equipment, like the mosquito netting and the overhead fan, Udorn had a few added starters. Like, for instance, the squat toilet and the splash bath. Because of the plumbing and water difficulties, the splash bath was a necessity.

The splash bath was like a little cement sink that stored water. From hours of standing, the stagnant water always had a scum on top of it. In theory, this was to be used for an emergency bath. In actuality, it was used as a flush for the toilet which had no mechanical flush. On the top of the splash sink stood a little tin can. This was to be used to scoop the scummy water out of the splash bath and pour it down the toilet.

During our first night in Udorn, we experienced a double tragedy. We were all of us feeling somewhat less than in the pink. In order to perk us up, Buddy—who was our across-the-hall neighbor—went hunting for a goody to eat. After combing the town, Rich came up with a can of peanut brittle he scrounged out of some local grocery store. We couldn't wait to open it. It may not sound like much, but at that very moment it was more exciting to us than caviar and champagne wrapped in mink.

The can had a key to open it, like a sardine tin does. Because of the heat, Buddy's hands were sweating and the key broke in half. In his anxiety to get at the peanut brittle he ripped away the top of the can. And at the same time he ripped away half of his thumb. The blood just gushed in torrents from his million dollar drumming hand.

We all had briefing sheets which listed numbers and names we could call in case of an emergency. I rushed him to the Thai doctor who was listed there. This doctor was the dearest man. He not only did a fine job in patching Buddy's thumb back together again, but he drove us to the show in his own car and remained there during the whole performance to watch over his patient. In the true Thai spirit, he refused to take any money. "You Americans are so kind," he said bowing to us, "that it is my great honor to be able to serve you."

Later that night, after we'd zipped Buddy into his mosquito tent, we came face to face with the second of The Great American Tragedies. We dragged ourselves back to our own room, hurled our tired weary bodies into bed and tucked our netting in. Just as we rolled over and said good night, the whole damn rig collapsed on top of us.

You ain't earned your show business stripes until you've played the Thai hinterlands in the 100-degree temperature where the only way you can quench your thirst safely is via steaming hot tea or warm bottled soda. We subsisted primarily on boiled rice and vegetables that were very, very well cooked. For dessert there were two raw fruits we stuck to: bananas and oranges, because they had outer peels.

Arrangements were made to feed us in Udorn, since there was no such animal as a restaurant. Gordon Murchey, the very capable and very wonderful United States Information Service Officer stationed in Udorn, woke us up every morning with steaming hot thermoses of fresh coffee. The two days we were in town, his wife prepared them and he delivered them. We can never be grateful enough. He and his wife were the two most beautiful room-service waiters we've ever seen in our lives. One night, the friendly Thai Army fed us mess-style after we did a show for them. The second night, Gordon invited the whole cast to his home. His wife had thoughtfully tried to prepare a few dishes that stray, hungry Americans might recognize. While we were there—wonder of wonders— we discovered that the Murcheys had a real live, genuine, Western-type toilet in their house. It was the flushest evening that we ever spent.

You haven't lived until you've died in Thailand. The Thais

are a very polite people, but like our Afghan chums they know from nothing about applause. They fear that this gesture is loud and noisy and possibly interrupts the performance. Their reaction is one of delighted but stunned silence. Back home it would look like we were dying. In Chiengmai, they were loving us.

This lack of demonstration troubled me. I mean, I hated to ask my wife to finish her opening speech then rush into the audience to crank up the applause. I mentioned this to her one night when she was engaged in her usual nocturnal relaxation: massaging her mosquito bites. "In Thailand," I said, "I notice that the audience doesn't applaud until the head man does."

"You mean, if he does," she answered.

"At the Palace," I continued, "I noticed everybody had one eye on us and the other on the King. When he applauded everybody did. And since he was born in America he knows all about the applause bit. Therefore, since he liked the show we were a smash all around."

"Honey, I don't want to bother you, but the King's a little busy and we just can't drag him with us wherever we go."

"I know, but in each town it's the same. If the head man is the Lord Mayor, the General of the Army base or the fellow with the biggest rice field, nobody makes their move until he does."

"Well," she suggested, "stick the head man in the spotlight at each show and ask him to applaud with his hands over his head."

Y'know something? It worked! Would I lie to you? We stopped the show all over Thailand.

In Hua Hin we set up shop in a forest clearing and worked to 14,000 Thai soldiers for an audience. In Lopburi we brought our props and costumes right into the field where the Thai Army and the Thai Air Force were on maneuvers. In Korat, we did a show in a hangar where a jet plane moved out so that our performers could move in. In Udorn we also raised money for their hospital, which today bears a plaque with this legend: THE JOEY ADAMS VARIETY SHOW, AS A SIGN OF THAI-AMERICAN FRIENDSHIP, DONATED TO THE UDORN CHANGWAD HOSPITAL, 20,354 BAHT. SEPTEMBER 19, 1961.

We played the up-country of Thailand during monsoon season, which seems to last all year. In Udorn we were greeted by the news that the bridge was about to be washed out. It was ready to go to bridge heaven, or wherever it is good bridges go when they just ain't got strength left to hold up any more. Only this particular bridge we needed. It was the only connection between the hotel, where some of our people were staying, and the theater. Underneath was one helluva lot of water. Before the helicopters, PT boats or U.S. Marines could come to our rescue, some of our troupe had to tramp five miles through swamps and waist-high water to make the opening curtain.

Mike Manieri, our vibraphone player, and Dave Lucas, our bongo boy, showed up weary and soggy. Mud-caked though they were, everybody was sure glad to see them. We cleaned them up a little and sent them onstage.

This show was for the benefit of the Udorn Hospital and nothing would stop us. We'd have forded an ocean, we'd have crossed a continent, we'd have climbed an Alp to get there. Because that's show business. And under any circumstances, the show must go on. Certainly no bridge, no swamp was too tough for me and my gang. It just so happened that my hotel was on the dry side of the bridge, right next door to the theater.

None of this ever bothered us seriously. The lack of de luxe accommodations never really threw us. Oh, there may have been a gripe or two. Maybe even three or four. But griping is healthy. It's nature's way of throwing off what's bothering you. Griping is good for you. For you—not me. I had to listen to it.

Considering the tough schedule and the rough conditions, our gang did very little beefing. In fact, they were great about the whole thing. Like the time in Hua Hin when we couldn't get any dinner. We did two shows that night for the army at an installation quite a distance from the hotel, which was the only place in the whole town that could feed us. When we got home, the dining hall and the chef were locked up for the night.

The only food we'd had that day were some bananas and tea laid on for us by the Thai Army between shows. You might say we were hungry. A couple of us fanned out to see if we could scratch up the cook or a reasonable facsimile, or at least somebody who had the keys to the breadbox. We finally found a fella who knew a fella who knew someone who knew where the cook lived. We eventually scared him up, but by then it was already on the dark side of midnight. I still don't know what he made for us. I only know it was between two pieces of bread. From the Gourmet Society it wasn't. But who cared. We were satisfied. We went to bed fed. And happy.

The cook who got up in the middle of the night to prepare something for us was typical of the kindliness of the Thai people. They all tried to make us comfortable. From the very first moment we set foot on Thai soil—on that morning at 2:30 when we arrived in Bangkok from Calcutta—they gave us the best they had. Binich Sampatisiri, Chief of the Traditional Arts Division, Department of Fine Arts, Ministry of Education for The Royal Thai Government, who was in charge of us the two weeks we were in Thailand, met us at the plane. Binich, who became a dear friend, and a delegation from the Thai Government and Thai Army had stayed up half the night to welcome us with flowered leis and the "wai" salute. The "wai" is equivalent to our handshake. It's a courtly bow combined with the gesture of clasping your hands in front of you in prayer position.

The Thais couldn't have been nicer. The trouble we had was with a couple of Americans. Where we went downhill was with our own. There were two officials assigned to us in Bangkok. The junior officer had been stationed in Thailand for about five years. The other was a newcomer who had just been imported to act as head man over him. Both were trying to exert their authority and both were pulling in opposite directions.

And the one on whom they were trying to exert their authority was me. And the one both were pulling in opposite directions was also me. These two big bosses had an even bigger boss who was over them, and all three of them were bosses over me.

Junior wanted to impress the big boss that he was running the show. He wanted to prove he was a good general. The only trouble is that I was the one he was proving it on. He was a general over one. I was his whole army. Without consulting me, he set up an impossible and inhuman schedule.

I explained to him that I was the one who had upped the standard Cultural Exchange contract from six to eight shows a week for our troupe. I explained that we were all not only willing but eager to do as many shows as they could find audiences for. I explained we all, voluntarily, wanted to go to the hospitals, the schools, the orphanages and any other place where we could bring the friendship of America. We didn't have to be conned into doing this. This had been my idea from the very first. This was the reason I took this trip. In fact, I was the one who cabled ahead and told him to find us as many places as he could.

Ambassadors Byroade and Stebbins also cabled Thailand that we were unusually cooperative and wanted to go all out in every country all the way down the line.

But this was too simple for Junior. He wasn't interested in showing how much we could do. He was interested in showing how much *he* could do. First he scheduled the maximum number of regular shows. To this he added a television show, a Command Performance and a documentary film that we had to make separately. To all this he added the extra benefit performances that we'd agreed to do. On top of that he added an impossible number of extra shows that he personally guaranteed he would make us do. And over and above all this, there was the usual number of receptions and official functions which we were required to attend.

We agreed to all of it.

On top of this Bangkok schedule they added an out-of-town itinerary, which meant we had to take some pretty rough plane trips almost every day. We weren't aware that we'd have to travel daily. Plans had been made for us to work the two weeks in and around Bangkok. But if this was important to our Government, it was important to us. We agreed to it.

But then our American pal arbitrarily arranged a plane schedule that was a killer. Every plane left at 7:30 in the morning. This meant we had to get up at 5:30 A.M. to pack, have breakfast and make the hour's trip to the airport. This was ridiculous. It was also unnecessary. Each hop ran about an hour and a half, which meant we'd arrive wherever we were going by nine in the morning. This is all well and good if you have a 9:00 A.M. appointment there, but we didn't have a date to be in these places until eight o'clock that night. Even when we had three shows a day to do, the first one never started before 5:00 P.M. So what was the point in making us get up at 5:30 in the morning when we'd worked very late the night before and traveled the day before?

We had our own aircraft at our disposal. Strictly for us. Since we were doing many shows for the Royal Thai Air Force, they had arranged to place a Royal Thai airplane at our beck and travel. It was a big, beautiful ship. And there it sat on the airfield with nothing to do but wait for us to take us where we wanted to go and when we wanted to go. Our schedule made no difference to the pilots either. Or to the head of the Fine Arts Department. Or to the Royal Air Force. The only one it made a difference to was Junior.

"You're coddling your people too much," he answered when I complained about the unfair and unnecessary early morning schedule. "You need some discipline in your troupe."

"But," I explained, "our kids are willing to do anything

you want us to do. And more. Why kill us if it's not necessary? Why can't we leave at noon every day?"

"Because," was his answer, "you can't change the schedule once it's already been made. It's impossible. The Thai Air Force won't do it. And if you insist, I'll write Washington. I'll have your tour cancelled."

I hated to go over his head, but I had to take one more stab. I had to see if it was true that the Royal Thai Air Force, which had placed our own plane at our disposal, wouldn't change this schedule. I spoke to his boss. "We're here in Thailand for two weeks," I explained. "After we leave you, we have another three and a half months to go. We'll never make it if you kill us before we start. We want to do just as good a job in all the other countries as we're trying to do here. Why can't we change this schedule?"

I sat in the boss' office while he made a couple of phone calls. That's all it took. Just a couple of phone calls. "The Royal Thai Air Force is very happy to change it," he said. "They'll take you where you want to go and when you want to go. The only reason they hadn't changed the arrangements is because nobody ever asked them to. So, tomorrow morning you're leaving at eleven o'clock instead of 7:30."

Junior was now doubly steamed because I had gone over his head. He now had a good, throbbing resentment going for me. But one thing I have to say in his favor. He's a man of his word. He had promised to write Washington and blow the whistle. And he did.

"Isn't this murder?" I said to Cindy as we sat up until five one morning in Hua Hin talking about our problem. "He threatened to write to Washington and cancel our tour. He also said the only reason I didn't want to get up early is because actors like to sleep late. Isn't this murder?" I said.

"Listen, honey," Cindy said, "we've only played three countries so far. In Afghanistan, the Ambassador reported that we all were the greatest personally as well as professionally. We know for a fact that our Embassy in Nepal cabled for permission to replay us again at a later date. And we know for a fact that even here in Bangkok they've already cabled Washington for permission to extend our stay. Naturally, it would be better if there were no sour note sounded. But I'm sure by now everybody in Washington is well aware of the good job that you and the troupe are doing."

"I have a 'demanding personality' he said, just because I wanted a car. How am I going to get around to do my business and make all the extra shows and even meet with him constantly if I don't have a car? And after I explained the whole reason for changing the schedule, all he can say is that I'm an actor and I like to sleep late. Suddenly I'm the heavy. Just me. I'm the one who has the responsibility of twenty-five people. I'm the one who has to save their strength as much as possible so they'll last out the whole tour. I'm the one who has to fight everyone's battles. So it ends up I'm the heavy."

"Would you rather be like your brother?" Cindy asked.

"What does that mean?"

"I mean your brother, the letter carrier. Don't you remember when they offered to make him an assistant superintendent at a higher salary, but he refused because he didn't want the responsibility?"

"So?"

"So you have a choice. You can either be like your brother, or you can be like a leader. And if you're going to be a leader, then you have to take the responsibilities and the knocks that go with it."

Dawn was breaking and I was still pacing up and down.

"You're damn right it's my responsibility," I said. "And I'll take it. I came here to do one job and that is to win the friendship of the Afghans, the Nepalis, the Thais and the people of Asia. If I have to lose the friendship of a couple of Americans in the process, then what can I do about it? It's just that it breaks my gut that after all we've tried to do and after all we've accomplished—and this goes for everybody in the troupe—one fella can write one letter and threaten to cancel our tour."

"What are you so upset about?" Cindy drawled from underneath her mosquito netting. "What are you making such a federal case about? There's good in everybody. Junior can't be all bad. I heard he's got a very good handwriting."

"That's good news," I said. "How's that going to help? So he's got clean underwear, too, so what?"

"So nothing," Cindy continued, trying to get me out of my black mood. "I'm sure basically he's a good guy. In fact, he's probably a wonderful guy. In fact, he looks to me to be the kind of guy who's wonderful to his mother."

"So what do you want me to do, throw a sweet sixteen party for him when he comes to New York?"

I was beginning to smile in spite of myself, and knowing Cindy I knew she'd never give up until she saw the whites of my teeth.

"I don't know from nothing," Cindy needled. "I like him. But then I like you, too, so what do I know!"

By the time we went to sleep, my crazy wife had me so coked up that I wanted to rush right out and buy Junior a Valentine—almost.

No one can stay mad for long in Thailand. The Thais are basically a happy people, and maybe their attitude is catching. Very few of these sunny 25 million people are susceptible to communism. This is because of the nearly universal ownership of land, the lack of intense poverty, their allegiance to the Monarchy, the absence during all of Thailand's history of foreign colonialism, and their devotion to the Buddhist religion.

Thailand recognized many years ago that the hungry power of the Chinese Communists posed a serious threat to its independence and security. It has been unhesitantly cooperative in the Free World's efforts to choke off this bully. For example, Thailand was one of the first to offer soldiers to swell Uncle Sam's contingents in Korea in June, 1950. Since then, Thailand has joined SEATO and has been a very active member of the Southeast Asia Treaty Organization, which has its headquarters in Bangkok. In many other ways, this country has proven itself a loyal and effective Free World nation. It has received heavy military assistance from the USA to bolster its security and that of the surrounding area generally.

Meeting the threat of Communist aggression and subversion, and thus preserving the country's independence and integrity, is Project A with the Thai Government. But every so often, the government is faced with a crisis created by nature that places an extra drain on the exchequer. This year the rivers had flooded, creating a large disaster area that needed help.

So we were going to do our show on television to raise money for flood relief. Our show was to go on after Thai boxing. The Thais are a very sweet, dear and gentle people—until they get into the ring. Thai-style boxing is a rough sport. It makes our fighters look like Arthur Murray dancers. In addition to their fists, the knees, elbows and feet will be brought into attack on any part of the opponent's body. Kicking, gouging, grinding, pulling, or almost anything we consider foul, they consider fair play. The fighters are paid small salaries, which includes stretcher and hospital expenses. As a result of its no-holds-barred nature, boxing kayoes all competition in TV ratings.

We showed up at the studio promptly at 6:30. We were due to go on exactly at eight. On the dot of 9:42 we went on. You see, Thailand is very hot. Nobody has the energy to rush around. To Thais, punctuality means approximately. Television works the same. If something's scheduled for 8:00 P.M., so what if it's a few minutes late? They just don't sweat over it.

My translator on the show was Pichai Vasnasong, the country's Number One TV hotshot. He's a combination Godfrey-Sullivan-Murrow who does five interview shows and as many emcee chores daily. He's also an executive of the station, their head art director, top English translator and sole researcher. His salary's 150 bucks a month. His office doubles as a dressing room, and when I arrived I had to wait in the hall because Bangkok's top video star was changing his pants behind a desk.

This was their first big, live American variety telethon. They therefore expected a peak audience. The Bangkok area has 80,000 sets and 600,000 viewers. Often a hundred people watch one receiver. They have "community sets" controlled by policemen. At certain hours the local cop unlocks it, flicks the dials, governs the tuning and from then until he padlocks it again he's the monitor of that monitor.

It was estimated we had about 600,000 viewers. One of them was the King. As we do here in America, His Majesty called up and sent his donation for flood relief—50,000 baht. (A baht is a nickel—you figure it out.)

Early the next morning—and it's always early the next morning—we left for the airport en route to Cambodia. We were escorted by my friend, Binich Sampatisiri. It was now 8:00 A.M. Binich was jovial as all hell. He'd been in business since 5:00 A.M. As a parting gesture of love he handed me a warm letter of thanks on behalf of his government.

At the airport I was rushed by hordes of friendly fans who'd seen me on television the night before. I posed for pictures, I gave out autographs with both hands. They took pieces of my clothes as souvenirs. "Isn't this thrilling?" I said to Cindy. "The people of Thailand love me. This recognition makes me feel like I'm home."

"Whose home you talking about?" Cindy asked, "Marlon Brando's?"

"Oh, yeah? Well, they ask for my autograph pretty good in the States. Remember that woman who was running after me just as we were making the plane to come out here? Remember she was wearing a gray hat and a blue coat?"

"I certainly do. You mean the handwriting analyst."

"What difference does it make what she does for a living?

Why must you get picky? She asked for my autograph, didn't she?"

"Yes, and I already sent her a check for the analysis."

"You did? What did she say?"

"She said you should be in show business."

I was so busy posing for pictures I couldn't answer her.

"Will you zip up that grin for a minute so we can get on the plane? Your smile is so wide it won't fit through the door. You look like you swallowed a banana sideways," Cindy said.

"But dear, I can't refuse to take pictures. These are fans."

"Yeah, but you've been smiling at everything. Including the cameras that are laying on the 'For Sale' counter."

"All I know is, this is thrilling. To walk down the streets of Bangkok and be recognized from TV."

"It should happen to you in the States."

CHAPTER 9

Split Week
in Cambodia

It was the beginning of our sixth week when we limped into Phnom Penh, Cambodia.

"Phnom Penh?" Cindy said. "We musta made a wrong turn some place!"

"Now that I'm here I still don't know how to pronounce it. Is it 'Nom Pen' or 'Fnom Pen' or 'Pnom Pen'? Everybody here mumbles it differently."

"Let me ask you a personal question," Cindy said as we were unpacking at the Monorom Hotel. "What difference does it make? I mean, when we get back home how many times is it going to come up in conversation? Sometimes you can spend a whole night back home and nobody'll mention Phnom Penh once. I mean, unless you bring it up."

"Oh, I don't know. You might bump into somebody you know while you're here and you don't want to sound stupid."

"Let me ask you another personal question. Just for the sake of argument, who do you think you're going to bump into here 12,000 miles away from home in Nom, Fnom or Pnom Penh?"

"Oh, I don't know," I said. "Maybe Judge Crater or Amelia Earhart or somebody."

Cindy laughed. That is, I think she laughed. It was either a laugh or a bloodcurdling shriek. She came bounding out of the bathroom like she'd been shot out of a cannon. "That ratty shower is bloody ice cold," she shrieked.

"Why don't you turn on the other faucet?" I said, to calm her.

"What other faucet? What have you been reading, *Holiday* magazine? Where the hell do you think you are? There's only one faucet. It's either hot, cold or come-as-you-are. But whatever it is it's only cold."

"Well, why don't you wait until it gets hot?"

"Friend," she said to me lowering her voice, "it's been running since we got here. They ain't got from hot water. They don't know from h-o-t. Hot water they don't have. Such a thing there isn't here. It's cold. Real icy cold. The Eskimos don't have it so cold."

"I guess what you're trying to tell me is that the water's cold."

"Now I know what happened to Judge Crater. He's sitting around here some place waiting for the water to get hot."

"Listen, I got an idea. Why don't you call up the clerk and tell him there's no hot water."

"You call him," she snapped. "I didn't take Cambodian in high school, so I don't speak the language so good. And furthermore, how am I going to call the clerk? We don't have a phone."

"Yeah, but *he* has."

We'd had trouble with water ever since we'd started on this tour. Mostly, there isn't any. If there is you can't drink it unless you boil it. Even the ice cubes are made from boiled water, which is then frozen. But my wife had the plan. It all started with her element.

She'd heard about a wire coil element that boils water. So she went to the famous shop in Manhattan that handles these things, Hammacher and Schlemmer. She tested every element they had in the store. She took an Instant Electronics Course. She became an expert on alternating current and direct current. From memory she could tell you which countries have 110 volts and which countries have 220. She learned that certain areas have two-prong plugs, some three-prongs and some four-prongs. So it shouldn't be a total loss, she bought 'em all.

For weeks before we left she was in daily communication with Schlemmecher and Hammer or whatever their names are. In fact, it got so that when they were having an electric problem they called her for advice. Just before we left I was looking for larger quarters so Mr. Schlemmer and his partner could live in.

We started on this trip with one bag just for the electrical equipment alone. We had another suitcase filled with canned goods like soups, stews, spaghettis, Sanka, instant coffee and stuff like that. On our first day in Bangkok Cindy blew all the equipment, including a television set she borrowed from an Embassy official. She also blew the whole right wing of the Erewan Hotel.

We now had one suitcase stuffed with food that was of no value to us at all. I'd have cheerfully traded three jars of Sanka and two spaghettis for one can of sardines. Because of this emergency, Jerry Bell made us a portable stove. He got us a can of Maxwell House coffee. He dumped out the coffee and, with an icepick, punched holes in the can to create a draft. Then he dug up a can of Sterno and a makeshift grating and in this manner we set up light housekeeping in room 501 of the Monorom Hotel, Phnom Penh, Cambodia.

Food and living were very costly in Cambodia. And since we all paid our own tabs, this was a problem. For instance,

Cindy and I had tomato juice for breakfast one morning. It cost three dollars. It's really not that I was cheap, but after that it got so that I enjoyed cooking spaghetti for breakfast in room 501 of the Monorom Hotel.

I sent a suit to be cleaned. It was not that stunning three-button herringbone tweed, which by now was laying in a grave some place in Nepal. This was an Italian silk mohair job that was now the proud possesor of some imported spaghetti sauce.

"They charged me fifteen dollars," I complained to my wife, "to have this one lousy suit cleaned."

"Well, what do you expect? This country has problems. It's a brand new country. It used to be French Indochina. It's only been on its own a few years—since it won its independence in 1953. And it takes a while until they build up an economy. They got problems."

"Yeah, well this solves the tailor's problem, but how about mine? Who ever heard of paying fifteen dollars to have a suit cleaned?"

"Well," Cindy said, bending over a hot stove cooking up a fresh batch of spaghetti, "maybe he's a French cleaner."

"He sure charged enough to ship it to Paris!"

Despite the food and drink problems, we were all gaining weight. In many of the countries we visited they don't slaughter cows or pigs. It's against their religion. Consequently the only meat available locally is chicken and lamb. And since these are not always too safe, the next step is to try to fly meat in. But the one-engined kites that service places like Kabul and Katmandu have no refrigeration, hence foodstuffs would be spoiled. As a result, the main food in those countries is rice, supplemented by dishes like tuna fish casserole, chicken à la king, noodles, bread and more rice. And even those clowns who claim that calories don't count would have blimped up on this trip.

The three Sylte sisters were slowly becoming a quartette. Our lady magician was having trouble with her biggest trick:

trying to make ten pounds disappear. And Cindy, who's usually a puffy size 8, was fast approaching a blooming size 12.

Cambodge, as the locals call it, is the only land in the whole world where you can be arrested for looking up at the sky. Here, betting on the possibilities of rain is illegal. But popular. Somewhere in the center of town there exists a drainpipe with a flat rock underneath it. They pay off on the exact moment the first drop hits the rock.

Rain is a serious consideration here. The people of Phnom Penh live with the constant threat of flood. They never know when the cranky Mekong River is going to act up. In addition to our regular performances, we threw in some extra ones for their flood relief. It was touch and go as to whether we could show up at the theater, because we, too, were almost flooded out.

The method of transportation down Cambodia way is not exactly what you'd call waterproof. In fact, you can be drier in your bathroom shower than you can in a Phnom Penh taxi, called a *ciclo* (see-klo). Like in any other major city, you sashay out of your digs, hold up a finger and along comes a cab. And that's where the similarity ends. These *ciclos* are bicycles pedalled by one man with a cabin for one in front where the handlebars should be. If it rains, they throw a wet tarpaulin around you, and the only thing it keeps out is your vision. In this Cinderella coach I, Prince Charming, splashed my way to the theater. In front of the Cine Lux Theater, East really smacks up against West. Here, against the backdrop of the sixth-century Buddhist temples, peddlers in local garb hawk bubble gum, U.S. Chiclets and tins of Nescafé.

Our American show was such a big hit that the scalpers sold the same seats three times. We played to the only three-tiered audience in captivity. Talk about hot tickets, they were paying ten times the box office price for ours. All moneys collected went to the Education and Scholarship Fund of the town. Here, as in every other place we appeared, Uncle Sam footed the bills, while every red cent raised stayed with the host-government for local benefits.

Opening night, we were honored by Her Majesty, the Queen of Cambodia. The head of State, who is her son, Prince Norodom Sihanouk, was off on an errand some place. Actually he was on a Cultural Exchange Mission of his own. While we were in his country he was in ours.

The Queen decorated Cindy and me. She had no difficulty pinning the peace medal on me, but when it came to my poor wife with the built-up dress it was a tense moment for the Crown. It didn't do poor Cindy any good either. It took Her Majesty eleven stabs before she finally drew blood. Wounded but happy, Cindy retreated to the dressing room to pet her medal and lick her wounds.

Me, I was walking around like Her Majesty had just conferred knighthood upon me. I jammed my hand in my blouse à la Napoleon, took a stance and admired myself, medal and all, in the mirror. "Sir Joey Adams," I thought. "So far," I gloated, "I've been honored by two Kings and three Queens."

"One more King," Cindy said, "and you can go gin."

Beautiful Cindy was really dressed for the occasion. She had rhinestones in her hair, sequins in her eyeballs and even her fingernails were made of bugle beads. For the occasion she even broke out her Crown Jewels. What she couldn't wear she was carrying. In contrast, the gracious Queen was dressed simply.

"I thought the Queen looked beautiful," I said. "How would you describe what she was wearing?"

"Well, she was wearing sandals, an overblouse and a sanpat."

"What's a sanpat?"

"A sanpat is the native dress. It's an ankle-length skirt folded in the center and hooked at the waist."

"It's beautiful. Why don't you get some?" I said magnanimously.

"I already bought three," she said happily.
"What do you need them for?" I said nastily.

Two days later, at eight o'clock in the morning, I was
awakened by a delegation from the Court. I received them in
my shorts. There were no phones in my room, so this delegation from the Court came at eight o'clock in the morning to
herald the coming of an extra-special delegation from the
Court who would be calling upon me at 8:30. They begged
me to make myself available. I was available. I mean, at 8:30
in the morning I don't usually have such a busy schedule. Let's
face it, I don't usually ride my first polo pony until much later
in the day. Boy, was I available. If I was any more available
I'd be sound asleep.

The second wave of couriers banged on the door at exactly
8:30. I received them in sartorial splendor this time. I bowed
low. They bowed low. Then they revealed their secret mission.
"We have a request from the Queen Mother," they said.

"Anything," I said, reaching for my medal. "Anything for
the Queen Mother. You have but to command. What is Her
Majesty's wish?"

"Balloons," they said.

"Balloons?" I said.

"Balloons?" Cindy said.

"Balloons!" they said. "Her Majesty liked the quality of your
balloons in contrast to the local product and we'd like to have
the texture copied."

The request was granted. We even sent a few hundred extra
for her grandchildren. I figured it was the least we could do for
Cambodia.

Our hour and a half show in Cambodia stretched to two
hours. The main reason being my Instant Khmer. Khmer being
the Cambodian tongue. Here, speaking the language wasn't
that simple. The Cambodge tongue is a very flowery, very
polite, very courteous one. I had to say four of their sentences
to every one in English. For instance, just to say "Hello," it

came out, "I beg your pardon. If it does not offend you, I would like to bid you all a very gracious good evening. With your permission."

When I said "Hello" before the Queen, I had to be even more polite. The four sentences became eight. In the Asian countries, the introductions are longer than the show.

Cambodians are not only a very polite people, they're a very friendly, helpful people. They tried everything to make us comfortable. We discovered that there was no powder room backstage. In fact we discovered that the nearest facilities were in Thailand. Our Cambodian chums went to work. Before you could say "Chic Sales," they nailed together a john. They made only one slight error. They put the lock on the outside. This was fine, but the only trouble is that the people on the outside had more privacy than the people on the inside.

In Cambodia, a gent may have seven wives. And, seems to me, if he can withstand the Cambodian courtship—which is like an endurance test—he's entitled!

Firstly, ladies hereabouts never go out alone, even in daylight. They're always chaperoned by parents, relatives or someone as incorruptible as a Canadian Mounty. Instantly, this lowers the odds on a sneak meeting betwixt the Cambodian Romeo and his Juliet.

If a boy wants to set his beret for a girl, he must be a long-time family friend, have attended the same schools, have the same kind of home and background, and his father must know her father.

For the first date, he needs permission from her father. Being there's no telephone, a week ahead he makes an appointment with the girl (who must be 18) for an appointment to see the old man. She gives him the address; he gives her the time and day he'll call. This whole date is merely for an okay for the date.

Once past the reviewing stand, they may go out the first time —but only to a public party—and only if her parents know the party-throwers. And there's no pulling the wool over Mr. and Mrs. Cambodia's eyes either. The party-throwers must personally call for the girl and her sheik. It's ixnay on hand-holding and first-name-calling. Even the formal French pronoun *vous* instead of the familiar *tu* is used.

Date Number 2 must include a group of friends, all known to mommy and daddy. The friends must come to be reviewed personally, and officially request the parents' permission and guarantee the offspring's safety. The witching hour is midnight, or Cinderella turns into a juvenile delinquent according to local standards. With afternoon dates, her deadline is dusk.

When the suitor is this far through the obstacle course, the third date may be a movie. Even at that, Pop might drag along. But no dinner. Dinner and movie is only if you're engaged. Later, dinner is permissible. But only if their kin are well acquainted. And then no movies. For some reason, the eats and pictures combination spells danger in these parts.

Like in the USA, boys play the field. Unlike our custom, girls can only date one suitor at a time. And only if there's some intention of marriage. If there's mutual affection but not enough for marriage, he's welcome at her house but not welcome to take her out.

No matter who the boy is, she sees him only twice a week. No matter what it is, any gift must be presented in front of Mama. When it's getting serious and his mama's looking to give her the once-over, it's at the girl's house. Going to the home of the boy, who mustn't be over five years riper than the girl, is 100 per cent disallowed.

When he's ready for husbandhood, the boy pops the question—but to his parents. Next to her parents. Last, to the lucky girl. She'll accept—because Cambodian daughters obey Cambodian mamas. Then, his parents and the soon-to-be in-laws arrange details.

Following a three-day wedding, friends wake the newlyweds the morning after by thwacking them with cocoanut strings.

This is good luck, and it's Cambodian style for "It's too late to back out now, Charlie."

Like I said, any fella willing to brave this seven times is entitled.

Cambodia is a country where radios are such a mark of prestige that they're tuned full blast so your neighbor will know you have one. It is important to know the customs of the country you are visiting. When you're on Cultural Exchange, your performance offstage is just as important as your performance onstage.

In each country we were under the auspices of the USIS, which is the United States Information Service, the overseas arm of Ed Murrow's Washington Bureau, the United States Information Agency. This is the new diplomatic corps of the USA. Many of its members are ex-professors, officers, radio personnel and newspapermen. They are there to peddle the Stars and Stripes to the host country.

It is their job to grab as much space for the U.S. as possible—in the newspapers, on the airwaves. They produce documentaries for television and movies showing America's best foot forward. They present Cultural Exchange Programs in the field of sports, with such attractions as the Harlem Globe Trotters . . . in the field of entertainment, with people like Louis Armstrong . . . or in the field of culture, with a Louis Untermeyer or the President of Harvard. They arrange exchange scholarships. And they build and furnish USA-style libraries. In short, they're on the road for Uncle Sam.

When you're a traveling salesman, you present a swatch or a sample to a prospective buyer. We were this season's samples. And we had to live up to our sales pitch.

In places like Afghanistan, Nepal, and Cambodia, the tourist rate is almost nil. Even the travel agents don't come through too often. To many, Americans were what they saw in the movies. They were gunslinging cowboys from Texas, rum-running gangsters out of Chicago and society drunks who shot their lady friends in the navel. The only real, live 14-karat Americans they'd ever seen were the Embassy and USIS personnel, the professional Americans, whom they figured were not exactly impartial, unprejudiced or particularly representative.

It's a constant battle for USIS to combat the usually clever propaganda of the Reds. One time the Commies' smears backfired, and they got bopped with their own hammer and sickle. They planted a picture of an American Negro being hit on the head by a white man. Their newspaper section read, "This is how Negroes are treated in America." They hoped with this to stir up some nice, juicy hatred of our country. But the reaction wasn't what they expected. The Asians who saw the picture said, "Those American Negroes can't be so bad off. Look, they're wearing shoes!"

So when the Embassies and USIS pointed with pride to the Joey Adams Show, I knew we were on the Red, White and Blue spot. The show had to be the greatest. The samples had to be as good as the product we were selling. We had to make good. And we did. The operation was a success, but in this case the doctor nearly died.

If you ever have an enemy and would like to hang him up to dry, make him head of a Cultural Exchange Group. With so many people to please in order to keep the show on the road, your "friends" end up giving you more trouble than your enemies.

Just traveling with your own wife on a week-end holiday can be a tough assignment. You want to sleep—she wants an early breakfast. You want to shop—she would like to go sightseeing. She's tired—you're raring to go. You're hungry—she's on a diet.

And you love your wife. Now add two dozen additional temperaments who are locked together on an eighteen-week tour. Not a week end. They don't love each other. In many cases they don't even like each other. In the States they might even cross streets to avoid each other.

Suddenly they're thrown together morning, noon and night. They eat together, sleep together, and work together. Like D.P.'s they're shepherded together into the same hotels, the same buses, the same planes. Coupled with that they miss a few meals because the shows are too late, and they miss a little sleep because the planes are too early and they miss a little comfort because the countries are too hot. And when they finally get where they're going—their home, sweet home is a hotel room with lizards on the wall.

One of my stars sulked for the entire trip because our Ambassador asked me to cut out one of his numbers. Another never forgave me because she didn't like her spot on the show. One didn't think we had enough room on the stage. Another was angry about the way his music was played. Some beefed because they had to wear ties and jackets in 110-degree heat. Tension was building, and we'd only been out four weeks.

Don't misunderstand, I know it isn't easy or pleasant to get off a hot plane into a hotter airport dressed like you're on Madison Avenue. I'm sure it would have been easier for the girls to wear slacks rather than dresses or high heels. There were many times I myself would have preferred shorts and a T-shirt.

However, this was the image of an American that I wanted to show: well-mannered, well-bred and well-groomed. This was a State Department request. But the State Department was 12,000 miles away, and I was right there on the firing line trying to enforce it. Three countries later, I came to the stark realization that the mutiny Mr. Christian started would be a hymn-sing compared to my mob unless this rule were relaxed. I had to decide which was better to live with: a group of neat Americans or a group of cranky ones.

One beefed that his billing was too small in Kabul. Another griped that his room rent was too high in Katmandu. One thought the floor was too "fast" for his act. Another thought it too "slow." Some were unhappy because they hadn't heard from home. Others were unhappy because they had heard from home and it wasn't what they wanted to hear.

No matter which way it went, Operation Mail often added to our woes. We'd left our itinerary with our families, but it was always subject to change. We were traveling so fast that by the time a letter caught up to where we should have been we weren't there any more. And when it comes to Special Delivery, forget it, Charlie! You go tell the camel you're in a hurry. Many a letter went through half a dozen countries before it reached us.

For instance, when we were in Katmandu, the procedure went like this: the poor little letter was bounced from one country to the other until it arrived in India. There it changed planes. It got off the jet and onto the firefly that deposited it at the local post office. And the local mailmen don't know from our Yankee slogan that "Neither rain nor sleet nor snow will keep these couriers, etc., etc., etc." When they're ready, they ship it to our Embassy, who then transfers it to USIS, who in turn bundles it off to the official who is in charge of us. He then carries it to our company manager, Jed Horner, who distributes. By then, of course, we're two countries away. Back it goes to the Embassy who sticks it in the diplomatic pouch for delivery to us at our next destination. But it isn't that easy. The diplomatic pouch goes to Washington first. There it gets rerouted on that same merry-go-round.

And getting letters out is also a cloak-and-dagger job. When I was in the up-country jungles of Thailand I had a very important letter that I had to get to New York as quickly as possible. We packed it in the luggage of a friend who was going to Europe on a three-day leave and then on to the United States. This way we were sure that the letter would get there in not more than ten days.

Each one of our troupe had his own problem. There were twenty-five plots going at one time. I had to be mother, father, and target for the whole crew. It was my job to keep everybody happy. Win, lose, or draw blood, I had to try to pacify the troupe, please the Embassy, work harmoniously with USIS, cater to the big shots in each country, and report to Washington.

And smile. No matter what, the object was to keep smiling. It's difficult to keep a tight rein on your emotions when a taxi driver takes you to the wrong destination or the telephone operator wakes you when you think you've left a do-not-disturb. It's tough not to get angry when you're starved and you can't get through to the waiter. You must remember at all times that you are the foreigner. It's their language and their country. So, even though your heart is breaking, laugh clown laugh.

But it was all worth it. No matter what the difficulties or indignities or even the abuses, it was all worth it. Sure, I left a little piece of lung in one hotel room, a little piece of gut in another, but I still say it was worth it. I was only interested in one thing: the over-all picture. And that was to bring the friendship of America to the people of the world. I had a mission to fulfill and nothing could keep me from fulfilling it.

Wandering around the airport in Cambodia, waiting for our plane to Laos, I was dwelling on all this, ruminating on the glory that is America, when I smashed head-on into two schoolteachers from Pennsylvania. Both ladies dropped their Rolleiflexes when they saw me. "My goodness," one of them shrieked, "if it isn't whatshisname!"

"I'll be darned," said the other. "It's Joey Bishop!"

With a little helpful prompting from my wife, who hasn't yet let me forget it, they recognized me. "Of course," the fat one said. "You're Joey Adams. I remember you so well. You once appeared at our Elks Club Installation Dinner in Pottstown."

"Is that murder?" I whispered to Cindy. "They always remember you from things like Elks Club dinners, confirmations and meat market openings. How come they never remember me from pictures and television?"

"Maybe," grinned Cindy, "it's because you're never in pictures or on television."

My two red hot fans from Pottstown had just come from Angkor Wat, the fabulous ruins of Cambodia's ancient capital, way off in the jungle somewhere. To me, everything I had ever heard about Angkor Wat signified majesty, the glories of an ancient civilization, one of the wonders of this part of the world. "How was it?" Cindy asked breathlessly.

"All I can tell you, honey," sighed the skinny one, heading for the ladies' room, "is that I had one drink of water there, and ever since I've had the trots."

CHAPTER 10

Exchanging Culture
in Laos

W HEN our plane taxied into the Vientiane airport
in Laos on October 5, 1961, we began to get butterflies. I
could actually feel my heart jumping. We were setting foot
in the middle of a headline as it was being written.

I think all of us had mixed emotions. We were half afraid
and half thrilled. Afraid because we didn't know what we were
in for. We didn't know who would meet us at the plane—our
own gang or the Communist guerrilla fighters. The fighting had
been so consistent and so close to home that it was touch and
go as to whether we'd be allowed into Laos at all.

For a while it looked as though Washington was going to
cancel us out for safety's sake. But when we got the go-ahead
we were thrilled because we were stepping smack into the
middle of the history books. Just the thought of being there
was exciting. It was like watching an accident. You don't want
to look at it, but somehow you're drawn to it.

We entered Laos during a temporary cease-fire. I guess they

figured with the Joey Adams Troupe in town they were in enough trouble already. All I know is, when our Royal Lao plane touched down, all was quiet on the eastern front. The day we arrived the three princes of the uneasy Laotian Government were meeting in that historic international poker game to find out who would win the pot.

"Guess what?" Cindy said, gleefully, when we arrived at the airport. "There are tons of correspondents here from every major newspaper, every single syndicate and every wire service all over the world."

"Natch. The word is out. The news traveled fast. They all heard the kid's in town," I kidded.

"Down, Fido, down," caroled Cindy. "No matter what anybody says, you'll still always believe they came here for you —right?"

"Let's face it," I said. "When I hold a press conference, I hold a press conference."

"Did it ever occur to you," Cindy said tapping her foot on my foot, "that Prince Boun Oum is a pretty good draw, too? And don't underestimate the other two members of this all-star Laotian trio, Prince Souvanna Phouma and Whatshisname."

"Gee, I hope the papers back home don't connect me with all the troubles coming out of here. I had nothing to do with it."

"Of course you're not responsible for the troubles here—yet," teased Cindy. "They haven't even seen your act."

So this is Vientiane, I thought. Here it was, a living, breathing community. Back home it was a headline. The gaping holes in the city's buildings bore marks of the recent tug of war. This new open-air architecture was courtesy of the Reds.

It wasn't easy getting around. We had to avoid the countryside because that's where the soldiers play hide-and-seek. And we had to steer clear of the border because that's where they played a new game called "Shooting Down Mail Planes."

Small wonder that the one letter I air-mailed from Laos took fifty-two days to get to New York!

Laos lies like a key in seething Southeast Asia. It is a long and slender country, completely landlocked, and its narrow stem separates Communist North Vietnam from neutralist Burma and pro-Western Thailand. At its head it has a common 225-mile frontier with Red China; at its foot lies neutralist Cambodia whose ports are the gateway to the Malay Peninsula and Indonesia. It is a land of mountains and jungles and fewer than two million people. It is a buffer state. And it was being buffed all right.

When we pulled into town that October day, they scooped us all up and drove us to the USOM (United States Operations Mission) mess hall for a briefing session. There we encountered our very first female Public Affairs Officer from the USIS. Her name was Bert Potts. She was friendly. She was efficient and she was a crackerjack. She had in her hand twenty-five mimeographed fact sheets for us. These tip sheets in every town served as our guide and our bible. In short, the United States Information Service was just that, and we'd have been lost without its information and its service.

Our tip sheets for Laos read as follows:

TRANSPORTATION: Vientiane is a small town and you can easily walk from one place to another. There are no taxis readily available. "Samlor" is the name of the three-wheeled bicycles which can take you around. The going rate for a "farang" (foreigner) is usually higher than for a Lao. The usual rate is from 10 to 20 kips in the downtown area.

MONEY: The exchange rate is 80 kips to $1. The currency is stable and there is no unofficial rate of exchange.

FOOD: Western-style (French) is available at rather high prices at the Settha Palace and Constellation Hotels. The *Plat du Jour* is usually not too expensive, however. You can get good coffee, pastry and snacks at Ancel or the Maison Suisse. The Royal Bar has good steak sandwiches and onion soup.

SIGHT-SEEING: Main points of interest include:

That Luang: The most famous Buddhist monument in Laos and a very fine subject for color photographs. It is about a half mile from the center of town.

Wat Prakeo: The National Museum. Near the King's palace on the Mekong River in the center of town.

Morning Market: Where you can buy anything from baskets to silk. This is good for early-risers since most of the activity takes place from 6:00 to 7:00 A.M., but it is well worth the effort.

Our tip sheets also cautioned us to mind our manners. Under "manners" we were not surprised to find the big *DON'T* about exposing the bottoms of feet or shoes. Ever since Thailand, we'd all grown as modest about concealing our soles as grandma was about her ankles. By this time we were dragging our feet—if nothing else—but good.

Our friend, Gordon Murchey, had been loaned to us from Udorn. Since northeast Thailand and Laos share the same border, it was just a canoe-ride across the Mekong River for him. He and the other Americans let us know how glad they were to have us there. And they did their best to help us along. Believe me, we needed it.

SOUVENIRS: Most people like to buy Lao silk scarves or skirts which are expensive but attractive. Color postcards are available at the Casa Lao bookstore next to the Constellation Hotel. Any stamp collectors will probably want some Lao stamps which can be purchased at the main Post Office. Try the Commissary first as merchants around town selling stamps tend to overcharge.

NIGHT CLUBS: The Vieng Ratry and the Lido are the best. Prices are quite high, however. A drink or a beer costs about $1.25 or more.

GENERAL: The restaurants listed (with the exception perhaps of the Chinese ones) maintain sufficient standards of cleanliness that you can drink water and eat anything served. Be very careful about drinking water anywhere else. Usually hot tea or a "Green Spot" (bottled soda) will serve the same purpose.

French, not English, is in use although some shopkeepers may know a little English. Just be patient and polite and you can usually get what you want. You can try to bargain for items you buy in the stores or in the market, but food prices are fixed. Beer and wine are not expensive but whiskey is very high in restaurants and bars.

The standards of service you find here will be lower than in many of the countries you visit, but please be patient and the Lao will be very grateful for the chance to help you in every way that they can. Standards of courtesy are as high as in America and everyone will respect your kindness and willingness to cooperate.

MAIL: Mailing letters through the Lao Post Office is very expensive although the stamps are impressive. APO mailing privileges are available with mail going out first thing Monday, Wednesday and Friday mornings. Give letters to be mailed to any of the USIS personnel assigned to you.

NOTE: The American Commissary is open for members of the troupe to make small purchases such as cigarettes, toothpaste, etc. Payment must be made in dollars. In cash. No checks allowed. The Commissary is in the USOM compound. Hours are: 10–2, closed Sunday and Monday.

The second page of our fact sheets was a guide to pronunciation.

Laos:—The name of the country.
Pronunciation: Laos rhymes with grouse.
Inhabitants of Laos are "Lao."
The language is "Lao."
The word "Laotian" is a French word used both as a noun and an adjective.

Vientiane:—The name of the city which is administrative capital of Laos.

Pronunciation: Vientiane—(Vyen-Jan)

Vyen—as in "I have a yen for you"

Jan—as in Jaw + n

The name of the city translated means "City of Sandalwood."

Sweltering Vientiane features two hotels. No matter where you stay you're subject to the power failures that occur several times daily when every bloody appliance this side of the Mekong blows. Then there are no lights, no fans, no ironing, no nothing. Everybody waits in hot blackness until some little man rattles over in his ricksha and shoves another penny in the meter or something.

In our room in the Settha Palace we were preparing for the opening show the following night when Paul Johnson, the Director of the Lao-American school, came to pay us a visit. Cindy was cramming her Lao and I was boning up on next week's Djakarta and we were crouched, all huddled together in the pitch-black darkness. The only light in the whole room came from Cindy's Bunsen burner, where she was cooking up a fresh batch of spaghetti.

Paul came to see us about teaching English in the Lao-American School. "About a year ago, in August 1960, when things got a little rough around here," he explained, "five hundred wives of our men stationed in Vientiane were evacuated to Bangkok for protection."

"This may have protected them but it sure must have murdered their husbands," I said sympathetically.

"These wives of American personnel stationed here," he continued, "were the backbone of our teaching staff. It is very important that we keep this school open, as it is the only one that teaches English rather than French. And English is a major link in Lao-American relations. In order to keep our program going, we pressed into service army officers, Embassy officials, an odd missionary or two, or anybody that was passing through."

They even shanghaied tourists. If you could say "Hello, how are you?" without faltering, you taught advanced classes. One photographer in town for the *National Geographic* magazine took a class. Some Yale fellow rattling around the world took a class. And though the Laotian tourist rate is smaller than that of Siberia, any American who made a wrong turn and landed just long enough to get out—took a class.

"It would be wonderful," Paul suggested, "if *you* would take a class."

"Be glad to," I offered magnanimously. "Anything I can do to help. No job is too small, no job is too . . ."

"Not you. Mrs. Adams," he said.

"I don't mind," I said. "I'm a pretty good linguist, y'know. I can say, 'Good evening, friends' in high-class Lao, low-class Parsi or crosstown Cambodian."

"That's your trouble, darling," Cindy said. "You've been so busy learning all the other languages, that you've blown your own."

"Why do youse say that?" I protested. "My English she ain't bad."

"You're perfectly right," Cindy said. "You sound better already."

"Oh, well, *Sabydeekanoi,*" I chirped. "Which means 'Good evening' in Laotian."

"And a happy *Sabydeekanoi* to you, too," Cindy called as she dashed out with the schoolbooks under her arm.

Teaching class in a little red schoolhouse in Maine may have difficult moments, but entertainers who double at cramming English into seven hundred Laotians in a little bombed schoolhouse in Vientiane are really put to the test.

The Lao-American Association opened its doors in September 1959. They nearly shut them in August '60 when our American men were left wifeless and our Laotian pupils teacherless. It's a draw as to who was hardest hit.

Prince Spencer, one of the four Step Brothers, Joan Chase, wife of our comedy star, and Cindy were pressed into service immediately. They were handed the lessons for the day and pointed towards the blackboard. Their pupils ranged in age from 10 to 50, from monks to civilians. Tuition is 600 kip ($7.50) for a three-month course.

The method of instruction is choral mimicry. This means the teacher recites and the class repeats aloud. Laos, which was part of French Indochina, has many French-speaking citizens. But our home-made teachers were cautioned to employ "direct" methods—meaning only English was to be spoken.

After the first session, Cindy asked me to come to class. "Ohhh," I said sarcastically. "You need some help now, eh? You're calling for the master. You want me to come and teach, eh?"

"No," she said, "I want you to come and learn."

"Funn-eeee."

"My class, 2-C, has had 180 hours of English and some of them sound like they've had more than you."

"Funn-eeee," I repeated.

"At least," she sniped, "they have a larger vocabulary."

Cindy sat me in the back of the class with her advanced students. She opened her primer and recited aloud, "Janet Taylor was ready 10:30 on the dot." The class repeated it beautifully. This looks easy, I thought.

"What means 'on the dot'?" somebody asked haltingly.

Utilizing her wrist watch, Cindy pointed to it and explained it meant, "exactly." Pretty easy, I thought.

Feeling confident, Cindy said, "Now give me a sentence with the phrase, 'on the dot.'" Grinning happily, the student announced brightly, "I want a dress on the dot like yours." Not so easy, I thought.

Cindy continued, but with less bravado, until her nemesis, "Janet Taylor," opened a can of fruit. The pupils couldn't understand the word "can." She started explaining in French. Then she recalled that it's taboo to talk French. Then she realized she didn't remember the French word for "can" anyway. The most important thing is not to panic, I thought.

She clawed at the twenty-six pictorial charts lining the wall. There wasn't a picture of a can anyplace. She pantomimed, she sketched a picture on the blackboard. Even Del Monte wouldn't have recognized it.

With that I raced out like a maniac, tore down the steps, clumped through the streets of Vientiane, grabbed a can of spaghetti from my suitcase and rushed back, just as the class was leaving.

"What happened?" I asked my tortured wife.

"What happened?" she repeated, frothing. "What happened? I told them their stupid teacher would bring one of the damn things tomorrow to show them."

It was a broiling hot day. We were drenched with perspiration and failure. Before I killed myself, all I wanted out of life was some iced tea. We found a restaurant listed on our tip sheet. But in the restaurant nobody understood me or my schoolteacher wife. I tried English, Lao and even threw in some Cambodian. I used sign language. I drew pictures. Nothing. I finally ended up eating my own can of spaghetti. Unheated.

Frankly, I can't wait to get back to Laos because next time I'll insist on taking a class. If only to bring them a can and teach them two words: iced tea.

Americans have concerned themselves with health as well as education in Laos. In a tiny church in Vientiane, we visited the late Dr. Tom Dooley's priest and confessor, Father Menger. He spoke intimately of his friendship with the young founder of MEDICO.

This Medical International Cooperation Organization, the group which provides direct medical aid to underdeveloped countries, was born four years ago right here in Laos.

"Tom was intensely idealistic," said Father Menger. "He dreamed of a hospital in every country. But he was extremely realistic. He wrote a book a year so that the proceeds would make his plan feasible. He'd be at work by five every morning."

"Dr. Tom," as he was known in the field, was a simple MD with a king-size dream, a dream powerful enough to make Scrooges the world over open up their hearts and their wallets. His was the zeal of a father fighting for the life of his child. "Tom was such an outspoken foe of bureaucracy that he made many enemies," continued Father Menger. "When he came to town he'd room with me because he'd antagonized so many of our Embassy officials that nobody would put him up. He'd always say, 'Ours is the only person-to-person medical aid without religious or political strings.' Red tape causes loss of autonomy. For one badly needed Band-Aid, you'd have to file reports and wait until someone twelve thousand miles away okayed them!

"Some say Tom Dooley was a publicity seeker looking for self-glorification. An egotist. That whenever he opened his mouth Dooley came out. Others say he was a saint. A man of the people. A devoted worker for mankind. I only know that in his three years here he established seventeen installations. And the work must go on."

And the work *is* going on. We know, because we saw it. We saw it in Kabul, we saw it in Cambodia and later on in Saigon. It is ironic that Dr. Tom's three installations in Laos— MEDICO's birthplace—came to an end about the same time his life did. His first creation, Moung Sing, was evacuated because it's too close to the Red China border. The second at Ban Houei Sai is already in Communist territory and, because of the difficulty in getting supplies through, the third hospital has fallen apart.

In Cambodia, we visited the installation hacked from the jungles of Kratie. It's a nine-hour drive by jeep, an overnight boat trip up the Mekong or a forty-five minute flight by a single-engine egg crate. Telephones, telegraph offices are nonexistent. The only way they knew we were coming was when the plane dipped and buzzed the building. Their jeep then met us at the airstrip, built by the Japanese during the occupation. And away we jounced to the hospital.

The cases Kratie gets are a little different than the ones Dr. Kildare has to treat. Like the head-on collision accident victim. The only difference between an American and Cambodian traffic accident is the conveyance involved. This man had been thrown from an elephant. The patient was banged up and pent up. He chattered furiously. But in some dialect nobody understood. Let's face it, Khmer isn't exactly an international language. When they finally broke it down from Khmer to Cambodian to French to English, his problem was, "If I'm laid up in the hospital five days, who will look after my elephant?"

Here in the hospital, originally directed by a "medicine chief," nestled amongst the prejudices and superstitions of the hill tribesmen, MEDICO set up shop. Every morning they see about 150 cases starting at 7:00 A.M. Some are burns inflicted during childbirth since these people believe women must lie over red hot coals for many days before and after delivery. Others are burns incurred as a result of home remedies such as the application of hot irons to flesh to frighten the evil spirits.

Another do-it-yourself treatment is the string in the ear. It's knotted on both sides so it stays securely and it is used to alleviate inflammation. Questioned as to why the string wasn't in both ears to alleviate it faster, one tribesman answered, "I tried, but it didn't work that way."

A preponderance of patients are overdose cases. Medicine is a new toy in backward areas. Therefore, if one patient's dosage is to swallow two shiny capsules daily, his jealous friend might chomp four, five, or the whole bottle in one bash. And they're injection happy. Each outdoes his next-hut neighbor. In Kabul one woman was getting shots. Her friend wasn't. The doctor finally jabbed the friend with plain water to shut her up.

On Saturdays MEDICO pulls teeth. One yowling, howling sufferer wouldn't allow the trouble-making molar to be extracted because of the excruciating pain. Yet, she wouldn't be deprived of the distinction that having a tooth yanked would give her in this dentist-free community. She selected a different tooth, a healthy bicuspid, explaining, "The other hurts too much. Pull this one."

It costs MEDICO approximately $2.00 per patient. Treatments are free, but some grateful souls give what they can. For a routine examination, one fisherman's wife handed the technician a strand of bamboo. On it were several live crabs strung together like beads. For delivering his beautiful eight-pound son, one farmer brought an orange. Another gave his surgeon a dozen eggs. Eggs being costly in these parts, this equalled a specialist's fee. In Malaya, some minor surgery won the doc a panther and a talking bird, a mynah which chattered strictly in Malayan.

Many patients can't believe they're actually receiving something for nothing. It's beyond their ken. They regard the doctors as spies who must have ulterior motives. But whatever the motive, it isn't money—or comfort—or perfect conditions.

Miss Dodie Stokes is twenty-nine. From Texas, she is a technician at Lomphat Village, the second Cambodian installation, in the mountain province of Ratanakiri. So primitive is Lomphat that for six months every year it is totally inaccessible. Her quarters? A six-by-six foot one-room tree house that can be reached only by ladder. It has bamboo floors, grass roof, stands ten feet off the ground in a hollowed-out tree trunk. Running water and plumbing—outdoor or indoor—is something she only dreams about.

Dr. John Jauregui, head of Kratie, is twenty-seven. He lives with his wife, four children aged five, four, two, one, several stray dogs and a monkey. The monkey was a gift. Jauregui once refused a present in order to stop the practice. The offended patient never returned. He now accepts all gifts. Even monkeys.

Often these expensively trained MD's double as architects, engineers, chambermaids, supply officers, carpenters, diplomats who can mesh harmoniously with local officials, and mechanics who can repair generators, fashion sewage disposals and coax weary truck engines to rouse themselves just one more time. Occasionally, they triple as veterinarians and crop-rotation consultants.

Always, they infiltrate the community, mix with the people, afford them their first glimpse of Americanism and in many cases do more to cement love and friendship between our countries than foreign aid ever could. It gave our troupe a thrill to feel that all us guys and gals were on the same team.

CHAPTER 11

Exchanging Friendship in Laos

I WAS DISCUSSING the problem of foreign aid with our Ambassador, Winthrop G. Brown, one evening in his residence in Vientiane.

"I'd like to tell you about some of the things we are trying to accomplish here even under the present difficult circumstances," he said. "For instance, I went to the royal city of Luang Prabang recently to be present at the opening of a small dam situated about five miles outside of the city. To those of us who think about the Boulder Dam at home, this one may not seem very impressive at first glance because it is only three feet high and sixty feet across. Yet to me it was very impressive because of what it signified in terms of practical results and active collaboration between the local people and their government and our government."

As we sat in his back yard, he explained that this dam is a simple concrete structure which will supply three neighboring villages with a constant flow of good water sufficient to irrigate

119

five hundred acres of land throughout the year. The basic design was done by an American engineer attached to USAID. The details were worked out by engineers of the Lao Government Department of Agriculture in consultation with the American engineer.

The work was done by the local villagers under the supervision of the Lao Department of Agriculture and with several visits by our American engineer for counsel and advice. The cement and some dynamite which was required was provided by USAID. Aside from the time our engineer spent in doing the design work and in his several visits on consultation, the total cost to the United States for this dam was $385.00.

I asked Ambassador Brown if the Lao are particularly proud of this little dam. "Very," he said, smiling broadly. "This is typical of the kind of thing we are trying to help them do in this country. We have to recognize that the area in which we can work is now limited because of the unfortunate security situation. Yet there are still substantial regions of the country in which Lao forces have control and the villagers can operate in peace."

In these areas, under the direction of a Lao who is Commissioner of Rural Development, a program has been worked out for rural development on this self-help principle. This means that the local government officials go to the villagers and say to them, "If you will tell us what you need and are prepared to provide the land, the labor, and the locally available materials necessary to accomplish the project, we will help you with the technical advice and with the materials which you yourselves cannot provide."

After a slow start this program is beginning to roll. The type of project which the villagers I met normally asked for was a schoolhouse, a small dam like the one the Ambassador described, a road to communicate with other villages or even a well. The schoolhouses are very simple, with cement floors, wattle walls, a plain wooden frame and perhaps corrugated iron roofing. Like MEDICO, which also began in Laos, this program is designed to help the Lao to help themselves.

Our troupe had a first-hand experience with one of the Laotian projects that was still incomplete. It was a half-built, outdoor sports arena. And we were the first sports to inaugurate it.

Our Embassy had received many requests from the Lao Army to see us. The military had been unable to get tickets to the scheduled performances because those had been sold out weeks in advance to the civilians. Besides, even had we scheduled an extra performance, the theater was not sufficiently large to accommodate all those soldiers who wanted to attend. The theater's seats numbered about five hundred. The soldiers' requests numbered about ten thousand.

Of course we wanted to do it. We wanted to do anything. We wanted to do everything. So, when it came to the Lao Army, we wanted to see them as much as they wanted to see us.

The largest place available to accommodate all the soldiers was that unfinished project—the sports arena. Actually, at this point it was only a couple of semicircular tiers of concrete set in an acre of mud. Like all over French Indochina, this was monsoon season. And when it wasn't monsooning it was raining, and when it wasn't raining it was flooding. All I know is, it was always wet. Here, we were grateful for the weather. Because it meant we were safe from attack, no matter what went on at the local summit meeting. There's always a cessation of hostilities during the monsoon because the enemy can't move along the muddy roads, can't transport his men, can't navigate the Mekong. But this rainy season was about finis. Time was running out. When we finally did pull out eight days later, it was felt we were amscraying none too soon.

Meanwhile, back at the ditch, the rains had stopped, but the ground was still submerged in water. The day of the army show, forty burlap bags were commandeered and thrown into the water holes. This sopped up some of the mud and gave us enough foundation to lay planks across so our girls could get to the stage in their costumes. The stage was a hastily built ramp which our boys pasted together, with the help of the Lao Army. The appreciative Lao soldiers even kept iced soda and cold towels backstage for us. The Lao Boy Scouts were our ushers and escorts.

The U.S. Marines who were stationed there also got into the act. A couple of them lent a hand and a hammer to build us a desperately needed john. Next to it they put up a dressing room. Around it they threw an honor guard. Ours was the only john in captivity with a private, uniformed doorman.

I wonder if it ever struck Kipling that East would meet West in Laos where a stadium full of Buddhists would someday clap their hands, stomp their feet and holler their heads off to a Yankee jazz band tootling, "When the Saints Go Marchin' In"?

Throughout this trip we worked under every condition. In order to be a hit in this part of the world, it's just as important to be a Daniel Boone as it is to be a Daniel Kaye. Once we even did a show during a dust storm. It had stopped raining just long enough to start dusting. The dust reacted like ground glass on our mikes. So they had to be swaddled in felt. This might've been good for our mikes, but it was hell on our singers. They sounded like they were yodelling into rain barrels.

Our stage manager, Jerry Bell, was called upon to do things way beyond the call of stage managing. His first job was as plumber *extraordinaire*. Whenever we set up shop in a theater, his number-one duty was to bring the outhouse indoors. Then he had to get fresh flowers each performance. And they had to be boiled. A good portion of Chaz Chase's act is to eat everything in sight. He chomps cigars, cigarettes, matches, his shirt front, even his boutonniere. But he won't chew up a flower unless it's washed. And you can't wash with water in Southeast Asia unless it's boiled.

Next, Jerry had to rope off a segment of backstage so that John and Bonnie Shirley could blow up their four hundred balloons each show. These are not the usual round balloons. They're long ones. And when they're inflated they're several feet in length. This area had to be protected against winds and dust because dust would bust our precious balloons. Invariably the entrance to the stage had to be widened so these huge crates of balloons could be brought out for the finale.

Another job for Jerry was the doves which Celeste Evans used in her magic act. He had to get the Good Housekeeping Seal of Approval for them country by country. Even if we were sweltering enough to die, he had to see that the fans were off when her doves were on. The slightest breeze on their feathers and you end up with ruffled doves. And this would have ruffled Celeste a helluva lot, too. And here there was always the danger that some local gourmet would cop one of them and have fried squab on toast for his midday meal.

The four Step Brothers are precision tap dancers. The smoothness of their act depends on the smoothness of their floor. Don't misunderstand. Radio City Music Hall we didn't expect, but most of these stages were about as level as Jayne Mansfield's profile. Consequently, Jerry had to Scotch-tape a stage together every show, and hope that the local wood would not have warped by showtime. Because each theater area was different, we couldn't transport the same tailor-made stage from place to place.

Since the musicians were onstage all through the show, Jerry had to see that each one was supplied with a cold bottle of pop, iced towels, and his own personal can of insect repellent. In these hot, moist countries, when the powerful stage lights went on they drew every insect this side of Pago Pago. This meant Jerry had to DDT the stage and our boys before and during every show. And he had to hose down our outdoor platforms nightly to clear the decks of dead bugs.

Another major headache were the peeping Toms, Dicks and Harrys. They were harmless. They didn't want much. All they wanted was to watch our beautiful 39–24–34 Sylte Sisters undress. Now that's not asking too much, is it? I mean, I can't say I blamed them. Who wouldn't? But it seemed to me—and to the Syltes—that there must be a more diplomatic way of establishing Asian-American relations.

Even in America the world of make-believe is a magnet. There are always stage-door Johns and Janes. There are always autograph seekers and photograph takers. There's no private life if you're in the public eye. It's always open season on show people.

Add to that people who've never seen our kind of entertainers before. Multiply that by people who've never seen our kind of people before. And you've got a mob scene outside our stage entrance that would make the subway at rush hour look like a night club in the daytime. Most of them seemed to be clustered around the Syltes' dressing room window, or a chink in the wall, or a tear in the canvas, or a break in the plaster or wherever the girls were changing. Periodically, ricocheting through our theater, could be heard the bloodcurdling shriek of "J-e-e-e-rrr-r-r-r-ryyy-y-y!" This meant, "Whatever you're doing, come quick! We found another pair of eyes!"

Jerry came quick. And he closed up the dressing room window or chink in the wall or tear in the canvas or break in the plaster or wherever we developed a new hole in our flank.

After a while we not only stationed guards outside, but inside, too. In one country we had a rash of souvenir hunters. They seemed to find things before they were lost. Like a couple of teakwood elephants that were given to us by the head of the Thai Army in Chiengmai. Once a couple of pair of shoes, tied together by shoelaces, mysteriously walked away—and there were no feet in them!

For the first seven weeks I used to do my big trick at the end of Celeste's magic act. I made a cane disappear. Only one night somebody made the cane disappear before I could. This cut short my magic career, but it probably started a whole new one for some sleight-of-hand artist in Southeast Asia.

One day poor old Jerry went out searching for our souvenir

hunters and returned with a hole in his pants. Some souvenir hunter had sliced off his back pocket—wallet and all. But in a way none of us really minded these involuntary contributions to foreign aid.

Considering the basic training we'd taken in all these other stops, the theater in Laos where we did our scheduled performances was pretty good. While we were putting on our show at the Natasinh Theater, the three Laotian princes were putting on a show of their own on a hill some place. I don't know who was winning across the bargaining table, but across the footlights we were way ahead.

We were way ahead offstage, too. I figured we reached a good percentage of the people and at least 33⅓ per cent of the princes. Our Prince Charming was Boun Oum. As a gesture of friendship, he tossed a swinging outdoor rice party for us at his palace. Boun Oum was the head of the Laotian Right Wing Government. But this night he put politics aside and it was right wingding all the way.

When the equerry invited us to this unexpected and unprecedented dinner, I was in a dilemma.

"I'd love to," I stammered, "but USIS is throwing a dinner for us at the same time."

"USIS *was* throwing a dinner at the same time," said the equerry.

"Was?" I repeated stupidly.

"It's been cancelled."

"Who cancelled it?" I asked.

"The Prince."

"In that case," I said, "we'll be there."

As he turned to leave, I said, "By the way, USIS has made a great deal of preparation for this party. Do they know it's been cancelled?"

"I'm on my way to tell them now," he answered.

This promised to be a big dinner because when I'm asked to a feed, I bring the whole family. When you invited J. Adams you invited twenty-five eaters. We always traveled as a team. These were the instructions I issued ever since we had an incident in Nepal. There, only twelve of us were invited to a certain function. This was on the way to causing a lot of disharmony until I found out about it. From then on we had a rule. If it's an official function and they want one—they have to take all. Unless, of course, somebody didn't want to go for reasons of his own. But that was his problem. I saw to it that everybody was always invited. Invariably, everybody always showed up. After all, it was the only game in town.

Besides food and drink fit for a king—or, rather, prince— Boun Oum served liberal portions of gorgeous girls who performed the traditional Laotian dances for us. For dessert, His Highness himself played the national Lao instrument which sounds like the word "cane" and looks like a bamboo bagpipe.

The members of the royal houses of Asia are all musical. In Afghanistan, the Crown Prince plays a swinging guitar and the younger son blows a cool sax, daddy-o. In Nepal, the King's brother, a jazz buff, collects everything on records from Rudy Vallee to Bix Beiderbecke. And when it comes to King Phumiphon of Thailand he's right up there with those other royal cats: Duke Ellington, Count Basie, and Nat King Cole. Prince Sihanouk, the Irving Berlin of Cambodia, is well known to tear off a snappy composition in between running the affairs of state. But, man, you ain't heard nothin' yet till you dig Boun Oum of Laos beat out a mean "cane."

Talk about Cultural Exchange, I could really make a pile if I could get all these boys together for one hot fortnight at Birdland.

The Prince was a jolly host. As we all arrived in our Sunday-go-to-meetin' clothes, he met us at the door in an open-collar sport shirt. "Did we arrive too early, Mr. Prime Minister?" Cindy asked in her busted French. That was the only language in which we could communicate because His Highness speaks no United States and we didn't exactly talk a Castilian Laotian.

"*Non*," he said in flawless French.

"What'd he say?" I asked.

"He said 'no,' " the interpreter said.

"He said 'no,' " Cindy explained, interpreting the interpreter.

"Oh, he said 'no,' " I said.

Then, according to my wife's translation, he either said, "My aunt is in the attic with her lawn mower and her bloomers," or "My mother-in-law is running around in her sneakers inside the dog."

"What'd he say?" I asked the interpreter.

"He said this was supposed to be an informal party so take off your jackets and ties and make yourselves comfortable."

"What did he say?" Cindy asked.

"What'd he say? He's speaking English! Don't you recognize your own language? What's your native tongue?"

"I've forgotten. I've been living with you so long."

My gang, who lo! these many months had been hammered on the head to wear ties and jackets at all times, did look at me a little strangely when I sauntered in tieless and jacketless. "When in Rome . . ." I said to the boys. And before I could say, "Julius Caesar," they unraveled down to their shirts and slacks.

Not that I want to be a Prime-Minister-dropper, but it reminded me of a similar incident with David Ben-Gurion when we were in Israel in 1952. I was excited about meeting the Head of State, because up until then the only Head of State I'd ever known was my mother-in-law.

When I dressed for the occasion I not only had starched collar and cuffs, but starched lapels as well. I don't have to tell you about my wife. She makes a visit to the A & P a formal affair. You've heard of Jackie Kennedy's underdressed look? Well, Cindy hasn't. We looked like we were ready for a coronation. When David Ben-Gurion greeted us at the King David Hotel in Jerusalem, he wore an open-collar sport shirt—with a

figured design, yet. I said to my wife, "Forget it. I'm not wearing any more ties for the rest of the trip." Two weeks later we
were in Haifa at the Megiddo Hotel on top of Mount Carmel.
They were advertising a Saturday-night dance. I thought it
would be fun if Cindy and I went to the dance like any two
sabras in Israel. No interpreters, no photographers, no guides,
no nothin'. I paid the admission like everybody else, presented
my tickets at the door and a man stopped me. "You can't come
in," he said. "You gotta wear a tie."

"You kidding?" I screamed. "David Ben-Gurion, the Prime
Minister of Israel; David Ben-Gurion, the head man, never
wears a tie."

"I know," he said. "But David Ben-Gurion never comes to
our Saturday-night dances."

Prime Minister Boun Oum had thrown together a very
snazzy spread. His attire may have been informal, but his
larder wasn't. He doesn't exactly rough it in Vientiane. Behind
a high fence and a cordon of guards, he lives in an enormous
mansion set in acres and acres of grounds. In every corner of
the garden he had a table piled high with foodstuffs, and
there were some gorgeous dishes dishing it out, too.

"Did you ever see so many different exotic foods?" Cindy
said happily, licking her chops.

"First prize," said I, "goes to anybody who can tell me what
they are."

"Listen," Cindy warned, "leave us have none of your picky
eating. We are guests of the Prince. And whatever he offers
us we will eat. And we will enjoy it. And we will smile . . .
won't we?"

"You know me," I groaned. "Kill me, shoot me, beat me,
stab me, I'm a lamb-chops-and-broccoli man."

"Oh, I know you, all right," she snapped. "You go in a
Chinese restaurant and order an American cheese on white
bread. It's not the Prince's fault that you're a wacko on food."

My wife, who loves this kind of eating, had long since

abandoned her spoon and was now working with a shovel. There was one little goody which His Highness personally prepared for my Cindy. It was a whole bunch of chopped stuff served on a leaf. The idea was to wrap the leaf around it and eat it whole—bush and all. Then there was another tasty called glutinous rice. This I altogether never saw before in my life. It's gummy like an eraser. You pick it up with your fingers and pinch, squash, and knead it into whatever size ball you want. This then is sloshed around in peanut juice—and a good time is had by all.

My wife was up to her elbows in sauce while I was starving. "What can I tell ya?" I said. "I'm a man what has traveled. I've been to Germany, I've been to Turkey, I've been to Africa, I've been to Greece, I've been to Philadelphia. I have never seen such food. I don't know what to refuse first."

"Obviously," Cindy said, rolling another lump of glutinous rice, "you are a peasant. There are five hundred people here and every single one of them is lapping up the food like mad. It's delicious. It's positively terrific. I'm loving it."

"Why don't you ask the Prince for the recipe?" I needled.

"Leave us not forget why we are here," she said, stuffing another leaf in her mouth. "No sacrifice is too great for your country."

"Not even heartburn?"

"Oh, shaddup," she said, "and eat something. I'll see that you get the Purple Heart."

"Better I should get a ham sandwich," I muttered, reaching for a leaf.

The palace was overflowing with gaiety. The Lao are a happy people. And the gayest and happiest of them all was the Prince. He's about 6 feet 2 inches tall, has silver hair and an infectious smile. He's big, he's jolly, and he's round.

The Lao respond to joy easily. I will always remember the love that filled Boun Oum's garden in Vientiane that Friday night. It was for this reason that Cultural Exchange was born. This was the reason for our visit. This is why the official receptions were mandatory, and it was written into the contract that they had to be given and we had to attend them. At these functions, we had a chance to look each other over and we liked each other.

All I know is, every place we went they liked us. And they liked America. We saw no "Yankee, Go Home" signs. There were no anti-American demonstrations. I believe the people of Southeast Asia are not motivated by hatred for our country, our leaders or our people. But they are afraid.

Everywhere they are peppered with the Red propaganda that Americans are rich, bloated with power, and spoiling for war. They're afraid those "warmongering bullies of the West" might drag them into another fight.

That's why our tour was more than a Cultural Exchange. We exchanged far more than culture. We exchanged friendship and ideas and customs and laughter. As General Clay said so well, "When the tensions are eased, there's always a better atmosphere." We were there to ease those tensions. We were traveling without portfolio, armed only with friendship and fun.

Foreign aid is a waste of money unless the people of each country get a chance to meet the Americans who are giving it to them. You see, they think we're loaded with money and, therefore, it's the easiest thing for us to give away. It's like a wealthy father who sends his child to boarding school, supplies him with all the loot he needs, but not the love. Sending a fat check is not enough. It's nicer to give it in person, and to give some of yourself along with it.

When we went to the wards to do shows, the blind touched us, the sick reached out to us. No paved highways can buy that. We were showing them we cared. And they certainly appreciated it. They were overflowing with thanks.

As a parting bouquet we were treated to a ceremony which is the highest offering of Laotian love, the *baci*. The *baci* is a traditional gesture of Lao friendship given at weddings, the birth of a child, or the arrival and departure of good friends. In the *baci*, the honored guests sit on the floor around a centerpiece of flowers which have been placed in a silver bowl. An older, respected member of the community chants verses in honor of the guests and then he ties their wrists with cotton string.

When anyone's wrist is being tied, all the others, who sit around the guests in a circle, must touch the person beside them or in front of them so that the "good spirits" flow throughout the group. Eventually, everyone in the group will have his wrists tied in this manner. The "good spirits" that we took away will remain with us as a symbol of Lao-American friendship.

In line with the ritual, the twenty-five of us removed our shoes and sat cross-legged on a deep pile of carpeting. We were ever mindful to hide the soles of our feet. One of the highlights of the ritual is the *lamthad*, a Lao song which alternates between chorus and solo and which is tailor-made for each special occasion. Each singer, given the general topic, makes up his or her own verses, like the Calypso singers of the West Indies. In our honor they chanted:

Chorus: Think of the lovely smell of these flowers, full of the fragrance of the sun, that even shine in the evening.

First solo, sung by Miss Dok Mai: We wish to pay respect and love to the troupe of Mr. Adams and all his guests who join us here.

Second solo, sung by Miss Chanla: The Natasinh School of the Fine Arts Department wants to thank the Joey Adams Show for coming to show us the civilized nation.

Third solo, sung by Miss Nilavan: Everyone enjoys seeing all the wonderful abilities of the troupe. Singing songs, playing music, dancing in a wonderful way, making jokes, making balloons, making magic!

Fourth solo, sung by Miss Ohoam: We all put our palms together to wish the Joey Adams Show well.

Finale: Good luck and a safe voyage. Have a happy journey. Have long life and happiness forever. If you do, you will obey our wishes!

Amongst Asiatics, hands clasped as in prayer at chest level is a greeting of respect. At lip level it's greater respect and at the forehead it's supreme reverence. They placed their palms together and we placed our palms together in prayer position before the forehead and we all of us bowed to one another.

The more exalted the guest, the more numerous the strings. Around our wrists they'd looped so much cord that we looked as if we were handcuffed. Everybody was cautioned not to remove these—under penalty of broken friendship—until they fell off naturally. Or, at the very least, to keep them on a minimum of three full days. Every single one of us kept to the tradition. Not one removed our bindings until the third day was up.

The last morning of our stay in Vientiane, Bert Potts, Gordon Murchey and Paul Johnson, Cindy's principal at the Lao-American School, came to help us pack. All of us had cotton strings on our wrists. We were all bound in friendship, Lao-style. It made me a little sentimental.

I started to think of my friends and family back home. And what they were doing at this very moment. And why hadn't I heard from them. Then I remembered they were cautioned against sending letters to us in Vientiane because of the odds against the mail getting through.

"Oh, I forgot," Bert Potts said. "I have a letter for you." I grabbed it out of her hand, tore open the envelope and ripped out the letter.

"Who's it from?" Cindy barked. "What does it say? What's happening back home? They must be so worried about us. What's the news? Is everything all right?"

"It's from your mother," I said.

"Oh, the poor darling!" Cindy said. "She must be so worried about us. What does she say?"

" 'Dear kids,' she says. 'The whole country is in an uproar. Everybody is all excited about the sensation of the nation. Everybody is doing it. Children and grownups alike. It's a new dance craze. It's called the Twist.' "

If we had been on Mars we couldn't have felt further away from home. But really way out, and on another planet. The Twist! Back home they're shaking behinds . . . and here they're shaking worlds.

As we were checking out of the Settha Palace, our Ambassador, Winthrop Brown, brought us the news that Prince Boun Oum, our friend (who was still a prince and still our friend) had been ousted as Prime Minister. "I wonder whether this event will make as big a splash at home as the Twist," I said to Cindy. "It's hard to tell from here what's really important any more."

CHAPTER 12

Command Performance
for Sukarno

Ever since we amscrayed the USA to play the
Afghan-Lao-Cambodian circuit—which is the Asian version
of New York, New Haven and Hartford—we've played the
Palace more often than Nora Bayes. So, although another
Command Performance was routine, sharing a rice bowl with
President Sukarno of Indonesia wasn't.

We were scheduled to present our court jesters at 5:00 P.M.
at Sukarno's country palace in Bogor. There was only one
tiny, little problem. Nothing important. We just didn't have
any instruments, props, costumes or luggage—that's all. We'd
arrived the day before from Laos via Bangkok and it seems
either Royal Air Lao or Garuda Indonesian Airlines or some
Thai skycap mislaid our stuff—although how anybody could
just mislay 3,009 pounds of equipment, not including personal
luggage, I do not know.

When we changed planes in Bangkok, we found ourselves
in the usual predicament. They couldn't take all the equipment

134

and the luggage and the people like they promised. This was S.O.P. in every airport in every city in every country. As always, everything was all set up and checked in advance. They knew we had 125 pieces of personal luggage, not including hand baggage. They also knew how many pieces of hand baggage we had. They also knew we had 3,009 pounds of equipment—not including the Wurlitzer electric piano that the Wurlitzer people had donated to this tour. They knew there was a complement of twenty-five persons. They knew the size, weight, and color of every piece of equipment, every hunk of luggage, and every single passenger.

They had our passports and our blood count. They knew where we were coming from and where we were going to. But whenever we got to an airport "they couldn't take all the equipment and the luggage and the people like they promised."

Many planes couldn't accommodate our full load since invariably we had to land in airfields too small for jets. Often we would have to split up. Our crew would fly some Kitty Hawk job whilst our cargo rode another. Take, for instance, our big crate of lights. This held everything. It carried generators, handmade fuses, flashlights, power batteries, transformers and everything so that American voltage would fit Asian wattage and Asian amps would fit American bulbs and so altogether our two worlds would fit plug-to-plug with their sockets.

This big crate of lights which was so important to us backstage was a pain in the butt to every airline. On one hop this crate was just exactly two inches too fat for the belly of the antique C-47 we were hitching a ride on. We all had to wait around the field for three hours while this big mama crate got busted down into four little baby crates.

Another time, for two and a half hours, our sound man rode through a storm standing up in a cargo plane which had no bucket seats, no safety belts, no nothin'. We'd learned by now somebody had to guard the equipment. If it wasn't waylaid or mislaid, it usually got busted. Heavy transformers were almost always piled on top of glass props, and underneath everything you'd be sure to find my little Yankee Doodle straw hat.

At every airport there was organized confusion. Personal stuff had yellow tags marked "P." Stage gear had pink labels with "S." All was numbered. All was counted. In theory it worked great. In reality what took place was the mad mix-up of a Marx Brothers' comedy.

Luggage was always a big problem. If we had to make an eleven o'clock plane, our wake-up call was at 8:00 A.M. But our luggage call was for 6:00 A.M. This meant we had to have our luggage packed, marked and lined up in the lobby by six o'clock. We couldn't stash it in the lobby the night before because there was nobody to watch it. And you couldn't exactly check 125 pieces of luggage in the parcel room— even if they had a parcel room.

Cindy finally came up with the answer. "Jerry's got to get up early with the luggage anyway on account of he's in charge of it. So how's about we all stick all our luggage in Jerry's room the night before? This way we can all lay around in bed till 8:00 A.M."

"Yeah, let's all stick all our luggage in Jerry's room the night before," chorused everybody but Jerry.

That solved our problem. But now Jerry had one. His room became an alley. All through the night all sorts of stray humans were dragging in valises, car sacks and shoe boxes. Poor old Jerry never complained. The night before every trip he went to bed with 125 old bags. Personally, I think it's the best thing that happened to him on the whole tour.

When we stopped off in Bangkok on our way to Indonesia, it was the same old story: "They couldn't take all the equipment and the luggage and the people like they promised." If I hadn't had to make a plane I would have killed myself. Oh, they were very polite. Thai people always are. Of course, I've never seen a Thai whose luggage was missing or who couldn't get his equipment on a plane, but they are the politest people in the whole world. They speak softly. They smile a lot. And they never hurry.

The Thai stewardess behind the check-in counter was as beautiful and fragile-looking as an orchid. She smiled wide and bowed low. "I'm sorry," she whispered politely, "but it seems they couldn't take all the equipment and the luggage and the people like they promised."

By now my nerves were screaming inside me. We'd gotten no sleep the night before. We had been ready very early to make the plane from Laos. It was hot. It was always hot. And I didn't even have any money to get a cold drink. That is, I didn't have any Thai money. My pockets were jingling with Laotian kips, Afghan afs and Nepali rupees. In one pocket I even had a couple of yards of Cambodian riels. But not one baht to my name.

I was ready to explode. I was just about to blow my top when the words of that first briefing rolled around in my weary brain: *DON'T* raise your voice to a Thai, *DON'T* point or shake your finger, *DO* keep smiling . . .

I managed to separate my lips just enough to let my two front teeth peek through. "You see," I whispered and smiled, "we have a command performance for President Sukarno tomorrow afternoon in Indonesia and we can't do it without luggage and equipment."

The Thai stewardess smiled and bowed and called in her superior who bowed and smiled. I, too, bowed and smiled. By now my back and jaw muscles were beginning to ache. Eventually, the officials did the only thing possible under the circumstances—they got rid of us. They turned us over to the representative in charge of the Garuda Indonesian Airline. They figured, let *him* worry.

The name "Sukarno" was magic here. These people immediately went to work. They took some seats out of our plane to make room for our equipment and baggage. Then they didn't have enough seats for all of us, so they replaced the seats and took out the baggage and equipment. It looked like we were back where we started. But not quite. It was now three hours later.

They finally decided that their main problem was to get us the hell out of the airport. We looked like DP's. Our troupe was sprawled out all over the terminal. So they arranged to put us on the first plane out and ship our luggage and equipment the first thing in the morning. We arrived in Djakarta on schedule. Exactly five hours late. It was now 2:00 A.M.

Outside of two night watchmen and an insomniac, there wasn't the usual large delegation to meet us at the airport. But we were lucky, at that. Because we had no luggage and equipment we went through customs in only two and a half hours! We figured we'd worry about our gear the next morning. And we did.

It is said that everything looks different in the light of day. The next morning everything did look different. It was worse. Now we were not only missing our stuff but a Garuda Indonesian airplane as well. Nothing serious. It just didn't show up.

"Don't worry," chorused the airline officials. "Fear not," we were told. "It's coming this afternoon."

It was now twelve noon. Just five hours before we were due to appear before President Sukarno at Bogor Palace. And still we had no bags, equipment, make-up, clothes, props—no nothin'.

Everybody in our group was in a funk. That is, everybody except me. I was calm, cool and numb. I mean—let's face it —who stands up a President? I don't work good in front of a firing squad. The most important thing, I kept saying to myself, is not to panic. A fat little man with a wide tie and beads of sweat on his top lip was the spokesman for Garuda. "They said you shouldn't worry. They said it's coming this afternoon."

"Who is 'they'?" I asked. The beads of sweat were now showing up on my upper lip. It's always "they." "They" say that falling in love is wonderful. "They" say I shouldn't worry because my luggage is coming this afternoon. Who the hell is "they"?

Cindy smiled and whispered to me, *"DON'T* raise your voice, *DON'T* point or shake your finger, *DO* keep smiling." Cindy overlooked one small point. *She* isn't a Thai or an Indonesian. So naturally I took all of this out on her.

"DON'T butt in!" I shrieked, *"DON'T* nag me, and *DO* leave me alone!"

I turned to the fat little man with the wide tie and the beads of sweat on his top lip. "Who is 'they'?" I queried softly, controlling myself. "I want to speak to the 'they' who are in charge of my luggage and equipment. Will you please take me to 'they'?"

The beads of sweat on his top lip rolled down. He now had beads of sweat on his lower lip. And so did I.

At 2:00 P.M. the missing 8:00 A.M. plane arrived from Bangkok. Everything came off but our luggage and equipment. "They" just hadn't put it on the plane.

Now our luggage had reached the proportions of an international incident. The time for making with jokes was over. The fat little man with the wide tie, and the fat little comedian with the thin smile were no longer the principals in this drama. The Embassy of the United States of America and the Government of the Republic of Indonesia took over.

A priority cable was sent from our Ambassador in Indonesia, Howard Palfrey Jones, to our Ambassador in Thailand, Kenneth Young. Couched in diplomatic talk, the gist of the message was, "H-E-L-P!!!!"

For years President Sukarno had been suggesting to our Embassy that they sponsor an American Variety program here. The Joey Adams Show was the first one to come through. He'd looked forward to it for months. As we learned later, he had been scheduled to fly to Vienna for a kidney operation and had postponed it a week just so he could see our show. He had invited five hundred of the top four hundred of Indonesia to be present at the command performance. The importance of our appearance was, at this point, completely out of proportion.

Nobody cared about us any more. We were just the pawns in an international chess game. We were dummies who had to have clothes, props, and instruments. The major concern of two governments was just to get us ready, wind us up and point us toward the stage.

Our Embassy in Thailand chartered a Royal Thai Air Force plane and sent a cable to the tune of: "Keep your tuxedo on. Baggage arriving 7:00 P.M."

The plane was an hour late. This was great because we were due at the palace at five. The show was scheduled for six. Now the seven o'clock plane wouldn't be in until eight. It was still an hour's drive from the airport in Djakarta to the President's country place in Bogor. This meant we couldn't start dressing or begin to get our stage ready until nine. Which meant showtime was penciled in for ten o'clock.

Somewhere around seven o'clock, Sukarno himself had gotten into the act. He stationed his army at the airport to unload our equipment. He had aides on hand to whisk it through customs, plus trucks and official motorcycles standing by to careen the fifty-five miles to Bogor. It was the first time in history that a bunch of saxophones and microphones ever had a military escort.

Meanwhile, back at the palace, the natives were getting restless. They'd finished dinner and small talk and had been sitting around for hours waiting for the main event. The calmest and most gracious of all was the President himself. For the major portion of the evening he sat off in a corner with me swapping traveling-salesman-type jokes and sentimentally crooning Negro spirituals with our Sylte Sisters.

The President was in a jovial mood. We soon found that he loves to sing and he loves to joke and he seems to have a great capacity for enjoyment. Referring to himself in the third person as he is prone to do, the President said, "The best description written of Sukarno is that 'He's a great lover. He loves his country. He loves his nation. He loves music and art. He loves women. And he loves himself.' "

"In that order, Mr. President?" Cindy asked.

"Yes," he smiled widely, "in that order."

That Sukarno's personal magnetism emanates even from the set of his shoulders, from the back of his neck, is known to Sukarno himself. He generates electricity. He's dynamite from the top of his *beji* to the tip of his gleaming black boots. It is an image that he is aware of and strives to maintain.

He carried the gold-headed walking stick presented to him by the army and wore his trade-mark: powder-blue uniform and *beji,* that dark velvet cap, now the symbol of nationalism, which he never removes. ("In our society it is unpolite to remove one's cap. Besides, I am getting a little thin on top.") Minus the horn-rimmed spectacles, he looked far less than the sixty years he admitted to.

"The President seldom wears civilian clothes," he explained, in answer to the question, "because as Supreme Commander of the Armed Forces, the people like to see the President in uniform."

"Could it be, maybe, that the President likes to see the President in uniform?" asked my fearless wife. "Or maybe that the President knows he looks handsomer in uniform?" He threw his head back, flung his arms over the back of the chair and laughed loudly. Then, "I use your American expression, 'No comment.' "

The waiters were passing around refreshments of every sort, but the President stuck to cigarettes and black coffee. "I diet constantly," he sighed, lighting another cigarette. "I never touch one drop of alcohol because it doesn't belong to those five great loves of my life, but smoking keeps your line. You eat less."

Admittedly vain, he playfully thwacked his midriff. "I don't have many suits and every time I get a little fat I have to let them out."

At this point, Madame Sukarno, a wifely look on her beautiful face, pattered over and whispered quickly. Immediately, the President of the Republic of Indonesia did what any husband—president or pants-presser—would do. He minded his missus and got up to mix and mingle with the guests. He went from table to table entertaining his friends, Indonesians and countrymen, with an almost professional skill. President Sukarno turned out to be the most high-class social director in the business.

The First Lady of Indonesia, Hartini—whom the President calls "Tin" for short—would be a First Lady anywhere. She's attractive, she's gracious and she's regal. Madame Sukarno was wearing native dress because the President does not like her to wear Western clothing since, as he puts it, "I prefer her to reflect the Indonesian identity."

She had on an ankle-length red and black batik sarong. Batik is the hand-painted cloth that is a specialty of Indonesia. Over this she wore the traditional finger-tip length black lace tunic with long sleeves. "The President prefers me to wear black," she told us. "In fact, he prefers all women to wear black. It's his favorite color. The President is very interested in my clothes," she continued in her perfect English. "He buys much of my material. Even when he's abroad he brings me many different kinds of material. And for important functions we select my wardrobe together."

Hartini Sukarno had black hair pulled back into a bun, just like Cindy. And she wore big gold ornaments in her bun, just like Cindy. In fact, when they were sitting together, the wife of the boss of Indonesia and the bossy wife of Adams looked like sisters.

As befits a State occasion, all the guests were resplendent in their silks and satins. Our gang was bewitched, bothered and bedraggled in their three-day-old drip-drys. As usual, we had had to leave our luggage with Jerry the night before, so we had worn these stunning traveling outfits the last day in Laos, the whole day traveling to Bangkok and now this long day in Indonesia. By now we looked like we could use a couple of CARE packages.

Cindy couldn't even get her hair done for the big night. She has coal-black hair. She's what you call "a bottled brunette." The dye was in the bottom of her suitcase and without it she was out of luck. In Asia, everybody's got black hair. So the hairdressers are equipped to make you blonde, red or bald. But they ain't got no such thing as black dye. That would be coals to Newcastle.

You might say our outfits clashed somewhat with the magnificence of the President's summer palace. It's set in acres and acres of lawn on which roam countless head of deer. Bogor is all white. It's decorated with priceless tapestries, portraits of the President, statuary, and hundreds of pieces of *objets d'art* which were personally selected by Sukarno. In fact, the entire palace—marble floors, crystal chandeliers and all—was decorated by the boss himself.

"Unfortunately, the President has very little time for play," Sukarno sighed deeply. "Sometimes I screen movies privately. I love your Greer Garson and Rhonda Fleming and Martha Hyer, whom I've met. But my favorite I've never met. Her name is Sophia Loren. But Hollywood smoothed her out too much. Outside of that, my only other relaxation is simply sitting in a chair and gazing at my art treasures. All of which I personally collected. Someday I shall leave them all to the people of Indonesia."

The screeching of the sirens, the glare of the headlights, the gnashing of trucks' gears suddenly announced that our equipment was making its belated appearance. All hell broke loose. The soldiers were rushing the stuff to the theater. The actors were rushing backstage to change. The guests were rushing into their seats to watch.

I thought it would be a good idea to allow the guests to watch us unpack the equipment and set the stage. They'd been kept waiting so long that I figured this would be a good diversionary tactic. All of us piled into the theater which was just another of the rooms in the President's king-sized bungalow.

I MC'd the proceedings with the help of President Sukarno, who was my steady heckler. The only thing that annoyed me was that he was getting bigger laughs. "I don't butt into politics," I kidded the leader of ninety-two million people. "So stay out of my racket."

"If you need a good comedian," he answered, "I'll be glad to travel with the show."

"I'll be glad to have you join us," I said, "but remember it's the Joey Adams Show and I get top billing."

"That's all right with me," he shot back, "just as long as I get top pay."

While this banter was going back and forth, all kinds of gnomes were behind me, in full view of the audience, nailing down flats, pulling up carpets and generally busting up the President's stage.

Indonesian dancers feature hand gestures. Their foot motions are secondary. Therefore, the big border of footlights along the bottom of the stage might have been good for his country's dancers, but not mine. It obscured the footwork of our Step Brothers. So we had to rip it out. In its place we set up our own system of lights. The lush rugs that covered the stage were fine for the delicate dancing of the Indonesians but they would have muffled the taps of our quartet of Yankee-type hoofers. So we had to rip the rugs up and, instead, lay in our own plywood floor.

Then other problems developed. The President's entire theater was equipped with Japanese machinery. Our men couldn't savvy the labels and dials so they couldn't tell how our equipment was functioning. Cindy had to sit out front through the whole show directing the volume of the sound and the intensity of the lights by hand signals.

Sure death for a performer is too big an introduction. The worst pox you can put on a star—even worse than a black voodoo curse—is to give him a twenty-minute build-up. By now our show had had a five-hour build-up. Nothing could follow that. If Jascha Heifetz were directing a five thousand piece orchestra for Frank Sinatra and Bing Crosby while they crooned to Liz Taylor making love to Elvis Presley as Grace Kelly was dancing a ballet on the back of an elephant with Sir Cedric Hardwicke—it still couldn't follow this five-hour build-up.

It's times like this that I'm sorry I didn't open a candy store.

But God was on our side and the show was just terrific. In the finale where we shoot out the balloons, Sukarno stood up and shot them back. When Chaz Chase ate his boutonniere, the President then handed him a corsage to eat. We could only hope that the flowers were germ-proof. When the Syltes sang, he clapped his hands in rhythm. The President beamed happily from the time Cindy made her opening speech—which he had taught her—straight through to "The Saints Go Marchin' In."

The President was so pleased with his American visitors that he granted Cindy the first and only formal interview he's given any American reporter in years. As he said in this exclusive meeting two days later:

"I hope you write something good. American newspapers always try to put a hook on their stories about Sukarno. They only try to give the President trick questions. Never to hear his answers.

"Look here, I'm an open book. No President makes more speeches than Sukarno. I even wrote a whole book about my emotions, called *Sarinah*. My parents were freedom fighters. They were very poor. My mother was Balinese. She had to cook and wash clothes, so I was brought up by this village woman named Sarinah. She had a powerful effect on my life. She taught me to love."

He'd kept this appointment with Cindy in his Djakarta palace to which he traveled by helicopter. The lawn, with police, soldiers and photographers, looked like a subway platform come rush hour. Cindy was ushered past the foyer with its Sukarno photos, through the anteroom with its Sukarno sketches, and into the drawing room where, underneath a life-size oil portrait of himself, stood Sukarno.

During their conversation, he agreed that the Lion of Indonesia was a Lamb at home. "I'm the most lovable man in the world," he chuckled. "My wife calls me 'Mas' meaning 'Gold.' Living with the President is very easy because he is not a difficult man. He is very understanding. He can be very soft.

"My birthday is double six—June 6. It is my great luck that I'm Gemini, twins. And that's me. Two extremes. I'm very emotional. I can cry in a sad mood or I can be exacting. I am hard like steel and I'm poetic. Because I'm two halves I can exhibit all shades and lead all peoples. I am the All-embracing."

A starched aide-de-camp arrived at the end of their first half hour, rattled off some quick Indonesian and received an answer which meant the same in any language. The President had canceled his next appointment. The startled aide vanished, leaving the two of them alone again.

"I am also a very good husband," he continued. "I always remember my wife's birthday and our anniversary . . . but do you think you should print this? I don't want American women mad at me. What will they think of a President who discusses such unimportant things?"

Assured that our women adore snooping into the private lives of public figures, the President—who speaks Indonesian, Central Javanese, Sudanese (which is the language of West Java), English, German, French, and Dutch—beamed and flashed even white teeth.

"I am a very good father, too. My children love me very much and I love them. Of course, there is not much family time for the President. He can't play cricket with his son. Or baseball. But I kiss my children every time I have the occasion to. And I never punish them. Maybe a little angry look, that's all. My children will have the fullest opportunity to follow their own desires because too much help makes them dependent. My third child, a girl of ten years, is a great dancer. But no rock and roll. None of that new craze—the Twist—either. I have outlawed that here. It is mad."

Another aide brought coffee. The President drank it with a drop of milk. "Ego? Of course I have ego," he said pleasantly in answer to Cindy's question. "I lead ninety-two million people scattered over three thousand islands. Nobody can weld such people into nationalism without a burning will."

A devout Moslem, he was asked whether it was Allah's will or Sukarno's will that had molded his life. "It is not personal with me. I never had ambition to be a President. For me this is almost a . . . a . . . ," he struggled for the word, "a religion." (This last was breathed, not spoken.) "It's my duty. What a man serves his whole lifetime for. When I hear my people cry because they're hungry I must fight for them. It's an inner . . . an inner . . ." The rebel, whose convictions won him twelve years in a Dutch prison, shook his fist. "An inner obsession to get this country free, happy, prosperous, honored by the world."

Sukarno ("Some American newspaperman made up the fact that my first name is 'Achmed.' But it is not true. I have no first name. I am just Sukarno.") explained that he rises at 5:30 even if he's gone to bed at two or three in the morning. He then gardens, inspects his house or walks on the verandah while answering urgent mail and receiving his most important visitors informally—in pajamas. Sukarno, whose boyhood idols were Washington and Jefferson, says simply, "My tensest hours are 6:30 to 9:30 in the morning."

"And does Your Excellency sleep in 'py-yamas' as you call them?"

"No!" he exploded and his face crinkled into a cheery grin. "I sleep à la Gandhi. With all windows and doors open and no fans or air conditioning, no matter how hot it is, because the President likes God's air. Around midnight he reads himself to sleep with books that are light to read and light to hold. I even read the book your husband wrote about you, called *Cindy and I*."

My wife hastily mentioned that she hoped that wasn't one of the things that put him to sleep.

And how does the President of the Republic of Indonesia want to be remembered for posterity?

"I want something special written on my tomb. You know what I want written? Not 'Here lies buried His Excellency, Sukarno, the First President of the Republic of Indonesia,' but, 'Here lies Bung Karno'—Bung means brother—'The mouthpiece of the Indonesian people.' I come from them. I love them. I speak their language. That is the secret of my success."

As the starched aide arrived for the third time in the unprecedented hour-and-a-half interview, Bung Karno, one of the most powerful leaders of the free world, made a gift to his guest of four pieces of batik, escorted her to the car, kissed her on both cheeks and waved bye-bye from the top of his stoop—just like any other well-brought-up president might do.

Our regular scheduled performances were at Senajan Sports Hall, a brand new badminton stadium which seats ten thousand people. And we proved it every night. The indoor stadium, built like Madison Square Garden, was set up as if for a prize fight. Our stage was in the center. And working in the round to ten thousand people is like getting it in the neck. It's a big, fat pain. Wherever you stand, your back is to three-fourths of the audience. For an act like Celeste Evans', this was murder. How can you work sleight of hand when 7,500 people see where your hands are?

We tried to solve the problem by suggesting that we move the stage to one end of the hall so that we could face the whole audience. A logical solution. But, go fool around with Gene Autry . . . We were given three thousand reasons why this couldn't be done—none of them valid. You kind of got the feeling that Khrushchev's comrades from Afghanistan were in again, messing up the staging.

Of course, to be true-blue, honor-bright and honest-injun, I can't truly say that the theater was infiltrated. I only know that the sound and light boards must have been manned by hostile gremlins. And I only know that when we wanted a blackout they turned the lights full up, and when we wanted the sound up the mikes blew altogether. And if you think it's easy to do a show to ten thousand people without sound— good luck to you!

And, of course, I didn't have Mickey Spillane to sniff out the clues, but every night we'd have to nail down the boards of our specially built stage and every afternoon they'd be pried up again. Their explanation was that they needed to dust. I mean, even Mr. Clean doesn't suggest you dust *under* the floor!

We were using our own transformers to help our light and sound situation, but the second night our electric tube blew. Their engineers reluctantly offered to replace the tube. It was very nice of them. The only trouble is, their tubes had no parts in them.

Despite the obstacle course we ran every night onstage, the shows were very well received. We went away with a lot of satisfaction while our backstage "friends" were stuck with a lot of busted tubes. Their kind of trouble I could handle. But I was soon going to have to face a problem within my own troupe.

CHAPTER 13

Showdown

in Indonesia

THE FIRST THING I saw when we chugged into Dja-karta were big billboards and large newspaper ads advertising: "Joey Adams, top pelawak America, versus Bing Slamet, top pelawak Indonesia." The first thing I wanted to know when I got to the Embassy was what is a Bing Slamet? The second thing was what is a top pelawak? Whatever they were I seemed to be pretty mixed up with both of them.

Howard Palfrey Jones, our Ambassador to Indonesia, explained that "pelawak" means "comedian" and Bing Slamet was the top pelawak of Indonesia. "Bing Slamet," said the Ambassador, "has been billing himself as the Joey Adams of Indonesia."

"Even without seeing him, Joey is now a fan of his for life," piped up Cindy.

"He must be a funny fella," I said. "From now on I'm going to call myself the Bing Slamet of America."

From the very beginning, even before we left stateside, it

had been my idea to work with entertainers from each country. This would prove to be a true cultural exchange. I had sent word ahead to all the countries in which we were to appear that I would be proud to include any of their top artists on our show. In some of these areas they had no performers who could fit our program. They had no such thing as a vaudeville or variety theater. The only variety most of these places had ever seen was the Joey Adams troupe.

The thought of sharing a stage with local entertainers was my idea of hands-across-the-sea, show-business style. What better way to learn to know each other than to work together, laugh together and play together? What better way to show another people you want to be their friends?

The ads and the publicity in the newspapers were full of glowing accounts of Andi Mulya and her sister, Tuty Daulay, Radio Indonesia singers—who were also going to share the spotlight with Bing and me. In turn, we were scheduled to be the guest stars on a special program at Radio Indonesia.

Everybody was very happy about this except the Bad Boy. He didn't want to do the extra show at Radio Indonesia. He claimed this wasn't one of the regularly scheduled performances and it wasn't in his contract.

Most Cultural Exchange contracts list six performances per week. The day you travel five hours or more you don't do a show. The day you first arrive in a new town you don't do a show. That day is reserved for the official reception which was as much a part of our job as working onstage.

This was a written regulation of Cultural Exchange. It was mandatory for each foreign post to arrange this reception the first night so that we could meet and mingle with the press, the local entertainers, officials and the rest of the people. Almost always we did an ad-lib-type show there which was the best way of introducing ourselves. In short, it was a chance for everybody to get acquainted.

There was never a week when we just did the shows our contract called for. Some of us were going to hospitals; the

Sylte Sisters were singing in church; Jed Horner, who was a stage director, addressed little theater groups; others of us were going to orphanages and schools. Some of us were even setting up shop on the street corners. The hospitals we visited didn't exactly come equipped with a central theater so we went through every single room and every single ward. For instance, at the Bir Hospital in Nepal, we did about twenty shows.

The truth of the matter is we looked for these extra opportunities to offer our friendship. Everybody wanted to do them. Everybody, that is, except the Bad Boy. He didn't want to do anything beyond what was in his contract.

It was Ambassador Jones who explained the importance of Radio Indonesia to the United States' effort. It had been an uphill fight for him to get the United States on the airwaves. He wanted the President's speeches or the stories of Lincoln, Jefferson and Washington or an hour of American music or a USA-type newscast included in their broadcasting. He was just beginning to succeed. And this was the first time they had ever asked him to cooperate in a joint Indonesian-American program.

"When Howard Palfrey Jones became Ambassador to Djakarta," a prominent Indonesian said in *The New York Times* recently, "the United States didn't have much of a policy— except for the Jones smile and the Jones personality." And the *Times* continued: "Soon afterward, relations between the United States and Indonesia were improving. New United States aid agreements were signed and the United States began a small program of arming and training units of the Indonesian army."

What the Communists in Djakarta dislike most about Howard Palfrey Jones is that he is so popular with everyone else. He is an informal, gregarious man, easily recognized by his bald head with its fringe of white hair and by his impeccable white sharkskin suits. He tackles his task with zest. One night in a village of three thousand he sang a solo at President Sukarno's request. He shows the same zest when he does the Indonesian scarf dance at a diplomatic party. His great progress with Radio Indonesia is another example of his hard work and soft-sell diplomacy.

Cindy and I were staying with Ambassador Jones and Mrs. Jones for our seven days in Indonesia. We got to know them and love them. We got to know that he was a soft-sell guy, that he always underplayed, that he never pressed the panic button. So, when he gently suggested that we cooperate with Radio Indonesia, we knew it was a top-priority assignment.

As always, everybody jumped at the opportunity to do an extra job. Everybody, that is, except the Bad Boy. We'd been having trouble with him straight along. He refused to come to official functions. If he did show up, sometimes he'd come in Bermuda shorts and sneakers to show his defiance. He refused to wear ties and jackets when the weather was hot. He caused strife within the company by picking fights, challenging members of the cast and hurting some of them professionally on-stage. He made impossible demands for cars and living quarters. In some cases he checked out without paying his bills.

For a while I coddled him. I babied him. I thought possibly that the rigors of this traveling were a little too tough for him or that maybe he was lonesome for home. He is a great performer. Because of his talent I didn't want to lose him. In the beginning I even made allowances for many of his eccentricities to myself and to the rest of the cast.

In our business we are prone to allow talent a few extra liberties. When Academy-Award-winning director Billy Wilder was asked why he was using the late Marilyn Monroe in his movie when he knew she was always late on the set, he answered, "I got an aunt in Peoria. She's never been late in her life. She's always on time. But who would come to see her?"

So, I took as much as I could for as long as I could. I was only interested in our over-all program. The personal abuse I had to endure was unimportant. For a while I thought I could win the Bad Boy. I certainly tried hard enough. I nursed him when he was sick. I consoled him when he didn't hear from home. I comforted him during his tantrums. When he complained about the food, Cindy cooked a can of soup for him over her Bunsen burner. When he asked for money, I loaned it to him. Cindy and I stayed up all night listening to his grievances. When he complained about his room, Cindy invited him to stay with us, so he would feel that he had a family.

I worked so hard trying to win him that I almost lost the rest of the cast. When he created dissension in the ranks, I automatically took his part and tried to smooth it over with the others. I knew he was wrong. I knew the others had a legitimate beef. I couldn't even blame them when they started to turn against me. But I felt if I agreed with the rest of the gang and salved their wounds, even though they were right, they would tear him to pieces.

I was beginning to hate myself. I was embarrassed in front of my wife. I was catering to the Bad Boy more than I was to her. I was losing respect for myself. The rest of the cast were beginning to look at me like I was weak. Or, if not weak, afraid. And if not afraid, just plain stupid. One of the troupe, an old friend whom I've known since I started in show business, said to me one black day in Djakarta, "Why are you always on his side? Why don't you get rid of him? Why don't you get wise to yourself? Everybody in this cast is beginning to hate you and that goes for me, too! Why don't you fire him?"

My heart was in a sling. How could I explain that I couldn't fire him? If we were in Pittsburgh on a commercial date, I'd have paid him off a long time ago and kicked him all the way back to New York. But when you're twelve thousand miles away from home and your booking agent is the United States Government, it's not that easy.

First of all, every single member of the troupe was advertised in every single one of the countries. They were in brochures, in pamphlets, on billboards, in local newspapers. This had been arranged months in advance. Their backgrounds, pictures, credits and biographies had been sent ahead to each country. Each member of the troupe was an important part of the whole picture. The locals knew so much about each one of us that it would have been a personal disappointment if even one member of our family were missing—or replaced.

If I fired him, I'd have to tell why. Between American wire services and Asian news syndicates, there were reporters everywhere ready to spotlight anything we did. And either his distorted version or my unpretty one would have to get into the papers. It was more important for me to protect Cultural Exchange than to salve my battered ego. How could we be good will ambassadors spreading the word if we couldn't get along with each other? Maybe our one little troupe couldn't help Southeast Asia singlehandedly, but one wrong move could sure hurt our efforts there.

So the State Department wasn't about to let one dancer put his foot in it or one magician have something up his sleeve or one acrobat pull one lousy trick or one musician hit one sour note. They weren't about to let one person knock down what they'd spent years building up.

The State Department had given me all the power in the world but warned me not to use it! They cabled me to control the situation and then followed it up with cables telling me not to make waves. "It's all in your hands," they said, but then they handcuffed me. Why? Because the government was afraid. And they had good reason. Our State Department, our embassies and the USIS had worked very hard to erase the picture of *The Ugly American*. It was to counteract this false impression of the U.S. that we were sent on this mission.

Meanwhile I was the only heavy. I was the heavy with Washington because I couldn't seem to control my troupe. And I was the heavy with my troupe because I was trying to protect the Bad Boy. And I was the heavy with the Bad Boy because I was beginning to turn on him. When I saw the serpent was becoming a dragon that was creeping beyond the confines of our family, and Indonesian-American relations could be harmed as a result of his attitude toward Radio Indonesia, I put my foot down. There was no more room for appeasement.

I discussed the situation with our Ambassador, who was keenly aware of what was going on. We knew the time had come for everybody to stand up and be counted. I drove over to the Dharma Nirmala Hotel where most of the cast was staying. I asked Jed Horner to round up the whole group and call a meeting. Three of the musicians were bunking together and theirs was the largest room, so that served as Convention Headquarters.

One by one they straggled in. "What's happening?" each one wanted to know. "What's up?"

"I'll explain," I said, "as soon as we all get together."

Jed and some of the others went out and brought in chairs from the other rooms. Some of the troupe sat on the floor, some sat on the bed, some on the window sill. With twenty-five people in the room it was very hot, but it was going to get even hotter in a little while. I stood up in the center of the room. I was tense. I was tight. I was determined. "We are here for one reason," I started. "To bring the friendship . . ."

"Are you going to start that love crap again?" the Bad Boy interrupted. "Are you going to tell us some more about we should all love each other and about having harmony and friendship and affection and all those other tinny phrases you throw around?"

Maybe my way was wrong. I don't know. Maybe I'm not a realist. But all my life I've looked for movies and books that have happy endings. Maybe this can be construed as weakness, but even if it can, I'd still rather be my way. I looked him straight in the eye. "Don't mistake goodness for weakness," I said grimly.

I laid out the plans for the program at Radio Indonesia

plus the Indonesian-American show we were going to have onstage. Right on cue the Bad Boy pulled out his contract. I told him pretty fast what he could do with it. As usual he was peppering his objections with four-letter words and belching smoke and breathing fire. I snuffed out that fire pretty fast with the news that anybody who didn't cooperate in the Indonesian-American effort would be on the next plane back to the States. I'd even pack his bags and make sandwiches for him.

There were no more sides. Not his side. Not my side. Not the troupe's side. Not the State Department's side. Just the side of what would show the United States to best advantage. And doing a performance at Radio Indonesia and standing arm-in-arm with the Indonesian entertainers was that side. And anybody who wouldn't cooperate in our community effort, anybody who wanted to be in business for himself, could get on the first plane the hell out of here. I was beyond worrying about making a scene. I was ready for any battle and any storm.

"Every last damn one of us," I said quietly, "is going to do the show at Radio Indonesia like we planned, and every last damn one of us is going to be onstage at Senajan Hall tonight working his heart out with and for those wonderful Indonesian people."

And we did!

It was apparent that everybody felt relieved. The throbbing that had been going on inside the troupe eased off. It was as though a boil had just been lanced and was draining.

The show was a big smash. Our cast was never greater. Out front nobody knew the Civil War that was going on inside the tired old comedian. The show was scheduled to go on at eight o'clock. By six o'clock Senajan Sports Hall was packed to capacity. I still don't know when these people work. From noon to five everybody siestas. The stores are closed, business is shut down and there's nothing moving but the tourists. Here it was six o'clock and everybody was ready to enjoy again.

Bing Slamet, top pelawak of Indonesia, and Joey Adams, tired pelawak of America, met in the center of the ring and made funny for the people in two languages. Between his English and my Indonesian, Bing and Joey had more laughs on The Road to Djakarta than Bing and Bob.

We'd rehearsed a pantomime comedy bit which we did at the beginning of the show. Audiences have always loved it when the overdog gets the pie in the face. In this case, Bing was the underdog. He was 5'4" to my towering 5'7½". He's a cute little guy with a crew cut and a lovable pixie face. The Indonesians are crazy about him. Bing and I had a mock battle over the affections of my Cindy. When he won and walked off with a beaming Cindy, I looked crushed and the audience cheered.

What more could I sacrifice for my country? He wound up with my best girl and my best laughs.

From the opening strains of "Angin Mamiri," "Indada Siririton" and the "Bengawan" sung by Bing Slamet, Andi Mulya and Tuty Daulay to our finale of "The Saints Go Marchin' In" the audience was with us all the way.

The best review we received was from First Minister Leimani of Indonesia. After the performance he said to our Ambassador Jones, "If the price of rice goes up, we're likely to have riots in Djakarta. But if the price of tickets to Joey Adams goes up, everybody would pay without complaint."

As one Djakarta paper put it, "Tickets to the American variety show are selling like fried bananas." I guess this is the Indonesian version of hot cakes.

But the Communist paper in town, *Harian Rakjat,* was a lone dissenting voice. It headlined its critique of our show: "All Crazy." As they would with anything else made in the USA, they gave us the well-known rap-eroo. Let's put it this way: Fans of ours they weren't.

The reviewer complained, "Adams acted superfluously

when he repeatedly waved his arms and cried, 'All crazy.' It seemed that Joey Adams does not intend to increase his Indonesian vocabulary. He used the word 'crazy' several times through his crazy performance." What this pinko didn't mention was that this was one of the catch phrases of the show. For instance, whenever Chaz Chase did something particularly wild, I would say, "He is crazy." When I attempted a magic trick and it didn't work, I would say, "I'm crazy." When the audience laughed, I said, "We are all crazy." It was a funny bit. It was always a funny bit. It had been funny in Afghanistan, in Cambodia, in Thailand, Nepal, and Laos— and it was funny here, too. It was just not as funny as Communism, that's all.

Wherever we went, in every town, people would take great delight in saying to us, "I am crazy, you are crazy, we are all crazy." Wherever we went it became a catch-phrase like Joe Penner's "Wanna buy a duck?" or Jackie Gleason's "Away we go." It was just one of the many bits we did in the local language.

The comrade on the *Harian Rakjat* summed us up this way: "The performance by the Joey Adams Variety Show is nothing more than a recreation." Obviously our "recreation" must have made some dent with the Commies. It wasn't long afterward that the Russians sent a similar troupe along to the very same areas we'd just opened up.

Soon after leaving Djakarta we received a letter from Ambassador Jones. He said, in part: "The other night Marylou was sitting with President Sukarno when the Soviet Ambassador's wife, referring to the Russian show, needled Marylou and asked, 'Did Indonesia ever have anything like this?' President Sukarno interjected, 'You should have seen the Joey Adams Show!'"

The nicest compliment came from my pal, Bing Slamet, who literally gave me the shirt off his back. Before I left he peeled off the brown batik he was wearing and presented it to me.

And so with a song in my heart and a new batik on my body, I reluctantly left the warm, friendly people of Indonesia.

And what happened to the Bad Boy? Well, he's still a great performer. It's just that under tough conditions some temperaments create bigger problems than others. Thank the Lord he's no longer my problem.

CHAPTER 14

Where Are the Slings of Singapore?

SINGAPORE wasn't what I figured at all. I think my main problem was that I'd seen too many Clark Gable pictures. I seem to remember him as a gay soldier of fortune swiveling through the dark, mysterious streets of Singapore. In my mind's eye, I remember him in sailor's garb running his hot hands over the rump of a gorgeous Chinese broad who was busting out of one of those cheongsams which was slit all the way up to the armpit.

I envisioned Eurasian-type sexpots in water-front cafes. To me, Singapore was full of booze and broads and junks and opium-smuggling and jewel thieves and spies and all-night fleshpots and all the other foreign intrigue you can stash into a "B" picture.

Forget it. It never happened. Since the war it's only a memory. By twelve midnight Singapore is closed tighter than Philadelphia on Sunday. Singapore just ain't the honky-tonk I envisioned, that's all. It's beautiful and lovely and has handsome hotels, elegant restaurants and it's as residential as Milwaukee or Portland or Atchison, Topeka or Santa Fe. If it hadn't been for one good rousing fight with my wife, I'd have had no excitement in town altogether.

Ever since Afghanistan, when I heard we were going to hit Singapore, I couldn't wait to taste a Singapore Sling. This is a drink I remembered Clark Gable ordered in a picture once. I remembered him with Jean Harlow in one hand and this Singapore Sling in the other. I can just see him now tilting back his hat, swaggering over to the bar and snarling at the slant-eyed dragon-lady barkeeper: "Gimme a Singapore Sling, baby."

This was one of the first things I wanted to do when I hit town. I dragged Cindy into the nearest dive and I swaggered over to the bar. I tilted back my hat, put my foot on the railing like I'd seen all the big boys do and I commanded, "Gimme a Singapore Sling, baby, and make it a double."

This was a mistake right away. The "baby" behind the bar was a 6-foot 2-inch gorilla whose name was Sol. "Give ya a what and make it a which?" he asked.

"I'll have a Singapore Sling, pal," I said in a tone that was now more Donald Meek than Clark Gable.

"Never hoid of it," he said.

"Whaddaya mean, you never hoid of it? Clark Gable always drank it here with Jean Harlow."

"Well, he never drank it in this joint, Mac."

I settled for a cup of Sanka.

Singapore was the first town where we could get any kind of food we wanted. We could sink our molars into anything from a thick end-cut of English roast beef to a New-York-type sirloin. You could get Malayan dishes, Indian dishes, or even Malayan dishes from India. I was so desperate by now I'd even have settled for a ham on rye.

I knew only one thing. I didn't want rice. For the past ten weeks I'd been feasting on boiled rice, fried rice, curried rice, brown rice, glutinous rice, saffron rice, white rice and burnt rice. I didn't want to see another rice as long as I lived. I was so satiated by now that I figured even if I ever went to a wedding, I'd throw noodles.

The Singapore Junior Chamber of Commerce, who acted as our sponsors in town, treated us to dinner the night we arrived. They whisked us to Singapore's Chinatown which is the most densely populated one-square-mile in the world. They were very loving. And they figured by now we must be so sick of roast beef and so tired of sirloins that they wanted to give us a taste sensation that was indigenous to the area. You'll never guess what the main dish was. It was the most savory, succulent, tantalizing, titillating moo goo sub gum hunk of rice you ever saw.

Like the good hosts that they were, Arnold Mannering, the Britisher who was Secretary of the Junior Chamber of Commerce; Ronald Chang, their Chinese President; and W. Wolfe Reade, our USIS officer, asked us what we'd like to do our first night in town.

"I'd like to see the wild, frenetic, sexy, lewd, lascivious night life," I said, slobbering.

"Willya get a load of the Errol Flynn of The Stone Age," said Cindy, wiping my chin.

"What kind of Errol Flynn? What's with the Errol Flynn jazz? He's dead," I said.

"Well?"

Her point was well taken. As a matter of fact I was looking to lay my poor, old, rice-laden bones down altogether.

"What are you carrying on?" Cindy said. "What's with you with the night life with the sexy girls with the lascivious? You'll lay your tired, rheumy eyeballs on one sexy Chinese girl and I'll have to apply liniment to you for a week."

"Issat so?" I said. "Just because we're married ten years you're beginning to take me for granted. Don't be such a big shot, Big Shot. Just let me loose at one of those red-hot Oriental babes."

"At your stage in the game," my jealous wife yawned, "better you should curl yourself around a red-hot water bottle."

"I'll have you know that before I was married I was very big with the ladies. I used to stay up all night howling and hooting and tumulting. They called me the Nightmayor of Broadway."

"You mean, the Nightmare of Broadway, don't you?"

Now the gauntlet was down. Tired though I was, I had to take up the challenge. I insisted that we go to a sin-filled, wicked nightspot. Preferably one of those low down dance halls where Clark Gable used to have his big fight scenes.

"I know just the place," Mannering said. "I've never been, but I know where it is."

We all piled into the station wagon. We went up little narrow streets and down dark alleys and past the section of town where the Death Houses are. These are rows and rows of little buildings that look like stores. But they have a most macabre inventory. Instead of selling real live merchandise, these shopkeepers deal in death. Here the aged and infirm go to wait to die. As we do when we pay our respects at a good rousing Irish wake, the family and friends and loved ones have a collation in the front room. Only difference is, that at these wakes the guest of honor is still awake and waiting in the back room.

A little beyond the Death Houses we circled past the bazaars which are spread out for blocks and blocks, and are open every night. Here there are hundreds of stalls where you can buy anything from one unmatched button to lingerie to the ingredients for shark-fin soup to milady's handbags. In short, it's an open-air five and ten.

A few chopsticks away we stopped off to listen to my biggest competitor: the Chinese storyteller. These storytellers sit cross-legged out in the open on the ground around a brazier and spin their tales. Their rapt audiences consist of venerable Chinese elders with wispy white beards who are yearning for a touch of the homeland, and young Oriental workingmen who stop by to pick up one for the road. Some sit on the ground smoking a pipe. Others are sipping their tea or rice wine. Some are standing around nibbling at their rice bowls. Under a starry sky, with the noise of the city in the background, only the voice of Honorable Storyteller is heard. On into the night he weaves his fables of mystical lands far-away-across-the-sea to his enraptured listeners who thirstily drink in every word.

Being of a practical mind, I turned to my Chinese host. "Mr. Chang," I asked, "who pays these men? Do they belong to a union like the American Guild of Variety Artists?"

"No," he answered. "After the storyteller is through he takes up a collection."

"In other words, the better he is the more money he makes. Is that right?"

"That's exactly right."

"What a wild idea," I said. "I can't wait to tell Myron Cohen, Alan King, Bob Hope, and all the guys back home. No more bothering with theaters, night clubs, agents, managers. When I get back to New York, I'll dust myself off a piece of corner on Times Square and set up shop and start to make with the stories and collections."

Squawked my ever-faithful second, "Listen to me, kid. I've heard your routine. Better you should make the collection first."

We drove past Change Alley which is a narrow, covered version of the outdoor bazaar and is the most famous shopping sight in all of Asia. To Change Alley go the richest ladies and poorest coolies to bargain for their wares.

And we drove past Raffles Place. "Hey, we got to go into the Raffles Hotel!" said the walking guidebook I married.

"What's with the Raffles Hotel?" I said. "We're going to that sinful, wicked, lascivious, lewd all-night dance hall where Gable used to carry on."

"Peasant," she said. "Don't you ever read anything besides

your tired old joke books? Don't you know from Somerset Maugham?"

"Sure I know him. What do you think I am, stupid or something? All us writers know each other."

"Well, do you also happen to know that the Raffles is the famous hotel he made immortal? Do you just happen to know that this is the exact, precise spot where Mr. Somerset Maugham wrote some of his greatest stories?"

"That's all very nice," I sniffed. "I ain't one to knock Mr. Maugham. I mean he's a pretty good writer, too, and all that. But if he and Mrs. Maugham were in Brooklyn, would they give a look in on the candy store where I wrote *The Joey Adams Joke Book?*"

It was five minutes to twelve when we pulled up to the lewd, lascivious dance hall.

"Perfect timing," I said. "At midnight this joint will be at its jumpingest. Clark Gable always had his biggest fights at midnight."

"Yeah," snapped Cindy, "and if you don't stop acting like George Raft we're going to have one, too."

"Hurry up, c'mon," I said, shoving Wolfe Reade, Arnold Mannering and Ronald Chang ahead of me. "And watch yourselves because they can roll you pretty good in these joints and if any of these broads approach you, just be careful what you drink. Just follow my moves."

Like Gable I shoved my way through the double doors and entered the biggest, noisiest, roughest silence you ever heard in your life. The quiet was deafening. In one silent corner of this big, dark, empty barn, a middle-aged Chinese female was sitting all alone cracking litchi nuts. On the huge floor one lone couple were swaying halfheartedly to an even more uninterested four-piece Malayan band who were tootling a Guy Lombardo-type waltz. The long bar near the door was decorated with one stray sailor. He wasn't being hustled, rolled or sexed.

"Where's the action?" I hollered to the Chinese man at the door. "Let's have some booze. Let's have some broads."

"What are you, some kind of clazy nut?" he said. "We crose at twev o'crock!"

Singapore is a rainbow of all races. It's a melting pot. A chop suey of all languages, nationalities, and customs. It has venerable Oriental gentlemen who still figure their accounts by the beads of an abacus, yet pull out a Diners' Club card to pay their restaurant chits.

It features Indian women in native dress with priceless jewels in their foreheads who drop the expression, "Okay," into a normal conversation. It has English ladies wearing Mandarin clothes, Sumatran females in Thai silks, Chinese beauties sporting Indonesian batiks, Japanese women in gold-threaded Malayan weaves, Singaporean lovelies in drip-dry blouses and American wives like mine who try to inveigle their husbands into buying all of them.

Singapore was the first cosmopolitan city we'd hit since Bangkok. And it was a mad dash to glamorize ourselves. The girls wanted manicures, pedicures and any other kind of cures. And me, I had hair grown so far down the back of my neck that it looked like I was wearing my wife's mink stole.

Although most of the guys resembled unmade beds after they traveled an hour or more, our girls had some kind of magic going for them so they always managed to look pretty good when they tumbled off a plane. They each had one outfit which they wore when traveling. It made no difference where they were going to or where they were coming from. They always wore their same "Flight Outfit." For the first five weeks I thought maybe it was a coincidence that they wore the same ensembles, but by the ninth week I thought they were painted on.

The Syltes had a Jacob's Robe-type number. It was a gaily-colored three-quarter length cotton jacket underneath which was a black sheath. They'd selected it because they didn't have to worry if dirt or wrinkles or their tummies showed. The Jacob's Robes hid a multitude.

Cindy wore a white washable turban which camouflaged her hair problems. Her flight outfit was a black and white striped job. A drip-dry. It didn't show dirt. It didn't show wrinkles. And it didn't show up after Singapore. When we arrived there I personally set fire to it.

But I must admit that our gals always looked reasonably smart and ready for the photographers when they pulled into any new place. And so, all in their flight outfits, without even taking a moment to change, everybody piled into the hairdressers.

For a girl, traveling under the best of circumstances can be rough. And Cindy is a glamour girl. She's the type that would look Fifth Avenue if you set her down in the middle of a Laotian jungle. And she did, too. She ain't exactly the simple type, either. Her slogan is: "When in doubt—add!"

And she does. She adds necklaces and bracelets and pins and earrings—and that's just to go swimming. Whatever she can't wear she carries. She has custom-made fur coats just to go to the furriers. When I let her out at night she's a work of art, but at home she's a slob.

She trots around the house wearing Doctor Dentons which are full-length pajamas with feet in them and a trap-door. For a kid of five or under, it's fine. For a kid of thirty or over, it's grotesque. Since she's always cold, she adds to this ensemble anything that's handy. Like, for instance, maybe my evening socks or an old sweater or a torn shirt. In short, around Chez Adams, Madame Adams looks like a bundle of wetwash.

Cindy's hair is jet black, parted in the center and pulled back sleek and tight into a bun. She doesn't go to a hairdresser to have it shampoo'd, she goes to a bootblack to have it shined. People say she has a wide-eyed surprised look all the time. They should see her at night when she loosens the bun. Her eyes clamp shut altogether.

When we got into the Cathay Hotel, she washed her face,

loosened her bun and made herself at home preparatory to darting downstairs for the beauty transfusion. "With your make-up off," I said to her, "and your hair wild and in that clown of a flight outfit, you're about as attractive as a condemned building. But, obviously, there must be something wrong with me, too, because I love you. But then I always did dig Salvador Dali, so what can I tell you?"

"That's the dirtiest, meanest, foulest truth I ever heard in my life," Cindy answered, "and I resent it. I don't deny it, but I resent it."

"Darling, I'm only joshing," I said. "With your blue black hair, your snow white skin and your ruby red lips, you are the most beautiful girl in the world . . . and the brightest . . . and the sweetest . . . and the wittiest . . . and . . ."

"Aaaaahhhh, whadda you know?" she stopped me.

Cindy and I enjoy each other. You see, there are only two of us. We have no children. Maybe it's because I have a very strict mother-in-law. And maybe it's because, as Cindy says, "You're at the age where a good hot cup of tea and the Late Show and you've had it!" Maybe it's because I flunked biology and zoology at school, I don't know. I only know that at our house we got nothin' that grows; no plants, no dogs, no kids.

We've always been very close, but this trip brought us even closer. For most of the four and a half months, we clung to each other like two Arabs in the Bronx.

We have one important thing in common: my mother-in-law. By that I don't mean to say my mother-in-law is common. It's just that she's more common around our house than I am. My mother-in-law and father-in-law live three houses away from us. That is, in theory. In practice, it seems like they're living with us but their clothes are three houses away. At best Jessie, my dear mother-in-law, isn't too cheered when Cindy trudges away for a week end. This four-and-a-half-month separation was a real wrench for both of them.

Cindy and I have traveled quite a bit, as have her parents,

but none of us have ever been quite so far away before or for so long a time. Maybe Jessie could have taken this with better grace had she known we were going to be in Palm Beach where she could pick up a phone every twenty minutes and reach us, or where she knew the worst thing that could happen to her baby was a bad case of sunburn. The headlines about Laos and Vietnam frightened her. And the closest actual contact she could have with us for eighteen weeks was a piece of paper with our itinerary on it.

Cindy and Jessie's main source of sustenance is not air or food like it is for the rest of us. For them, it's a phone. Their lifeline is a telephone line. Jessie's phone bills run forty dollars a month on wrong numbers alone! So you can imagine her frustration when her kid is off in the wilds of Asia some place and she can't get a call through. It's not that easy to dial Rangoon 6. . . .

So, when my itchy-fingered wife swished into the Cathay Hotel and saw a real live telephone in the room, she immediately placed a call to her mama.

"Honey," I said, "remember, there's twelve and a half hours difference. It's 5:00 P.M. here in Singapore which means it's 5:30 this morning in New York. If the call goes through now it's the middle of the night back home and you'll wake up your poor old mother!"

"What poor old mother?" Cindy squeaked. "She's only two years older than you."

"Four."

"Two, but who's counting. Willya get a load of Dorian Gray. You've been thirty-nine longer than Jack Benny. You're older than Chippendale. I ain't the one to blow the whistle on my dear, middle-aged husband, but if, as and when my mater and pater should buzz off to an old-age home, you are going along as a package deal."

It took us hours to get the phone call through. There are only certain times when the circuits to the United States are open. And then if the overseas operator has reservations booked ahead of yours, you just have to wait your turn. But this was my lucky day. Must be I live right.

"Boy," Cindy said gleefully, as she hung up, "we sure are in luck. The operator says she'll be able to put my call through."

"That's the finest news I've heard in years. At twelve bucks for the first three minutes and four bucks each additional minute, this kind of good luck could break me altogether."

"So how much could it cost for ten minutes? A paltry forty dollars."

"You kidding?" I said. "When you and your mother get on the phone you clear your throat for more than ten minutes."

When the call finally came through, it fortunately did not wake my in-laws. It woke us instead. It was a lovely 3:30 P.M. in New York, but it was 3:00 A.M. in Singapore. Cindy got up like a shot. She started to jump up and down and bounce around and carry on like a mad woman.

"Mommy," she screamed into the phone. "Mommy, darling, how are you, what's new, I haven't spoken to you in ten weeks, I miss you, we're in Singapore, I hope we didn't wake you, how's Dad, how's Grandma, Joey sends his love, have you gotten my letters, oh Mommy it's so wonderful to talk to you, the shows have been doing wonderfully, what's the weather like there . . .?"

Before Jessie even got a chance to answer I blew thirty dollars. We had just rolled up about $42.50 worth of phone call when they settled down for some serious conversation.

"So listen," hollered Cindy, "what do you want me to bring you? How about a cheongsam . . . A cheongsam . . . C-h-e-o . . ."

"Forget it, willya," I crabbed. "Just to explain it will cost me eleven dollars. Ask her does she want a blouse. It's simpler."

"Mother says silver is cheap in Singapore. And she says how's about we get her some silver."

"Silver shmilver," I yelled. "Promise her anything and give her Arpège and hang up. It's costing a fortune."

"Stop yelling. I can't hear . . . not you, Mother. What'd you say? . . . Sterling silver grape shears?"

"Sterling silver grape shears?" I repeated. "Maybe they could use something more practical like monogrammed croquet balls."

"What kind of sterling silver grape shears, Mother?"

"Sterling silver grape shears?" I shouted. "That goes with white-gloved butlers and polo ponies. Your parents not only don't have polo ponies, they don't even have a cat."

"And suppose I can't get the sterling silver grape shears? . . . Oh, then you want a King George sterling silver bun warmer."

"Bun warmer?" I squawked. "A bun warmer! Your mother wants a bun warmer?" I was turning purple. "A bun warmer goes with kippers on a sideboard and servants and things. Your father don't have no servants. Your father don't eat no kippers. He eats puffed rice on account of four boxtops win him a set of steak knives."

"Do you just please mind shutting up," Cindy snapped to me. "I call my mother and all I can hear is you. Now, do you just mind? Will you please let me talk to my mother a few minutes in peace? You I can talk to any time of the day and for free, yet. This is my first chance to talk to my mother and . . . what'd you say, Mother? Get you a sterling silver what?"

"Tell her to go to Tiffany's and tell her to charge it. It'll be cheaper," I said huffing and puffing. "And hang up!"

"Mommy, darling," Cindy said gently, "we're halfway through the trip. We'll be home before you know it." She caressed the wire and hugged the phone. "It's October 23rd already, darling. We'll be home Christmas Eve. That's only two more months. Give Daddy a hug for me. Kiss Grandma for me."

"Tell her," I said, "we'll be in India on December 5th and I'll personally see to it we'll call her on her birthday. And tell her I love her, too." Cindy delivered the message and with a lifetime of love in her voice, she said good-bye.

There was no sleeping after this. We were both too excited.

We celebrated by going to the faucet and taking a drink right out of the tap. It was the first time we'd been able to do that in ten weeks. And to think, we could even brush our teeth with this water without boiling it. This alone was worth the seventy-five Malayan dollars we were paying for our suite. It's roughly three Malayan to one American. So when you smooth it out we were paying twenty-five Yankee dollars per day.

And another thing, we had hot water for bathing although we were cautioned to turn the spigots tightly when we were through since Singapore was facing a serious water shortage. And we had air conditioning. And we had the morning papers and morning tea free of charge.

Singapore was like an oasis for us. We really pulled ourselves together here. Everybody had their lost buttons replaced, busted zippers repaired, broken heels fixed, clothes cleaned, make-up replenished and we sort of got wound up and ready to go again for the second half of the trip.

By the time we reached Singapore everybody was broke. The last time we'd gotten any money was in Bangkok. Before we left stateside we were given five weeks' expense money in advance. The rest of our salary was sent to our homes every week to pay the rent, feed the kids, and keep the home fires burning.

In Bangkok, we'd been cabled four weeks' advance expense money, which, of course, was deducted from our salaries. But we blew it on such luxuries as rent and food and living expenses. This wasn't such a catastrophe except that if we wanted to continue to live and eat and sleep, we needed some cash PDQ. But it's not that easy.

It works this way: the State Department is your boss. But they are not a booking agency for show people. Therefore, the theatrical arm of the State Department is ANTA, the American National Theater and Academy. ANTA in effect was the liaison between Uncle Sam and Uncle Joey. It was ANTA's job to arrange for visas and passports. It was ANTA's job to negotiate our itinerary and transportation. It was ANTA's job to okay my selection of people and to get them cleared through the State Department and the FBI.

What Dean Rusk is to the State Department, a gal called Gertrude Macy is to ANTA. Gert was the traffic cop for the whole shooting match. ANTA on the other hand is not a licensed theatrical booking office. Therefore, in turn they had to give the whole package over to a legitimate, franchised theatrical booking agency. This is where we inherited the well-liked Joe Glaser and his Associated Booking Office and my good friend, agent Jackie Green. It was the State Department who sent our pay to Gert Macy who sent it to Jackie Green who sent part of it to our families on the home front and the rest to Jed Horner, our company manager, who then parceled it out amongst us.

The reason we weren't paid from week to week on the road was because not every country was a free port where you can lay your hands on American green. Some countries have frozen assets and you can't get dollars since the only commodity they'll pay off in is local currency. Hence, ANTA figured out in advance we'd get paid in Bangkok, then four weeks later in Singapore. These cities worked on a free international money exchange.

Jackie Green cabled our money to the Nationale Handels-bank in Singapore. That's when the fun began. Oh, the Chemical Corn Exchange cable arrived at the bank okay. And all of us arrived at the bank okay. The only thing that was missing was the dollars. They just didn't have any. Our passports were okay. Our visas were okay. Our identification was okay. The only thing that was missing was the dollars. They just didn't have any. The poor skinny little manager of the bank was faced one 9:00 A.M. on October 23, 1961 with twenty-five hungry humans. And there he was with his dollars down! He scurried around to every bank this side of Mandalay trying to scratch up every Yankee buck he could lay his sweaty fists on.

Nearly twenty-four hours and eleven banks later he scared

up all the dollars we needed. And I do mean dollars. Because that's how we were paid off. In single dollar bills. Did you ever try paying off twenty-five people four weeks' money in advance in single-o dollar bills? When the poor skinny little manager piled up the greenbacks in front of us we lost sight of him altogether. As we left the Handelsbank with our pockets bulging with dollars, we may not have been the richest folks in town but we sure were the lumpiest.

CHAPTER 15

At Bat for
Uncle Sam

Opening night at the Victoria Theater was a real shock to our nervous systems. The theater was plush, the stage was smooth. We actually had footlights and spotlights and overhead lights and dressing rooms, stagehands, curtains, wings. We even had a grand piano. I was so thrown that I fluffed my opening lines in Malayan which was okay since this was one state where everybody speaks English. Whereas foreign lands are trying to teach English to their countrymen, Singapore is trying to uproot English and make Malayan the native lingo. As a result the audience and myself were in the same class. We were all beginners in Malayan.

The price of admission had gone from three Malayan dollars up to eight Malayan dollars. The proceeds went to the Jaycee Scholarship and Welfare Fund. We did one special matinée which was free of charge to children from the various youth organizations including members of the Boy Scouts, Boys Brigade, the Federation of Boys Clubs, the Federation of Girls Clubs, Boys Town, Salvation Army Home and other social welfare homes for underprivileged children.

It was at a children's hospital that I lost my heart. I had courted my wife for two years until she convinced me that I was in love with her. But with Lalida and me it was love at first sight. Lalida was sugar and spice and everything nice. Lalida was four years old. I met her when I entered the St. Andrews Orthopedic Hospital for children in Bedok.

I had a sure-fire lay-'em-in-the-aisles routine for children whenever we visited a hospital. I used the cane trick as an opener. They were always surprised when I produced a cane from out of a handkerchief. And so was I. The crummy thing didn't always work. I followed that with my high-class chicken bit. This was that stale rubber fowl that, following a few abracadabras, I pulled out of my straw hat.

When somebody heisted my cane, my smash number became the Eddie Cantor imitation. Even though the kids didn't know what an Eddie Cantor was, they did like my jumping up and down, clapping my hands, rolling my eyes and fluttering the handkerchief. This got them hysterical. I could never understand the laughs here. I mean, I was serious about this imitation.

The kids giggled at the William Tell bit with John Shirley, and screamed when Chaz Chase bit a big hunk out of my straw hat, but they particularly loved the big finish when I danced with the Steps and fell flat on my face and had to be carried out.

As we were ushered into the first children's ward, a huge airy room with about thirty beds lining all four sides, we were all set to jazz 'em up with our bag of tricks—when I saw Lalida. Before I could don my straw hat and sing out my first greeting, Lalida led the other children in a cheerful chorus of "Good morning, Uncle Adams, welcome to our home." Although the little doll was crippled in body and was tied to the bedpost so she couldn't fall off, her hands reached out for me. My arms and my heart reached out for her. She had the big-

gest, darkest, dancingest eyes and the widest, happiest laugh I
have ever known. I could have eaten her up. The two of us
just held onto each other like we could never let go.

For the next hour there was nonstop laughter in the Home
for Crippled Children. While each performer was doing his
turn, I came back to the bedside and clung to my Lalida. As
she was pouring her joy and gratitude into me, I was pouring
my strength and love into her.

I have entertained at a good many hospitals down through
the years. After each one of them, I left with a depressed feeling. Except this time. Here the children were all so full of
joy. Before I could cheer them up they had already cheered
me up. These kids are all physically handicapped—all of
them—yet they are able to be happy. How many of us are
plagued with unhappiness although we're physically fit. The
troublemakers of the world with their healthy bodies and sick
minds could really learn a lesson from my little Lalida. "And
a little child shall lead them . . ."

As John and Bonnie Shirley; Chaz and Joan Chase; Maceo,
Prince, Flash and Al of the Step Brothers; and Deanna, Deanda and Joan Sylte and myself went from bed to bed distrib-
uting our lollipops, I promised each of my newly adopted children that America would never forget them.

"As soon as I get back," I promised each one, "Uncle
Adams will send you a houseful of the nicest toys we have in
America."

And Uncle Adams didn't forget. It took a couple of months
to get home and it took a couple of months to ship it, but
right now at the St. Andrews Orthopedic Hospital for Crippled
Children in Bedok, Singapore, there is "The Joey Adams Toy
Library" which was christened by the children, and is in perpetual use.

When you think of Singapore, you don't readily think of an
underdeveloped, underprivileged state but rather a cosmopolitan, metropolitan one. However, the reason the Joey Adams

Show was sent here was because Singapore is a tinderbox. The Red Chinese have their athlete's foot in the door of Singapore. The border is thirteen hundred miles away, or roughly the distance between New York and Miami.

This one-time Crown Colony is a tiny island at the foot of the Malay Peninsula. It had become an independent member of the British Commonwealth two and a half years before our visit in October of '61. And it still had one major problem: it was not unified. Singapore's main population is Chinese, some of whom speak Cantonese, Mandarin, and dozens of other dialects. Another large segment of Singapore's citizens are Indian who speak a diversity of dialects like Tamil, Hindi, Punjabi and so on. Many of their other citizens cling to the language and customs of Malaya, their next-door neighbor. According to one of their high government officials: "We will lose out to communism if we do not quickly unite our people in a common loyalty. We're a new country and our first duty is to pull our nation together before we can build it up. For that reason, our first step is to designate Malayan as the language of the land."

Oddly enough, they are looking toward the entertainment media to bring cohesion to their nation. Mr. John Duclos, who is the Director of Broadcasting for Radio and TV Singapore, told us, "Many of our countrymen are illiterate. That's why television is so important. We must get our people used to seeing the flag of this state. We will fly it often on television. We must get our people accustomed to seeing the faces of their government leaders and hearing their words. We must accustom our people to seeing in one room, on one show, Chinese faces in close proximity with darker Hindu faces and white children's faces. We must by means of video get these people used to the feeling that the government's arms are around the black, the white, and the yellow."

And here again is why the Cultural Exchange in general and the Joey Adams Show in particular was born. Our show had white and black, Jew and Gentile, with added assists from the Indonesians, the Singaporeans, the Moslems, the Buddhists and the Hindus—all working together, all laughing together.

Because the radio and TV of Singapore is under government direction, their programming plays hop-scotch between the two great powers. They try to get the best of both worlds. They like to keep everybody happy. They feature the best programs of Russia and Red China as they do of England and America.

A good percentage of our whodunits, variety shows, stick-'em-ups, cowboy 'n' Indians and situation comedies which are gassing the people from Long Beach, California, to Long Beach, Long Island, are strictly thumbs down in Singapore.

"We are leery of your Westerns," explained Mr. Duclos, "because in order to picture your way of life to the best advantage, we mustn't ever indicate to a very unsophisticated audience that people in the Western world bump people off. We must not promote the feeling that an American feels the solution to every problem is to shoot his enemy.

"And we cannot use your variety shows or your situation comedies such as 'I Love Lucy' since the preponderance of our nationals are not Western-orientated. The 'Lucy' concept, in which a female is not only equal to the male but superior, is outlandish and unthinkable to the Asian mind."

Cindy and I asked him how an innocuous variety program like the "Perry Como Show" could injure our effort.

"Because on such programs the women are dressed immodestly. Brief or low-cut attire is considered highly improper in our society. Seven-eighths of our women have never worn such dresses or such shorts. This is for their private life. And we do not wish our people to think that such improper attire is the norm in America.

"Furthermore, most of your comedians depend upon sex situations for their comedy. They bring sex into every point. If it's not blatant, it's relative to a woman's dress or attitude or even something about the comedian's wife. Sex doesn't play such a big part in the Asian's life since if he wants five wives, he simply goes out and gets them. He doesn't have to dream about it all the time."

And how do our whodunits or private eye programs fall short?

"I saw a sampling of your 'Sunset Strip' recently," continued Mr. Duclos. "In one segment a married man ran away with a woman. And we were treated to thirty minutes of such sin. In another, a man became involved with a prostitute in a low dive. Your stories should dwell on adventure not wickedness."

Anything or anybody that carries the United States label to the world market has an obligation to be an ambassador for his country. We knew from the moment we left the shores of the USA that we had a job to do. It figures Uncle Sam wasn't sending us on a pleasure cruise. Like the Peace Corps and the Embassies and USIS and the branches of the foreign aid tree such as USOM and ICA, we had a job to do.

Parts of that job took me right back to our kid days when we played cowboys 'n' Indians and cops 'n' robbers. The whole world today is divided up between the good guys and the bad guys, just as it was in our games. It's communism versus freedom now. And today's bad guys aren't about to give up until they've pulled every foul in the book. They're the masters of the kick in the groin.

And these bad guys have a pretty good trick, too. It took me about four press conferences in four different countries to get wise to them. They throw you a curve. A question with a big, fat hook on it. And then they leave before you get a chance to answer. It's like the wise guy who heckles, "When did you stop beating your wife?" Before you can tell him you're not even married, he's two cities away, and with him went your reputation.

At almost every press conference we ran up against one such fink. Take Singapore, for instance. We weren't five minutes into our questions and answers in my living room in the

Cathay Hotel when a short little guy with a bow tie started pitching to the left. And this joker wasn't a southpaw, either. He tried for a headline by asking the four Step Brothers how it felt to be a Negro in the USA.

Now there are some of us who are passive Americans and some of us who are passionate Americans. He just happened to fall into a pot of four passionate Yanks. "Listen, pal," Prince Spencer said quietly, "outside of heaven there's only one place I want to be. And that's the USA."

I figured now was the time. I walked across the room and stood by the door before he had a chance to leave and crawl back under his rock. This guy was going to get the full answer.

"Ever hear of a guy called Joe Louis?" asked Maceo Anderson, another of the in-Step Brothers. "He was a Negro out of Detroit who became the champion of the whole world. And Willie Mays is a Negro, chum. So is Jackie Robinson. They're two of the greatest baseball players who ever lived. Ever heard of them? Why don't you go ask them what it's like to be a Negro in the USA? Why don't you go ask them how it feels to be cheered by millions of fans—white and black?"

Al Williams cut in. "I got a little news for ya, Mac. It just so happens that we got thirty-five bona fide Negro millionaires in the United States. Ya hear me good? Thirty-five. Negro. Millionaires. United States."

"Some of the richest men in the United States are Negro entertainers," said Flash. "Like Eddie Anderson. And Marian Anderson. And Harry Belafonte and Nat King Cole and Lena Horne and Johnny Mathis and . . ."

"And Sammy Davis, Jr., who ain't a millionaire, but he sure lives like one," cracked Prince.

I wasn't certain, but I thought the other reporters smiled. The Comrade was beginning to turn the color of his politics. He looked longingly at the exit, but it was blocked by all 5 feet 7½ inches of me.

Flash went right on. ". . . And you ever heard of Dr.

Ralph Bunche? He's a Negro. He just happens to be Under-Secretary for Special Political Affairs at the UN, that's all. And how about Congressman Adam Clayton Powell?"

"Sure we got problems," admitted Prince. "Sure we got Little Rock. Sure we got integration troubles. We're not too happy to play the South. In fact we avoid it. But we got laws and we got courts and we got millions of Americans of all races and all creeds and all colors who are willing to lay down their lives to make possible the freedom set down by a man called Abraham Lincoln a long time ago. Did you ever hear of him? Man, let me tell you something. We got it made in our country."

"You got any other questions?" asked Maceo.

Propped up against the door, I was really beginning to enjoy this. Our four boys were sitting on the couch sipping coffee from a table in front of them. On the other side sat the reporter. But there was more than a coffee table separating them. Calmly, coolly, without pressure, without being hurried and without raising their voices, our boys were slowly but very surely screwing this bastard right into the ground. He was going to have one fine bunch of quotes to take back to his propaganda chief.

The bow tie bobbled up and down. He made one last feeble attempt. "How come America is always preparing for war? How come they use all their money to buy arms and ammunition?"

Now he was all mine. I left my post at the door and stood right in front of him. "I guess," I said, "you don't know the history of our country. We are farmers, mechanics and actors. We are bricklayers, bookkeepers and even bookmakers. We are doctors, lawyers, and Indian chiefs. We're rich men and we're poor men. We go about our business enjoying our freedom—until it is challenged. And then we all get together to fight to preserve it. And we keep on fighting until the battle is won.

"But when it's all over we all go back to our farms, our

tools, our businesses and our stages to enjoy the freedom we fought for. So, you see, friend," I said, "we're not always preparing for war but an American never could take a bully."

"Not even at a press conference," whispered Prince, as he opened the door and ushered the reporter out.

CHAPTER 16

SRO in Hong Kong

HONG KONG is the kept woman of Asia. And like every other kept woman she has her glamorous side and her tawdry side. She's sexy and she's seamy. She has a beautiful façade and she has a back street. She's a mixture of two worlds.

The silks and satins of our kept woman's façade are the made-to-measure beaded shoes you can get for fifteen dollars; the I-can-get-it-for-you-wholesale handmade brocades out of Red China; the custom-made clothes you can get slapped together overnight for a fraction of stateside cost; the green and white jade which is the best in the world and is piled up on counters like bubble gum in a candy store; the cashmere sweaters at 2-for-1 price; the transistors and radios and cameras and wristwatches that are duty free; the pearls that come to you straight from the oyster without a middleman. This is the tinsel of Hong Kong.

The back street of the lady known as Hong Kong consists

of the refugees from Communist China who exist on the fringe of starvation; the opium that's smuggled in and out of here to all parts of the world; the ladies in the tight skirts and loose hips who hawk their wares to any Tom, Dick, or Wong; the coolies, the laborers and the ricksha drivers who service the rich for a bowl of rice a day, the Chinese who live five deep in one-room huts. This is the tarnished side of Hong Kong.

This Crown Colony of Great Britain, which is considered the step-daughter of John Bull, is really the mistress of Mao Tse-tung. With one exception. Instead of his keeping her, she's keeping him. There's a polite word in our society for anybody who lives off a lady. But like any panderer who puts his lady friend on the street, Mao is cold and calculating. He's only interested in one thing. What he can get out of her.

You can be sure that a good hunk of tourist money finds its way back to Mao's wallet. And he's got his fist in the till of many a Hong Kong bank. And he's got his sticky fingers on every buck that your Aunt Minnie spends on that fancy Chinese brocade and jade. But he's got his company manners on when it comes to Hong Kong because Hong Kong's pretty sweet for him. However, if he ever decides to strangle his mistress, the lady that's known as Hong Kong will crumble like a fortune cooky.

Mao has even let the word out that the Chinese who are already squashed into Hong Kong can have relatives join them —for a fee. The going rate is from two thousand dollars to twenty-five hundred dollars per cousin. This is for relatives who are too weak or too old to escape on their own. The steady flow of Chinese who are trying to get the hell out of China is causing a serious traffic jam on the border. This traffic used to move only in one direction; it now goes both ways. Because the Crown Colony is full to overflowing, the Hong Kong *polizei* have been rounding up the latest batch of refugees— feeding them, giving them enough food to take on their way and hustling them back over the Red border twenty-two miles away. What happens to them after that nobody knows.

Of the colony's three million residents, two thirds are refugees from Red China. The reason we were in Hong Kong was not because the government thought I needed a new three-button blue mohair job or that Cindy could grab up a couple of good bargains in this shoppers' paradise. But because our practical Uncle Sam figured as long as we were in the neighborhood—so it shouldn't be a total loss—how's about we pop over from Singapore on the way to Saigon and show a little instant friendship to these refugees.

We did our first show in a new resettlement area at Wong Tai Sin which is deep in the heart of Kowloon, the part of Hong Kong on the mainland. This area comprises blocks and blocks and blocks of apartment buildings piled smack up against each other as far as the eye can see. Financed by British funds, it's built along the same lines as every low-cost housing project that any metropolis has slapped together to replace its slums.

Wong Tai Sin is teeming with humanity. Many a flat has more than one family crammed into it. And the Chinese have pretty big families. These people not only live there, they work there, too. This is where I was first introduced to cottage industries.

Because of the city's housing limitations, many one-room cubicles are shared by several families. Each cubicle, or "cottage," houses so much industry that, by comparison, the average factory seems as quiet as a British gentlemen's club. In one corner, a man may be making plastic flowers, in another, someone may be manufacturing jewelry while the womenfolk are hopscotching all over the place feeding the families, running after the kids and hollering to their neighbors. The whole scene is one of perpetual bedlam. Wong Tai Sin is like Times Square on New Year's Eve.

Right smack in the middle of this Babel is the American-built Community Center which is financed and maintained by us. In the courtyard of the Center, which is the only clearing for miles around, our show pitched camp. As the saying goes,

"Damn clever, these Americans." Because this provided a vantage point for thousands who could watch from sidewalks, gutters, and rooftops or hanging out of windows, fire-escapes and rickshas.

Being a whiz-bang at languages, Cindy and I immediately boned up on "A funny thing happened to me on the way to Wong Tai Sin" in Mandarin. Opening night nothing happened. We threw four more sure-fire type phrases in Mandarin. Nothing. They stared at me like we weren't on the same side. I dumped my pidgin Mandarin and asked our USIS men wha' hoppen? Twas then I learned that although Mandarin is the Number One Honorable Lingo of China, Hong Kong is ninety miles from Canton and these refugees spoke only Cantonese. And in thirty-two different dialects, yet. The next night we crammed Cantonese—with its nine tones. And better our Cantonese should have been thrown over a lobster because this time we hit an all-Mandarin group.

Cindy and I had to make another appearance directly after the show. So USIS had arranged for a local driver to meet us backstage and take us to our destination. After all, I wasn't exactly what you'd call a hundred per cent familiar with these streets. I mean, take a job as a guide in Hong Kong I couldn't. To tell the truth, I have difficulty separating Column A from Column B on a Chinese menu.

I knew we had to get out the very instant the show was over. Otherwise we could never make it at all. There were thousands of bodies everywhere. Every inch of space in every which way we looked was just crammed with eyes and ears and shapes. We knew we'd have to make our move before anybody else made theirs, otherwise we'd never reach the car.

And our move was timed to the last strains of "The Saints Go Marchin' In." There was to be no balloon barrage finale here. We couldn't shoot out four hundred balloons into this teeming mass of humanity or there would surely be a stampede. This we found out the hard way. In Afghanistan, the twenty thousand turban-tops almost ripped the stage down and trampled on each other in their frenzy to get at the balloons. It took a squad of police flailing their belt buckles to prevent actual mayhem. In Djakarta, at the Senajan Sports Hall, our crew couldn't even get the balloons off the stage and out into the audience because the audience stampeded the stage to get at the balloons. John and Bonnie narrowly escaped injury when swarms of Indonesians rushed them to claw at the precious cargo as it was being carted on-stage.

So, as soon as the "Saints" was over we made a mad dash for the car. Cindy made it okay. I made it okay. But the driver was nowhere in sight. The moment we slid into the front seat of the car, we were swallowed up in a quicksand of humanity. It was like a mob scene in one of de Mille's supercolossal extravaganzas. Before I could get back out to look for the chauffeur, we were sealed off completely.

There were Chinese to the right of us and Chinese to the left of us. Inquisitive eyes were peering at us from all sides. There were double-decker bodies piled up on the hood eyelash-to-eyelash with us at the windshield. For the first time in my life I could believe that one out of every four people on this planet was a Chinese. And the whole swarming mass of them seemed to be surrounding our car.

We felt like monkeys in a zoo. As a matter of fact, I was still wearing my monkey suit. I was in my tuxedo and Cindy was in her evening dress. Since this was just an open courtyard there were no facilities backstage for changing because there was no backstage. We had mixed emotions. It had been my feeling that we as Americans should always be well groomed and have that clean-cut American look. Anyplace we walked on-stage, no matter where it was, we would dress like it was a first-night performance on Broadway. The theory being that our audience was important enough to rate our party clothes.

Show business is a world of illusion, powder and paint and make believe. A magician is not a magician without his high silk hat and his cape. A dance team is not a dance team without tails and an evening gown. So, there we were. Me with my satin lapels and my Cindy with her spaghetti straps. On a stage with people in front of us it was glamorous. In a car with people surrounding us it was ridiculous.

These people had probably never even seen a tuxedo before let alone owned one. Hands reached out through the open car windows to stroke the silk lapels. From every side children and grownups were giggling, staring, chattering away in all kinds of dialects, and gesticulating wildly at the two freaks in the cage. None of them tried to open the doors and get at us. They were not a lynch mob. They were a controlled, friendly mob. But a mob nonetheless pressing curiously around us. And one with whom we had no communication.

Tension was building. We couldn't see streets or houses or anything beyond the layers of people. Our little Ford was beginning to rock. I was afraid we'd be crushed and the car would collapse on top of us. Our car was so completely hidden from sight that I was also afraid the driver would never be able to find us.

"Get a load of my lousy luck," I cracked to Cindy, trying to relieve the tension. "Here I am surrounded by thousands of experts who could teach me how to use my chopsticks and I ain't got a pair on me."

Cindy couldn't even manage a smile. She didn't think it was very funny.

We couldn't show these people we were afraid of them. They were trying to be friendly. We couldn't show panic. They were only trying to be nice. We managed to smile at them. Then we began to speak a few sentences which would have pleased them had they been able to understand us. We said, "Hello . . . Hope you enjoyed the show . . . Glad to see you . . . It's a pleasure to meet you." We knew they didn't understand what we were saying, but we hoped by the tone of our voices they'd know we weren't afraid and that we appreciated their gestures of friendship. Even a kittycat can tell who's its friend and who isn't. So we kept smiling and jabbering and jabbering and smiling until our driver finally fought his way through to rescue us.

A half hour later when we pulled up to the Ambassador Hotel, Cindy tapped me on the shoulder as we were getting out of the car. "Hey," she said, "that was very funny what you said back there about the chopsticks."

We were meeting Harry Odell, the local impresario, who was working hand-in-hand with ANTA and USIS in presenting our show in Hong Kong. Harry is Jewish, and was born in San Francisco, moved to Hong Kong and is now a British subject. His wife, Sophie, is half-French, half-something else. Such a parlay you never heard. The Odells were two important figures in the Resistance during the war. Harry sat out a hunk of World War II behind bars while Sophie's underground activities went on. At least one novel about this area has immortalized her fight for freedom.

Harry and Sophie, who love Americans and adore showpeople, acted as guides during our five days in Hong Kong. They were very loving. They wanted to show us everything. They wanted to show us Happy Valley, the racetrack, and Tiger Balm Gardens—the Oriental Disneyland—and they wanted to take us on the tram to the top of the Peak where you see the whole harbor. They wanted to drive us to Aberdeen, the fishing village on Hong Kong Island where you eat on a floating junk.

But who had time? Between our shows at the Queen's College Theatre in Victoria, the island part of the city, and Keswick Hall on the Kowloon side and our frenzied shopping on both sides, there was no time.

Hong Kong, bless its bargains, gave me a tic in my wallet. Cindy ran around like a maniac, going busted on good buys. Cindy figured she couldn't afford not to vacuum up everything in sight at these cheap prices.

For the Joey Adams Troupe, Hong Kong became a state of emergency. It was here that the whole crew fell apart financially. All of us went broke saving money.

"Lemme ask you a personal question," I said to my wife who was going through my next year's salary at a rapid rate. "What happens to all the money that you've been saving me all these years?"

"Make up your mind," Cindy said, shuffling my travelers' checks like they were a gin deck. "You want I should be a happy wife or a conservative wife?"

"In this paradise," I said, "a shopper like you could lose your mind and my bankroll in no time flat."

"Let us hope," she answered.

Me, I figure Hong Kong's like Vegas. Only here the one-armed bandits hold out tape measures. My dear wife now holds the world's record for inhaling thirty-six pair of shoes, eight suits, six dresses, fourteen bags—all matching each other —in one hour, seven minutes and two seconds flat. And the shops weren't even open.

"How about you and me, we play a new game called 'Let's unleash the wife's bank account'? How about separating yourself from the money you've been earning the last few years?" I needled.

"What kind of traitorous talk is that? That's communism if I ever heard it!" snapped my uncowed wife.

Cindy's been a model, comedienne and an actress. She's taken driving lessons, typing lessons, shorthand lessons, and sewing lessons. Whenever there was a full moon my dear wife used to go on a new kick.

One morning six years ago she announced she wanted to become a writer. Who could ever believe when she began foaming at the typewriter that in three years she'd be acclaimed by *Editor and Publisher* as "The brightest writing constellation to flash out from among the neon lights of the Great White Way in a long time."

My baby's column, "Cindy Says," is now syndicated in papers from Long Island to Hawaii. Her humorous features and celebrity interviews for the North American Newspaper

Alliance run in some two hundred papers around the world. Her byline is featured in top magazines everywhere.

Who would ever think when I married my gorgeous cover girl that someday they'd be whistling at her brains. Not even that gypsy with the garlic breath figured this would happen. Not one fortune cooky predicted it. Not one weighing machine warned us.

Oh, let's not lose our heads. So far the old girl isn't exactly dragging down royalties like Hemingway, yet. I mean, she ain't chipping in on the rent and all that. To be actually truthful with you, from her income I couldn't exactly retire. From what she brings home I couldn't even sit down! The fact is, her writing career is costing me a fortune.

Everybody wants to know is my wife tough to live with now that she's becoming a red-hot success. I can truthfully tell them, 'No.' She is not *becoming* tough to live with. She always was. Cindy was a snotty failure. She's the kind of a kid who was arrogant on spec.

Every hundred bucks Cindy makes she gives to me to invest for her. Our agreement is that I gotta pay all brokers' fees and guarantee her against all losses. I also gotta pay the income tax and guarantee her a profit. Naturally, this has nothing to do with her allowance that I fork over every week and the swollen bills she runs up in such supermarkets as Saks Fifth, Bergdorf's and Bloomingdale's. Anybody takes me for a fool . . . makes no mistake.

Now, for every one hundred dollars she earns I, personally, have to pay the government their cut. State tax on that clammy C-note is another few bucks. That, plus the broker's fee, her office expenses such as phones, stationery and stamps, which is also in our agreement, and the insurance against losses shoves me into another bracket altogether. So, no matter how you slice it, every hundred bucks she earns costs me about one hundred and sixty. Don't misunderstand, I don't object to Cindy being a big fat success—but who can afford it!

One morning in Hong Kong, Cindy woke up on the wrong side of her typewriter.

"Instead of crabbing about my spending, what's happening with all the fortunes of money I give you to invest?" she said crankily, handing me her monthly four-dollar salary check from the *Las Vegas Sun,* which had been forwarded to her.

"What're ya bothering me with this crummy four-dollar check?"

"Crummy check?" she squeaked. "Crummy check? That's a dollar a week. Some columnists only get $1.75 and my column runs once a week and theirs every day. So have a little respect."

"I don't want to bother you, kid, but your whole syndication embarrasses me. Every time I take your checks to the bank for deposit, the teller stares at me like I just robbed a poor box. With your one- two- and three-dollar checks I couldn't exactly crush Wall Street. Rockefeller ain't got what to worry."

"Maybe he ain't, but I have. Now I'm sure you're very humorous and very amusing and you're a comedian and all that, but what I want to know is, what are you doing with all my money?"

"What am I doing with your fortune? I'm keeping a woman, that's what I'm doing."

"I am greatly choked up with mirth. However, if you don't wish to handle my accounts properly, I shall take my business elsewhere. I am sure there are many reliable firms who would be happy to have a good customer like me."

"Now, what else can I do for you? I invested your paltry shillings in stock and this week alone your investments went up three hundred dollars."

"So where's the money? Gimme three hundred dollars."

"What three hundred dollars? Who's got three hundred dollars? I got no three hundred dollars. It's all on paper."

"Well, get it the hell off the paper and into my wallet."

I knew from long and costly experience that with my wife the shortest distance between two points is cash. So, I did what any other slob of a husband would do. I gave her the three hundred dollars. There's no other way to shut her up. I didn't always give in that easily. Years ago I used to reason with her, show her, try to explain to her. And *then* I gave in. Now I succumb immediately. It doesn't save me a dime, but at least it saves wear and tear on my larynx.

"So put this three hundred dollars away with all the other money I earned this year."

"Okay, if that's what you want, baby, and as soon as a good stock comes along I'll invest it for you."

"Meanwhile, how much interest do you give me on my money?"

"Interest? What kind of interest? What am I, a Federal Reserve Bank or something? I'm your husband! What are you bothering me with interest? I pay your income tax, I pay your state tax, I pay your expenses, I pay your brokers' fees and I guarantee you against losses. What more do you want from me?"

"4¼ per cent."

"4¼ per cent?"

"Yeah, 4¼ per cent. That's what the banks give. And that's what I want from you. I mean, that's fair. I don't want more from you that I can get elsewhere. I just want what the other banks give."

"That's very nice of you."

"That's okay."

And I think my wife is stupid! I've often said how bright and talented she is, but when it comes to finances she's stupid. I've just begun to realize that her stupidity is slowly bankrupting me while she is amassing a fortune. After I surrendered in the battle of the 4¼ per cent my enemy retreated to marshal her forces.

Financially speaking, hostilities had ceased and in our hotel room there was kind of a cold war. All was quiet on the home front while the enemy went along gaily building up her savings and tearing down mine. Just when I thought I'd won the peace, Cindy struck again. She marched in waving a local newspaper aloft.

"Lookit," she trumpeted, "here in the *Hong Kong Tiger Standard* is an ad from a bank which guarantees 5 per cent to all depositors. And they're so happy to have you that they even give you gifts and stuff. You can even win a trip to Brazil . . . what are you going to do about it?"

I did what any other self-respecting husband would do. I punched her.

The moment we stepped into our rooms at the Ambassador Hotel in Kowloon, my dear wife started to take inventory. This was so she'd know right away what she needed. How my wife knows she NEEDS a pair of ruby earrings or she NEEDS a silver lamé sheath or she NEEDS a white alligator bag, I'll never know. The one thing she's never in doubt about is the fact that she always needs something.

She took inventory as she unpacked so she'd know what she needed. My wife got busy immediately separating the nearly-new-but-slightly-used-clothes from the not-quite-yet-old-pile from the in-case-stuff. Since this was a long trip, Cindy had taken everything with her but our mosaic tile dining room table. She brought two suitcases, a make-up box, a hatbox, two train cases—and we went by plane—and a shopping bag. There were only six outfits that she wore regularly. The rest were "in case" clothes. She took one thing in case it rains, another thing in case it's hot. She took this in case it's a very dressy affair and that in case we had an invasion from Mars. She was ready for all contingencies. The dear wife was prepared for every emergency from a hurricane to a holocaust. She even shlepped along a three-piece ensemble for in case Scranton declared war on Pakistan.

The thing that bugged me the most was the Persian lamb jacket, the red rabbit stole and that hot, heavy, woolly, warm, itchy, wintry, black-and-white-checked coat. I hated them. I can't ever remember hating anything as much as I hated those three items. This was now the eighth country, the eleventh week and the twenty-eighth time we had packed and unpacked the Persian lamb jacket, the red rabbit stole and that damn, lousy, stupid, hot, heavy, woolly, warm, itchy, wintry, black-and-white checked coat.

"If I told you once I told you a million times, we are not going to Alaska. We will only be in hot territory, I told you. We will be in, around or near the equator, I said. Miami in August isn't so hot like it's going to be where we are, I said. The furnaces at U.S. Steel are considered tepid in comparison to where we'll be, I told you. Do you admit I told you these things?"

"Yes, sir, you did, sir," Cindy said. "I'll say. And how. Oh, boy."

"So how come you didn't listen to me?"

"You also told me Nixon would win. And you told me I could put money on Eddie and Liz spending their whole lives together. And in your top drawer I found recently some Willkie buttons. Any questions?"

"Yeah, what are you doing with these three heavy things in this hot, busting, broiling weather? If I told you once I told you a million . . ."

"Aaaaaaaah, who listens to you. Besides, you can never tell when just once in history there'll be one shot of unseasonable, freak weather."

When Cindy had emptied her last suitcase and stashed away her sequin gas mask, I unpacked the shopping bag which contained my extra suit, two pairs of shoes, three pairs of shorts and four oranges.

"So, okay, so let's go," she said.

"So, okay, so let's go where?" I asked.

"Shopping."

"Shopping?"

"I'll tell you one thing about you," she snapped. "You sure hear good."

"What are we going shopping for?" I asked. "We've only been here fifteen minutes."

"So what do you want to do, establish residence? We're shopping for clothes not a divorce. Let's get out of here."

CHAPTER 17

This Is How
the Money Goes

CINDY'S PLAN of attack took us to Nathan Road,
Cathay Road, Carnarvon Road, Connaught Central and Des
Voeux Road. Back and forth we sailed on the Victoria-
Kowloon ferry looking for bargains on both sides of the col-
ony. And the only real bargain was the Victoria-Kowloon
ferry. It's a ten minute trip across the bay from Kowloon which
is where the airport is and the tourists are and the high-class
Western hotels like the Ambassador, Peninsula, Miramar, and
Park are and where a lot of shopping is and where a good
hunk of my money still is.

On Victoria side, space is so limited that on most of the
streets leading off Queens Road—which is the main drag—
you have to walk sideways to snap up your bargains. Most of
the city is built vertically on the sides of mountains. There are
stores and stores in front of stores and double-decker push-
carts. Merchandise from brassières to dry noodles to jade
hangs off ceilings, walls, poles and clothes-lines.

This is such a congested shopping area that you've got to walk single file. Here, when an American tourist in a mink stole rubs shoulders with a Chinese lady in black flowing trousers or a Chinese gentleman with a black queue hanging down his back, they really rub shoulders. It's the only way they can pass one another.

The only way you can get from the Kowloon bargains to the Victoria bargains is via ferry. That is, unless you're some kind of swimming nut. The ferry is divided into two classes. Second class is directly over the boiler. First class is a little bit above the boiler. The rate of exchange is roughly 5.80 Hong Kong dollars to one U.S. buck and when you unravel it, the fare costs about four American pennies first class and two cents steerage.

As you chug back and forth you see Chinese junks, which house whole families, mingling with modern liners, rusty freighters, U.S. battleships and Malay fishing boats. The frenzied buying on both sides goes on well into the night. The neon signs blink on and off alternating between Chinese and English and beckoning to all us itchy-fingered travelers.

The only thing they got here that's more plentiful than pearls are tourists. Every tourist looks like a spy from "Foreign Intrigue," slithering around with their Polaroids, Brownies, movie cameras, still cameras and busted cameras. The women, regardless of the size of their *derrière,* are all wearing tight-fitting Chinese cheongsams with open-toed sandals and closed-toed socks. They top off this soufflé with straw hats and plastic handbags.

"You women look pretty ridiculous," I said to Cindy who was waddling along in her own snug cheongsam.

"We look ridiculous? We look ridiculous?" Cindy cackled. "In that comedy outfit you're wearing you don't exactly look like an *Esquire* ad."

"What's the matter with my outfit?"

"You saw Cary Grant wearing a neon shirt with a batik

jacket, snakeskin shoes, seersucker pants, socks with embroidered clocks and a baseball cap?"

"Who says he's a good dresser?"

"I've seen better ensembles on a shark."

"Just so happens, Big Shot," I said, "that this is what the
best-dressed men wear over here. The shirt happens to be Thai
silk which I snapped up off a classy men's shop in Chiengmai,
the jacket's from Bing Slamet in Indonesia, the shoes were a
handmade job in Singapore which is very big with the snake-
skins, the seersucker pants are an import from Madison Avenue in New York—you remember New York? Just so happens
that this is what's considered a man-of-the-world outfit."

"Yeah," said Cindy, "and you know the shape the world
is in right now."

My crazylegs wife was running around grabbing up every
bargain in sight like they were giving it away with green
stamps. And they were. Only these green stamps was American cash. In one shop where they were selling odd-sized
gloves, she bought up a dozen pair of size five wristies. This
was somewhat odd when you realize she happens to have a
six and a half hand. "But at these prices," she said, "how can
you turn it down?"

Everything in Hong Kong is custom-made. They can make
suits overnight. They can make shoes in a couple of hours.
And they can make a rich man into a pauper while you wait.
I went nuts with the custom-made bit. When I was a kid I used
to pay $2.95 for a pair of shoes. I had one pair of shoes that
went with every outfit. One of the reasons is I only had one
outfit. But these shoes were wonderful. I could walk in them,
I could stand in them, I could dance in them, I could even
run a little in them.

But how does it look to be here in Hong Kong and not get
custom-made shoes? I ordered six pairs of handmade, hand-
sewn, boot shoes made of the softest baby alligator. This alligator had a pedigree, yet. They were the most beautiful shoes

you ever saw. There was only one trouble. You couldn't walk or dance or even run a little in them. The most you could do was lean. After one wearing I developed hammer toes.

Undaunted, however, I limped over to my custom-made tailor. His sign says: "Made-to-Measure Overnight for $20." But that's if you want a sign made-to-measure. If you want a suit, it's more. You can get any one of your old suits copied exactly in twenty-four hours. From $20 to $65. According to the material. But not me, no, sir. I had to listen to a tailor tout.

"Cary Grant make suits here. Make Italian look, tight pants, short jacket. Look like Cary Grant."

The suit turned out magnificently. The material was the finest Italian silk this side of Lollobrigida. And it certainly looked like Cary Grant. It must have fitted him, too, because it certainly didn't fit me. The crotch was too tight and the arm-holes were too snug. The only way you could wear this suit comfortably was to walk around on tiptoe with your hands on top of your head. If this is the Italian look no wonder they hanged Mussolini. Between my custom-made shoes and my made-to-measure suit, I shook, rattled and rolled back toward the hotel. I might have been a first-aid case, but I certainly was well-dressed.

As I wriggled and writhed past a couple of tourists, I can swear I heard one of them say, "He certainly dresses very well for a deformed man."

There has been a foul rumor around the States that Hong Kong clothes don't last. That is a dirty, filthy lie. My suits lasted all the way to the airport. If only somebody would give me Cary Grant's address, I would send him six brand new, slightly used, Italian silk, Cary Grant–type Hong Kong suits absolutely free of charge.

We were five blocks from the Star Ferry. Being as how I was a hospital case and couldn't walk, I started to hail a cab.

"Let's take a ricksha," Cindy suggested.

"Not me," I said. "I can't bear to have some poor skinny little guy pulling me."

"But this is the way they make their living. Why are you trying to hurt their livelihood?"

"Who's hurting their livelihood?" I said. "Right away I'm the villain. Like I'm taking rice out of their mouths because I don't want to take a ricksha. I'm the president of the American Guild of Variety Artists, the largest theatrical union in the world. How will it look for a labor leader to . . . ?"

"Oh, knock it off, willya, kid. I voted for you."

"As the president of a labor organization, how will it look for a working man to pull me? It is my duty to . . ."

"What are you carrying on? These fellas don't vote anyway," said Cindy hailing a couple of rickshas since it's one to a customer.

"How can you do this?" I wailed. "The going rate for a man to pull you the first five minutes is only fifty cents Hong Kong or about nine cents American. I just haven't got the heart to have these two fellows pull us all the way to the ferry for eighteen cents."

"So give them a half-a-dollar tip apiece," suggested Cindy, "and they'll be very happy. After all, this is the way they make a living."

And so we jogged the five blocks to the ferry. I really couldn't enjoy the trip. Even the fact that it was downhill all the way didn't make me feel any better. I figured instead of nine cents apiece I'd give them a buck apiece and then at least my conscience would take a bath.

"How much?" I said magnanimously, stuffing my hand into my Cary Grant pocket.

"Twenty dollars," said Cindy's driver.

"Twenty dollars?" I sputtered. "What kind of twenty dollars? What's with the twenty dollars? Twenty dollars!"

A crowd was beginning to gather. My chicken wife had joined the crowd and left me there as a target.

"Twenty dollars?" I was screaming now. "What do you

mean twenty dollars? It says nine cents. Nine cents it says. Or fifty cents Hong Kong. Where do you get the twenty dollars? That's ten dollars apiece for five blocks. That's two dollars a block apiece. I ain't going to give you guys twenty dollars. Besides, it was downhill. No, sir, I ain't going to give you two guys twenty dollars."

"No two guys," said my driver. "Twenty dollars each."

By now we were surrounded by a mass of people, but it didn't seem as though it was time to make a speech on Labor Relations because everybody was looking at me like I was a dirty capitalist trying to cheat these two poor hard-working drivers.

All right, so what would you do? Even if I wanted to fight City Hall I wouldn't know where to find it. Go complain to the hack bureau. Where am I going to find my Congressman on a Monday afternoon in October in Hong Kong? I didn't even have my passport with me. I didn't even have my Diners' Club card with me.

So would you like to know what I did? Would you like to know what this imperialistic money-grabbing capitalist did to the two poor downtrodden, underprivileged peasant laborers? He paid them forty Hong Kong dollars, that's what he did.

I swore then and there that I would never knock another New York taxi driver again as long as I lived. To this day, every time I creep into a New York cab I have to restrain myself from kissing the meter.

And so, dear friends, if you ever see me on the street, talk to me about my trip, discuss politics, ask me for my latest joke, show me the pictures of your baby but *never, never* bring up the subject of the Labor Leader and the Ricksha Drivers. It's just too painful to talk about.

The day before we left Hong Kong, came the dark period in our tour called Operation Overweight Baggage. We'd been on the road from August 18 to October 30 and by the law of averages, the law of gravity, the law of diminishing returns and any other laws they got laying around, our baggage weight should have been lighter. We started out with forty thousand balloons and at four hundred per shot that load should have been diminishing. Celeste was carrying a couple of vats of bird seed and since, in many places, the birds were eating better than we were that should have been thinning out. Chaz Chase had his own private cache of special matches and edible shirt fronts. Figuring we'd be gone one hundred twenty-six days and at a rate of about three shows a day, he packed approximately four hundred shirt fronts. Considering we were gone in the neighborhood of seventy-seven days, his pile should have been lighter by around two hundred twenty-one shirt fronts and several gross of matches and match folders. We were carting a few crates of my books to give out—and because I'd been lucky enough to force about ten a week onto people, that should have been peeling off a few pounds.

But despite this, our luggage was gaining weight steadily. In Afghanistan our crew had picked up fur-lined sheepskin jackets and those Persian Astrakhan hats. In Nepal we all snapped up Gurkha knives for souvenirs and strings of beads like agates and carnelians and other stones grown locally. In upper Chiengmai and lower Bangkok we went nuts for Thai silk. We had cottons from Cambodia and gold-embroidered cloth from Vientiane and batiks from Indonesia.

Our whole gang had collected souvenirs for everybody they knew. We had the cigarette cases from the King of Thailand, walking sticks and cane instruments from Prince Boun Oum, wooden elephants from the Lord Mayor of Udorn and other gifts of assorted shapes, sizes and values from well-wishers. In Hong Kong we went nuts altogether. So, just before we left for Saigon came a frantic call from Jed Horner who had been computing the weights with a slide rule and had come to one conclusion: something's gotta go!

The State Department's arrangement had been that each person was allowed sixty-six pounds of personal baggage. The contract with the different airlines called for 3,009 pounds of overweight which included equipment. That's what they were responsible for, that's what they had contracted for and beyond that it was every man for himself. Furthermore, the heavier we got the tougher it was for the planes to leave the ground and the rougher it was for us to keep to our schedules. Either we were going to have to leave some of the wardrobe, some of the equipment or some of the troupe behind.

But this fact never really became clear to any of us until Hong Kong. Up until now we'd just been buying and stashing. Inside everything there was something else. In my straw hat laid a couple of pair of cufflinks in tissue paper. Inside the typewriter case was a pair of slippers we picked up somewhere and on the slippers was pinned a brooch we scooped up somewhere else. Inside the drum case was a camel saddle and somebody's shirts and ties. Even Wyatt Ruther, our bass player, was found transporting a couple of sheepskin jackets, an elephant minus one tusk and a wooden boat in his bass case. But suddenly, via Washington via ANTA via Jackie Green via the ruptured airlines via our company manager, Jed Horner, came the word to strip down to our bare 3,009 pounds before we took off for Vietnam.

Overweight has always been a sore spot in my life. But bubonic plague and those pesky irritations Moses loosed against them Egyptians were horseplay compared to the wars my wife and I have had about her excess luggage on other trips. Whenever we travel, I don't mind buying the tickets. I don't mind buying the luggage. I don't even mind buying the clothes that go in the luggage. But when you put them all together and they spell "overweight," I get the shakes.

"According to you," she shrilled, "anything apart from your toothbrush and scrapbook is excess baggage."

"Oh, yeah?" I ad libbed.

"Yeah," she screamed.

"Well, I call that traveling light."

"Well, I call that being a slob."

So, like everybody else in the troupe, Cindy and I went to

the post office to ship our excess tonnage home before heading for our next stop which was Vietnam. This is where the post office made their dread mistake. They weighed our parcels. We were $138 to the bad. I wouldn't say I made a scene, but I guess it did look funny auctioning off my wife's clothes in the middle of the post office.

"C'mon, sport," hissed Cindy, finally. "You might as well unleash the paper clip from your wallet and your mouth and pay us all off at the same time.

"You see, sir," Cindy explained to the postal clerk, "with my dear hubby it ain't the principle, it's the money."

CHAPTER 18

War and Peace in South Vietnam

V IETNAMESE Republic Army soldiers in major battle with the Viet Cong in Phuoc Thanh Province," screamed the headlines in the Vietnamese papers the day we arrived at Tan Son Nhut airport in Saigon.

South Vietnam had been declared "a state of emergency." We'd been hearing up and down Asia that this was a crisis area. In fact, the battle front had on occasion been brought as close as our hotel lobby. In one instance our Ambassador, Frederick E. Nolting, Jr., was on the receiving end of a home-made hand grenade which had been tossed into his official car as he drove along the streets of the city.

Right up until the very last moment when our Air France jet, loaded with Allied soldiers, set down in Saigon, we didn't think we were going to make it. None of us really thought that we'd be allowed to enter Saigon. All along the line, among our Embassy officials, the feeling had been that because this was a state of war Washington would pull us out of there.

207

We'd written our loved ones to keep in touch with Gertrude Macy at ANTA for any change of itinerary. I knew our families were even more scared than we were as they read the headlines that grew more frightening every day. Even well-meaning Americans who were dug in comfortably in safe cocoons like Hong Kong cheered us with, "So you're going to Vietnam, eh? Well, good luck to you, Charlie. Better you than me!"

We all knew the lay of the land. But none of us talked about it. We had a job to do. Uncle Sam at this point was our father, mother and guardian. He was responsible for us. If he thought we should go in, we were going in. So if we had any fears we kept them to ourselves.

There are not one but two wars being fought between the Viet Cong Commies of the North and President Ngo Dinh Diem's anti-Commies of the South. One was the war of armed terror and guerrilla warfare. This campaign of ravaging frightened, unprotected villages and strafing and bombing city streets could easily graduate to another Korea. This kind of war was easier to fight. The other, the war of subversion, is tougher to combat. The most powerful human forces on earth are those you cannot see. Hunger, fear and hate can be more destructive than an atom bomb. And the sneaky weapons of this warfare cannot be detected by radar or combatted by anti-aircraft. A well-placed lie can be more devastating than a well-placed bullet.

In order to function, subversion needs a cover. It usually operates under a cloak of propaganda. A slanted story in a newspaper. A cockroach on the airwaves. Poisoned leaflets. For this our troupe could be an antidote. This was one war *we* were equipped to handle. In this battle of communications, our arms were entertainment, friendship and affection.

When we arrived at Tan Son Nhut airport, we were greeted by the Vietnamese Frank Sinatra, Tran Van Trach, and the Ava Gardner Saigon-style, Miss Thanh Nga, and the local

Helen Hayes, Phung Ha. Tran was going to appear on stage every night with us as an added commercial for Vietnamese-American relations.

Our performances at the Hung Dao Theatre were dynamite. That is, almost. It could have been a show heard round the world. The third night we had an official visit from the bomb squad who entered with minesweepers. They'd been tipped that something was going to go off when the curtain went up. They scared the hell out of all of us. The audience never knew, because the bomb squad had done its house-cleaning before the doors were opened. Fortunately nothing happened. Either the bomb was a dud or the Commies, who hate the sight of joy or the sound of laughter, were just trying to harass us. If anything had gone off, I'd deny to my dying day that it was our show that laid that bomb.

The government was ever-mindful that there had been and might easily be again anti-American demonstrations by the Commies. There had been recent instances where Americans were killed in sneak attacks on the city streets and then there was the attempt on the Ambassador's life. We did two shows a night and at each performance the police patrolled the theater from roof to cellar. There were barricades backstage so that once the show began, nobody could get in or out. This was one place where the audience couldn't walk out on us.

Tran Van Trach, who shared headline billing with me, is a big favorite with the people. Tran opened the show with Cindy and later on did a bit with me. In his own spot he did some very good imitations of Bing Crosby, Frank Sinatra, the sound of an aerial battle and the sound of an automobile race besides singing some Vietnamese songs and presenting a puppet show. This wonderful talent is about 5'6", stocky and has a big, bushy head of black flowing hair practically down to his shoulders. He's referred to as "the singer with the lion-mane head."

We did a very funny bit together. And it wasn't too easy. We had to rehearse through interpreters. He doesn't speak United States and Cindy and I hardly ever speak Vietnamese around the house anymore. I mean, when we go to visit Cindy's grandmother in the Bronx for lox and bagels, it wouldn't exactly be appropriate.

I dug up this bit from my vaudeville days. I used to do it back in the Stone Age with my original partners, Tony Canzoneri and Mark Plant. Mark Plant would sit on a chair and I would sit on his right knee. He would put his hand up the back of my jacket and pretend he was manipulating my mouth in unison with the song he was singing. I was the only live dummy in vaudeville. I did this bit with many other singers like Sinatra, Dean Martin and Robert Alda.

So here I was a dummy again. Same bit, just a different country. And this time the lyrics were in Vietnamese. Tran and I became the Hope and Crosby of South Vietnam. Now, if anybody's interested in filming "Road to Saigon" we're available.

Security measures around us were pretty strict, since the city itself could be in a state of siege at any moment. We were cautioned to avoid side streets. We were told under no circumstances were we to venture forth at night alone. They insisted that we stick solely to the places named on our briefing list. And definitely no one was to wander outside city limits no matter what. Unless of course you wanted to be a target.

Cindy and I have a great capacity for joy. We can find something to enjoy any place. Even when there isn't anything. In Saigon we found onion soup. Until recently Vietnam was a part of French Indochina and the culture of France still remains. Especially their cooking. Every night after the show we used to play a little game. We'd scratch around until we found some little French *boîte* that would make us onion soup.

Maybe onion soup doesn't seem like a big deal, but we would look forward to it all day. Invariably I'd take some of the troupe with me. One day we heard of a little place that was just slightly off the briefing list and halfway down a side street. One of the policemen backstage told us that here they had the greatest *gratinée* this side of Maxim's. I weighed the warnings about Communist snipers at night versus the pleasures of hot onion soup with grated Parmesan cheese baked in a casserole. The hot onion soup with grated Parmesan cheese baked in a casserole won.

Cindy hadn't been feeling too well and tonight was like a special treat for her so we decided to go alone. Just the two of us. We found the place without too much difficulty and made it just as the man was closing up. Fortunately he'd seen the show and was a fan of Tran Van Trach, so he couldn't do enough for us.

The policeman was right. The soup was the greatest. If you ever plan to face a firing squad and you can have a last meal, you gotta have the hot onion soup with the grated Parmesan cheese baked in a casserole at L'AMIRAL Restaurant, 39 Thai-Lap-Thanh Street, off Rue Tu-Do, five blocks away from the Majestic Hotel in Saigon.

When we came out, the street was very dark. And you never heard such quiet. It was completely deserted in every direction. The only sign of life was a small knot of men hanging around the corner like they do back home in front of the neighborhood candy store. Only here when they hang around they squat around. They were sitting on their heels in a semi-circle passing the time of night.

As we slithered by they all stopped talking and silently turned in our direction. The only sound that could be heard was that of our hearts beating. It was like a scene out of an Alfred Hitchcock picture. Suddenly we remembered the warnings: Avoid side streets. Don't venture out at night alone. Stick to places on the briefing list. Just then a car backfired.

"What's that?" Cindy gasped.

"I don't know," I gulped, "but this is no time to play quiz games. Come on." So we grabbed each other by the hand and ran the whole five blocks home to the Majestic Hotel like two scared little rabbits. That was the effect of the psychological climate of Saigon.

Even aside from the war with the Viet Cong, the climate in Saigon doesn't foster the belief that you can live there to a ripe old age and pass on of natural causes. In addition to their other troubles, the South Vietnamese were suffering from floods from the Mekong River. Aware of President Diem's flood emergency declaration, we set up a booth at the Abraham Lincoln library, corner of Le-Loi and Charner Streets, to sell tickets for our shows at the Hung Dao Theatre. All proceeds were to be donated to the disaster victims in the Mekong delta. Not many days later our Ambassador Nolting handed over a check to the President of the National Assembly, Mr. Truong Vinh Le, in the amount of 675,000 piastres. All told, we racked up a little over eight thousand American dollars.

I had a great urge to see where our money was going. Also, I wanted to visit with these flood victims to let them know America cared. It was not that easy to arrange. The high flood area was not actually within Communist-held territory, but it was along the periphery. Also, in order to reach it we would have to pass through lonely miles that were ordinarily out of bounds to us because of the constant danger of Viet-Cong guerrillas.

The only man with the authority to grant us permission to go into this area was the high-ranking Government official, Mr. Ngo Trong Hieu, Minister of Civic Action. Kindly Mr. Hieu was not thrilled with the entire project. First of all, we were Americans. Secondly, we were civilians. Third, we were guests of the government. It all came down to the fact that he didn't want anything to happen to us. We were the personal responsibility of the Government and the burden of protection was enormous.

USIS arranged an appointment to see Mr. Hieu. Mr. Hieu is a heavy-set man with heavier problems. We were grateful that he was able to snatch a few precious moments out of his busy day to see us and so we went there with the idea that we would make it as brief as possible. But Asians don't work that way.

If you should have to make a very hurry-up, quickie phone

As we continued along the countryside, there were acres of grassy fields with one little hut in the middle of a rice paddy. Then acres of grassy fields again with another little hut in the middle of no place. This is where enemy guerrillas did their best work.

"This is our biggest problem," sighed Mr. Ngoan. "Our Government can not give each little villager protection at night. If we did this we would deplete the strength of our army. When a villager is at home all alone, undefended, at night, the Viet Cong comes with threats of murder to his family if he doesn't do as they bid. He is frightened. So he does it."

This means that these poor peasants in these doubtful areas are donating money and manpower to both sides as the bloody war goes back and forth like a pendulum. As President Ngo Dinh Diem said, "The Viet Cong strike our villages without warning and we must be able to send help immediately. Therefore the helicopters we are getting from the United States are so important. Second thing we need most is communications. That is the plan we are now following. It is hard to do some of the things we must do—for example, forcing villagers to leave their homes and move into the fortified, strategic hamlets. But it is the only solution. The encouraging thing is that the villagers, although they complain about moving at first, soon grow accustomed to the new life. It provides them with hospitals and social centers, and they come to recognize its benefits. As we create these new villages, provide them with their own defenses against marauding Viet Cong and establish communications among them, we are on the way to solution."

Every village we passed we had to pay our respects to the chief elder, called "The District Chief," who's the equivalent of a Yankee mayor.

"This is the Asian way," explained Mr. Dinh Le Ngoan who has been to the United States and is therefore very patient with the impatient American ways.

"It is protocol," he explained patiently. "When you were granted permission to make this trip, the information was sent ahead to the villages you were passing through so they would be on the lookout for us. The District Chiefs would be very offended if we did not stop by, thank them for their courtesies, show them we are safe, show them that the visiting Americans are very proud of the opportunity to pay their respects to the head man of the community, and bring them the regards of the Minister Of Civic Action."

As usual, tea was served. For about twenty minutes per stop we passed the time of day with the mayor, who, in each case, was wearing army uniform, as were the other members of his staff. On the walls of their offices were maps with pins indicating where the Viet Cong had struck last.

"The main trouble between our countries is the difference in our culture," said Mr. Ngoan, who is partial to the USA. "You don't know our ways and we don't get a chance to know yours. Our protocol and courtesies seem to make things agonizingly slow for the American. On the other hand an Asian pictures an American as rude and impatient. The truth is, we both underestimate each other.

"That's why it's good that you're here. It gives us a chance to know each other better."

When we arrived in the high flood area in the town of Cai Lay, which is about sixty miles southwest of Saigon, we parked our car and our escort in the city hall. After tea, the District Chief, who was an army captain, took us as far as we could go on foot. From then on we went by canoe.

The Mekong overflows at the same time every year. But this is the first time in one hundred years that it has been this high. In this particular village they'd lost one hundred people.

There was no land in sight. There were no streets. The entire village was under muddy, brown water. As we paddled along in our canoe, a grass hut with a roof of thatched cocoa leaves floated by alongside. On the other side a house made of bamboo drifted lazily downstream. Vegetables and clothing and hammocks sailed along what was once the main street. On rooftops were piled precious possessions: clothing, straw sleeping rolls, a loaf of bread, cooking utensils, a basket of rice. Men were fishing in what used to be their rice fields. One woman was perched on her kitchen table, fishing in her living room. Babies were splashing naked in the dirty river with garbage as their play toys.

Business was going on as usual. In a canoe a man was selling his fruit. One storekeeper had piled all his furniture in a heap and, from the top of the whole pile, he was calmly peddling his wares. Nowhere was there panic. There was no hollering, no moaning, no weeping. Orientals are stoics. Their Buddhism preaches it. Their lives portray it.

A little old grandmother, white hair caught up in a wispy bun, waded along hugging two oranges to her breast. Her cotton trousers were rolled up to her shriveled thighs. The water was knee-high. Through the interpreter I bid her greetings and passed the time of day. I commended her courage and that of her countrymen in the face of this disaster.

"This is decided by God," was her answer. "We must have done something wrong, and so we are being punished. If it is God's will to punish us, there is nothing we can do."

Cindy waded out to talk with a mother who was carrying a baby in her arms. "Why do you stay here when you know you're going to get flooded out every year?" Cindy asked.

"This is my home. I've lived here all my life. Where else could I go?" the woman said.

My wife asked the same question of a farmer whose land was under many feet of water. "After a flood the fishing is good," was his explanation. "And after a flood the land is rich for planting rice. There is no other such land anywhere in the country."

Back up on the high ground, in the Cai Lay Catholic church, the homeless were being sheltered. In one classroom, three hundred people were living. Another housed forty families. They were subsisting on rice and bread donated by the Students' Association. The nuns there wear scuff sandals. The

habit of their order is a floor-length black robe with the traditional Chinese mandarin neck and frogs all the way down the
front.

The nuns divided the chores among the people. The men
were out by day splitting firewood, carrying water, or seeing
after their lost property. The women were gathered together
chattering, sewing the few remnants of clothing that they had.
There was no worry about lost clothing since most of them
didn't have more than the set they were wearing. Their outfit
was a mandarin jacket, loose-fitting trousers and sandals.
When we arrived they were cooking the rice and bread outdoors over a makeshift brazier.

The classrooms were equipped with benches which were
pushed together to make beds. Those who didn't have benches
slept on straw mats or hammocks. Their possessions—whatever they could salvage: a broken bit of mirror, a ribbon, a
cup—were piled neatly next to each bench.

One emaciated little woman was sitting on the ground all
alone in a corner of the dusty courtyard. Her coal-black hair
was up in a coronet of braids. Her high cheekbones and the
deeply etched lines of her face framed a mouth which held
three black teeth. Two mangy, scrawny dogs with coats as life-
less as the dusty ground beneath them were kicking and biting
and clawing one another right beside her. She never looked up
from her sewing. She was repairing the long gash in her
trousers.

As Cindy approached, she unleashed a torrent of words. According to the interpreter, who had some difficulty since both
spoke different dialects, she said, "I am all alone. I am a
refugee from the north. I have left all my belongings there to
come here. Now I have lost all a second time. I am all alone."

When Cindy asked would she like to go to another village
so this wouldn't happen to her again, she said, "I moved twice
already. Once from the Communists. Once from the flood.
How many times can I move in one lifetime? This is my
home."

I asked one young man who was hauling wood, "Why don't you all do something to build up the delta with sandbags or dams or barricades so this tragedy won't hit you every year?" "That is not for us," he said, simply. "That is Government business."

Said another calmly, "The Mekong is very big, very powerful. It is too powerful to tame. It is some great special thing. We must just live with it."

As we left the one story, adobe church, the two nuns walked us over the dry, parched ground to our high car. I thanked them for their kindness in letting us visit. "Thank you," said the older sister, "for caring. And please thank America for their help."

We arrived in Saigon just in time to change and do the show. As we entered the city proper and drove past Cua Dong Cho-Moi, which is the block of the big bazaars, our Army escort veered off to the left and waved good-bye.

"Well," Cindy said, "we're home safe and sound. We certainly have a lot to be grateful for."

"Yes, and I certainly am," I said. "But I feel just a little bit guilty. We took twenty-five soldiers away from their post to guard us and nobody even tried to shoot at us or anything."

"Yeah," Cindy mused, "it does seem a shame."

Saigon is called the Paris of Asia. The second language of the people is French. And the second nature of the women is to be chic. The Vietnamese national dress is the most beautiful costume in the world. It's worn during the day and at night. It's worn on the streets and in the homes. It's worn by the peasants in the fields and the aristocrats in the city. By the old and the young, the tall and the short, the married and the single. It's the only dress worn by the Vietnamese woman.

This exquisite outfit consists of ankle-length white or black flowing trousers. Over it is worn an ankle-length tunic with high, stiff, mandarin collar and long, tight sleeves to the wrist. The brilliantly colored tunics are slit on both sides from the ankle all the way up to the waistline. This high-necked, long-sleeved, ankle-length outfit is worn even in the blinding heat of the day. The only concessions they make are open-toed sandals and parasol-like bamboo hats which are worn strapped under the chin to shade them from the sun.

Vietnamese women often wear their long black hair loose down their back. Their waists are about the size of a man's well-developed wrist. They're gorgeous. My wife who is a regular size 8 felt like an ox as all 115 pounds of her trotted along Rue Tu-Do, the main street of Saigon.

One night all the girls in the show dressed up in the Vietnamese national costume: the Syltes sang their song wearing hot pink tunics and white trousers; Celeste did her act in a flowered top and black pants; Cindy opened the show in a black-on-black embroidered tunic with the traditional black satin pajama bottoms and gold thong sandals. With Cindy's black slanty eyes and her long black hair loose she looked like a permanent part of the local scene. The audience loved the idea, but the girls loved it even more.

As usual our afternoons were taken up with hospital shows. These were arranged for us by USIS in collaboration with the Vietnamese-American Association, whose sole objective is peace, love, and understanding between our countries.

At the Cong Hoa General Military Hospital at Go Vap we divided our forces; half our cast went in one direction and half in another. We did a show in every single room even if it contained just one lone, solitary soldier. Our show had something for everybody. If we didn't win you with one act, we'd get to you with another. We left a little joy in almost every room.

But there was one little guy, a victim of the Phuoc Thanh battle, whom we just couldn't reach. He was in a room all by himself. He was a skinny little kid who couldn't have been more than high-school age. He looked like he should have been coming from a prom not a war. His thin, little body seemed to be lost in the big bed. As we entered the room he was propped up, ready for the show. I started off with the three beautiful Sylte Sisters who sang right next to his bed. They did everything from spirituals to jazz, but nothing moved him. It was like his face was painted on the pillow. I joined them in the one big song we do in the show and even tried my imitations which never failed. He didn't even know we were in the room.

Next came the Step Brothers. I've seen them stop the show in almost every country in the world. This afternoon they worked harder than ever. They danced on top of a table, they did knee drops from the top of the bureau to the floor. They used every show-stopping trick that they knew. Nothing happened.

Then I did my dance with the four Steps where I finish with a—you should excuse the expression—Russian kazotzky. As always, after ten kicks, the Steps, who have been holding me up, release me and I fall flat on my back. This usually gets a big scream from the audience. This time I did the whole thing with such exuberance, trying to win this kid, that I fell back so hard I hit my head on the bedpost. We weren't sure but we thought we saw a flicker of a smile cross the boy's face.

I repeated the bit. This time instead of the boys dropping me, they threw me a little. Our audience broke out into a grin. Now we really went to work. The boys kept bouncing me up and down like a basketball. The more the kid laughed the more I got bounced. By the time the show was over, the patient was cured, but the doctor was a busted-up bag of bones. Our audience looked like he was ready to leave the hospital and I looked like I was ready to take his bed.

At the end of the afternoon, our troupe combined forces in the big hall at Cong Hoa to do our entire program for the ambulatory patients and the staff of the hospital.

All the hospitals in South Vietnam are filled to overflowing. The Dooley Hospital in South Vietnam's Quangngai Province is so overcrowded they have to bunk three patients to a bed.

Many are casualties in the ceaseless war between the Viet Cong Communists of the North and President Diem's Nationalist troops of the South.

For the safety of the others, if a Viet Cong is brought in, he's chained to the bed. When we were there one had to be removed—but for his own safety: the other patients tried to massacre him.

The biggest problem for Vietnamese hospitals is not the patients but the relatives. If one soldier is confined, his entire family—grandma, cousins and all—set up light housekeeping on the doorstep until he's discharged. When the heavy floods washed away the hospital porch where they were camped, they still stayed. For months. And should the kinfolk take sick during their long, outdoor vigils, the hospital cares for them, too. This is what you would call the world's longest visiting hours and the world's friendliest hospitals.

The National Orphanage in Saigon had a big sign on the gate which said, "Welcome to the Joey Adams Troupe." As we drove past the entrance, the six hundred children of Co-Nhi-Vien orphanage at Quoc-Gia, Vietnam, held aloft hand-made signs in English which carried the legend, "Vietnamese-American Friendship Forever."

A twelve-year-old boy in a starched blue shirt and starched blue pants opened the show with this prepared speech. "How glad we are!" he began, as he introduced me. "Coming from a distant country, you have kindness to get here to our National Orphanage in order to give us, the miserable orphan children, many minutes of entertainments." The children topped our efforts with an exhibition of national folk dances to the accompaniment of their own orchestra.

As we left, they preceded us out the door. In their starched uniforms and arranged according to size, they lined both sides of the road. The first children were aged two, and they went all the way up to sixteen-year-olds.

Headlines were exploding all over Vietnam that morning,

but none was more dramatic than the picture of six hundred orphaned children standing at attention and in piping voices singing "God Bless America" in English to a handful of American vaudevillians in a tiny courtyard in a tiny town outside Saigon.

CHAPTER 19

Miss Killjoy's Poison Pen

I WAS SORRY Cindy couldn't have seen the orphanage show. But the rigors of the trip were catching up with her. Everybody in the troupe had had their turn, except Cindy. For a while we all thought she was an iron woman. But something hit her in Djakarta. We still don't know what it was. All I know is that she started to lose her hearing. First one ear then the other.

By the time we reached Saigon, she was almost deaf. She was hearing as though she were under water. Nobody ever knew it except Cindy and me. But now we had an added starter. Cindy had a high fever. She was at home in bed this particular afternoon trying to gather a little strength for the evening performance.

I rushed home to the Majestic Hotel to cheer her up with a blow-by-blow account of what I'd just experienced.

The small lobby leads to an open elevator which creaks its way up to your room. All rooms come with two meals a day.

For some reason, which I'll never understand, our particular room came without meals. But it did come with lizards.

All over Indochina you have lizards. We first made their acquaintance in Thailand. We got real chummy with them again in Cambodia. In Laos and Djakarta we were inseparable. Saigon, however, is where they really held their big convention. And most of them were in my room.

I know there must be a good reason for their being there. I know that wherever it's hot and muggy and sticky and mosquito-ridden, God provides his own built-in insect repellent. And in French Indochina it's lizards or chameleons or ghekkos or salamanders, or whatever they're called. They grow anywhere from the six-inch baby size to the full grown adult twelve-inch size. They're green, and they crawl all over the ceilings and the walls. They come out in full strength at night. When you put the light on in your room you can count maybe twenty or thirty of them on the walls and ceilings. Cindy used to go to sleep rigid with terror at the thought that one would fall down and share the double-bed with us.

The room had that old-fashioned, overstuffed, cumbersome furniture that your grandmother used to have in the old days, with doilies on it. The room had no closets as we know them. It had just a wooden wardrobe that had seen happier days.

Cindy was huddled up in bed lying against an enormous bolster pillow. The pillowcase was like cheesecloth and what was inside must have been kapok or hemp or whatever a taxidermist shoves into a stuffed bull. We didn't exactly sleep like a log here. It was more like sleeping *on* a log.

As I came in, my wife was staring pop-eyed at the ceiling watching the gathering of the clan. It was near dinnertime and the lizards were coming out for their early evening snack.

Between her hearing and her fever and the lizards and the garden-variety troubles we were having all along the way, my dear little wife was feeling sorry for herself. The best defense is an offense. Cindy is always happy. And she's always healthy. She was born to be gay. I knew no bug could lay Cindy low.

It was just that she was taking on my burdens too seriously. And trying too hard to fight my battles. The only thing to do was to take her mind away from her problems. Cindy fastens on joy very quickly.

I told her of our experience at the orphanage. "Y'know," I said when I was finished, "I really feel like a hero. I felt like a real ambassador for the USA today. Today I was really a comic in striped pants. I can just see myself back home when I come off the plane. I bet Kennedy himself will be there to greet me."

"Yeah," Cindy said, trying to play the game, "Sam Kennedy. From the delicatessen in Brooklyn."

I knew she was making an attempt to perk up. "I wonder," I said, continuing along in my own dream world, "Do you think they'll give me a ticker-tape parade? I can just see myself getting the Congressional Medal of Honor."

"Hey, AGVA Khan . . . hey, Joey of Arc . . . down boy. Here on the paper," my wife heckled.

No more was I trying to make Cindy feel good. I was really believing this now myself. "You never can tell," I mused aloud. "They might run me for Mayor of New York or Governor of the State or . . ."

"Look, Big Shot, when you visit my grandmother in the Bronx you'll still have to take the garbage out."

By now there was no stopping me. I was really off my nut. "Who knows," I whispered, in a daze, "you might wind up being First Lady of the land."

"Yeah, well," she said, crawling out of bed, "right now the First Lady has got to go wash your shorts because at this moment the future President of the United States happens to be down to his last pair of drawers."

Princess Valiant really made an effort, but she didn't have her land legs yet. So she stayed in bed and this time I did the family laundry. "All right, so I won't be President or Governor," I said, scrubbing my socks with Woolite, "but at least when I get home I'll be able to open my own laundry."

"When you finish the ironing," my wife called, "you can start vacuuming and then do the shoes. And if you're a good boy I may let you have next Thursday off."

When I had finished with my chores I noticed the letter shoved under the door. It was one hell of a thrill when I saw the envelope. It was postmarked New York and addressed simply: JOEY ADAMS SAIGON VIETNAM.

"Look at this," I screamed. "Am I famous or am I famous! It's just addressed: Joey Adams Saigon Vietnam. No hotel, no Embassy, no care of anybody, no nothin'. There are fourteen million people in South Vietnam alone—not counting the thousands of Americans here. This is a French colony which was taken over by the Vietnamese. They changed the original French street names to Vietnamese. The locals even have trouble finding each other. And *I* get a letter that comes direct to me all the way from New York that says, Joey Adams Saigon Vietnam. And I get it six days after it was mailed which means it didn't lay around here at all. It was just delivered direct to me."

Several clippings fell out of the envelope. "Can you just imagine," I boasted, "what the newspapers must be saying about us back home? Makes you feel it was all worth it, doesn't it, sweetie? I mean, to be appreciated by your own people. I don't think it's wrong, do you, sweetie, at least to want to be appreciated by your own? That doesn't make you selfish or hammy, does it?"

"No. It doesn't. It makes you truthful. At least you're not a hypocrite."

"You know what it's like, honey?" I said, groping for words. "It's like being a hit at Madison Square Garden with twenty thousand people cheering for you and then going home to a wife who couldn't care less. Every man wants to be a hero to his own family. Of course we didn't do this for publicity. You've got to be some kind of a crazy nut to leave your home for four and a half months and travel to the roughest countries in the world just for a line in a column. But now that we've gone through it all, I'd be a liar if I didn't say it would be nice to get a pat on the back while we were away."

Eagerly I picked up the clippings. There were eight columns. All by Miss Killjoy. The lady high executioner of a chain of American newspapers. They were the most vicious, malicious stabs in the back I have ever read. I'm sure she didn't vilify Adolf Hitler and Eva Braun that badly. I didn't know whether to laugh or cry. I didn't know what to do.

"Tell me," Cindy cried anxiously, sitting up in bed. "I can't wait to hear it. What do they say?"

I didn't answer her at first. I didn't know what to say.

"C'mon, what are you waiting for?" she said. "Read 'em to me, willya?"

"Well," I said reluctantly, "this one is all about what a big flop we are and how we're about the worst bunch of garbage our Government could send and what's wrong with our Government that they could do such a thing and that the State Department should recall us before we do irreparable international harm because if our country needs Joey and Cindy Adams then we're in real trouble.

"Another column calls us third-rate entertainers who are charity cases and who are taking a handout from the United States Government because we're no longer able to get a job in our own country. And she says here—quote—'I have contributed for years to actors' funds which are supposed to take care of performers when they're no longer able to get employment in their chosen fields.' So she wants to know why the Government is giving charity to us poor souls whom nobody else wants.

"Here's a beauty," I said waving a third one. "Here she says we've been on one beautiful, swinging joy ride—quote—'playing nothing but palaces, amusing the Heads of State and the elite of the various lands at the U.S. taxpayers' expense.' Another place she refers to us as a bunch of nobodies and that nobody ever heard of us anyplace."

I looked up at Cindy for comment. There was none. But not one word. Talk about frustration! I felt sick to my stomach. In New York we live eight blocks away from Miss Killjoy and she waited until we were safely tucked away on the other side of the world before she unleashed her methodical, calculated, deliberate campaign of hate against us. I didn't know whether I wanted to throw up or bang my head against the wall.

"Here's one dated November 1, 1961. It's a whole, full column of poison against the troupe, the whole Cultural Exchange effort, the State Department, our Government, and you and me. In it she quotes Mr. Heath Bowman, who is Chief of the Cultural Exchange Program for the State Department, and who said, 'This bouquet of variety acts has been requested by our Ambassadors overseas,' and that 'it was our feeling that this sort of thing brings them a little closer to the American people and enables them to laugh with us and demonstrates that we are not militarists.' And also, 'We are competing with the Russians. They are doing the same kind of thing. Only we do it better.'

"She disagrees with our Government completely. The one person with whom she feels she is in agreement—and she says so right here—is Nikita Khrushchev. And then she runs off at the typewriter that the Russians are doing better than we are in setting off nuclear bombs in the atmosphere, and in general she feels that Nikita's methods are better than ours and—quote—'If the Government in Washington thinks anything different we are in big trouble.'

"This last one is a doozey. It is a full, entire, whole column filled with hate for you. The headline says—And I quote exactly stab for stab—'Girl envoy hurts U.S.' Then there's a picture of you and then in about six hundred words she tries to smear you from one end of her column to the other. Here she says about you—quote—'Mrs. Adams is bombing around the globe sending home whole columns guaranteed to insult the Moslems, the Hindus and the Buddhists.' And—'Cindy

Adams can cause more global tension in an hour than the Peace Corps' Margery Michelmore could in a month of Sundays.' She calls you 'a secret weapon' who is going around hurting the U.S. effort.

"All this because you printed in your column the *DO*'s and *DON'T*s that were handed you in printed form by the State Department as something that every loyal American should know when they travel in these areas.

"What are we going to do about all this?" I asked Cindy. Cindy sat upright in bed.

"I'll tell you one thing I'm not going to do about it," she said very quietly. "I'm not going to get excited about it. I right now am broiling away with fever. For some reason I've already lost my hearing on this gay little cruise we've been on. This is now the third week that I can't hear. Joey, honey, I'm tired. I'm sick. And I'm worn down. I've given every bit of gut I can to this trip. I'm busted up inside and out.

"I've had to wash clothes—yours and mine—late at night when I'm so tired I couldn't stand up any more. I've had to smile hour after hour endlessly and try to be gracious when I'm worried sick about what's going on at home and when I haven't heard from my mother and father for weeks. I've never even complained about the lack of toilet facilities when I was sick as a dog. And if I've managed to put up with dozens of lizards that are crawling around only inches over my head, how do you expect me to work up a sweat over another lizard that's crawling around thousands of miles away?"

"Yeah, but what are you going to do about it?" I persisted. "You just going to let her get away with it? Aren't you going to try to get even?"

"She's gotten even with herself," my wife said. "She's done a better job on herself than I ever could. I don't hate this kind of a person. I feel sorry for her. I have nothing but pity in my heart for someone who's so bereft."

"I know, but . . ." I began.

"There is no but," Cindy said.

"But," I said, "suppose people believe this filth she's writing?"

"Suppose instead," answered my wife, "that people will believe what an Ambassador of the United States is writing? While you were doing a show at the National Orphanage this morning, here's what Ambassador Fred Nolting delivered to me. It's a copy of the cable he's just sent off to the Secretary of State in Washington, and it says, in part:

EMBASSY HIGHLY PLEASED WITH SUCCESS OF JOEY ADAMS VARIETY SHOW AS CONTRIBUTION TO VIET-NAMESE-AMERICAN RELATIONS. SHOW ITSELF AND ADAMS' PERSONAL GIFT OF CEMENTING US-VN RELATIONS MOST IMPRESSIVE.

"That," sighed Cindy dropping back on the pillow, "is good enough for me."

Cindy and I discussed the situation thoroughly and I got it off my chest and we decided to drop it. But our friend hadn't. The vilification continued. Since we'd been taking all this hammering without one peep of protest, she'd been getting more and more aggressive. A few days later Celeste Evans came to me with another column that a friend had forwarded to her. In this one Killjoy spewed her hatred toward the Cultural Exchange program in general and our show in particular.

"What are you going to do about it?" Celeste said.

"Nothing," Cindy said. "Let sleeping snakes lie."

This pot boiled around us for a full week while other members of the troupe were opening envelopes with other columns friends were sending them. Two weeks later, when we were in India and everybody was quieting down, John Shirley showed up with a new hate column. This one was against him, against Chaz Chase, the four Step Brothers and Cindy and me. Now Killjoy was going wild altogether. She was just striking out blindly in any direction—at the actors, at the Cultural Exchange, at the Government, at Cindy, at me.

"What are you going to do about it?" John said.

"Nothing," I said.

"Well, I'm going to answer her," he snapped.

"Be my guest," I said.

When we were in Madras in South India we got another letter saying she'd devoted several mornings of her radio program to knocking us. It was so vicious that even her husband defended us.

In Bombay we received a letter from our attorney who said we had a perfect suit against her because this was not one or two columns, but this was a steady barrage which comes under the heading of "Libel With Malicious Intent."

"What are you going to do about it?" asked our attorney.

In New Delhi, one of Cindy's publishers cabled her demanding Cindy break typewriter silence and defend herself.

"What are you going to do about it?" cabled the publisher.

The clipping that broke the camel's back was the one where the State Department publicly defended us in print. The headline in *Variety* said: "State Department Rates Asian Good Will Tour of Adams Unit as 'Smash Success.' " The dateline was Washington. It said, in part:

"State Department officials here point to a pile of reports from embassies and consulates throughout South Asia and proclaim that Uncle Sam's use of vaudeville as a good will Ambassador is a 'smash success.' The Joey Adams group has drawn raves from American diplomats where they have performed, messages rushed back to Washington attest. This has caused department officials here to fume over a recent syndicated column which said the Adams tour had been a flop. Department officials say her comment must have been triggered either by a grudge or faulty information.

" 'She couldn't be more wrong,' exclaimed one official. 'The Embassy in Cambodia cabled that our group was "a smashing success" and that the USSR Ambassador in Cambodia had asked Moscow to send a vaudeville show there, too.

" 'In Singapore the American Ambassador wrote the department that he "enthusiastically commended the effectiveness" of the troupe, adding, "All appearances singularly helpful in promoting American friendship." ' "

"What are you going to do about it?" I said to Cindy. "Now the State Department has even taken up the cudgels in our defense. They say she must have a grudge against you. What brought it on?"

"All I can think of," Cindy said, "is the first time she knocked me in her column—and that was a year ago. That was after I had written the *TV Guide* article on the make-up secrets of our television stars. All I said about her was that she toted her gear in a shoe box. Can you hate someone for that?"

"Well, what are you going to do about it?" I asked again. "You've even gotten letters from your mother and father wondering what you are going to do about it."

"Listen, sweetie," said Cindy, who by now was pretty tired of this whole thing. "I don't believe that evil can win no matter what guise it wears. I've done nothing to be ashamed of. Neither have you. As a matter of fact we've done only things to make us proud. So why should I have to defend myself? Defend myself against what? I haven't done anything to deserve it and I refuse to get down to her level."

"But, honey," I said very softly, "this is beyond you. It's beyond your own personal feeling and mine. All right, don't defend yourself. But do you love your Government? Do you have respect for your country? Do you believe in Cultural Exchange? Then say so. You've got to stand up and be counted."

Whenever Cindy is confused or in trouble, she has a long-standing habit of turning to the Bible. She opens it at random. She picked up the Bible that she always carries with her and opened it to Isaiah, chapter 54, verse 17, where it says: "No weapon that is formed against thee shall prosper; and every tongue that shall rise against thee in judgment thou shalt condemn. This is the heritage of the servants of the Lord, and their righteousness is of me, saith the Lord."

Then at last Cindy sat down and sent off a column to her
syndicate. It was an open letter to Miss Killjoy, making a few
pointed remarks like, for instance:

"You have repeatedly maligned the State Department-sponsored Joey Adams troupe which just completed four and one-
half months in Southeast Asia on behalf of President Kennedy's Cultural Exchange program. Through the New York
Times and an interview with *Variety,* the theatrical weekly,
our State Department officially went on record as saying the
Joey Adams Show was one of the most successful tours they've
ever sent out. As a result of our success, they are sending other
shows along the same route we have just broken through. As
a result of our impact, Russia is now assembling a similar
show to play the very same areas and, coincidentally, has in-
creased its budget for promoting entertainment units abroad.

"However, you figure you're more of an authority on our
effectiveness than the State Department. Or than our Ambassador in Nepal who cabled Washington for permission to extend our stay. Or than our Embassy in Thailand who cabled
Washington for permission to replay us again at the first
available date. You consider yourself an authority on our
doings in Afghanistan, Iran, Cambodia, Laos and points East
since you've garnered all your hot information . . . in New
York's poshest saloons.

"Whilst you, Mrs. Kollmar, were sitting ringside . . . and
yawning how we only entertained presidents and royalty, we
were working to 20,000 turban-tops a night in Kabul, Afghanistan in direct competition to the Russians who attracted 500
per night. And we were attempting to solidify friendship between our people by voluntarily adding extra benefit shows for
hospitals, orphanages, schools for the handicapped, institutions
for the blind, even a Beggars' Home in Chembur, India, where
the preponderance of inmates were leprous.

"And while the 'Voice of Broadway' droned on, the Joey
Adams troupe were thrilling to the voices of 600 children in
an orphanage in Saigon, Vietnam singing 'God Bless America'

in English and holding aloft signs saying 'Vietnamese-American friendship forever' as a result of the happiness this show brought them. And more important than your voice were the voices of American Ambassadors in eleven countries who considered our minstrels of inestimable value in breaking down the centuries-old wall betwixt East and West. And while you were elbowbending into the wee hours, we were using our free time in teaching English to Lao-American Association classes in wartorn Vientiane. And in performing for 5,000 refugees from Red China who can't remember when they smiled last.

"And while you, sour Mrs. Kollmar, were roughing it under the hairdryer at Dior's and burping about what a waste of the taxpayer's money our joyride was, we were catching planes at 5 o'clock A.M.; doing morning, afternoon and evening performances; getting dressed via candlelight; going without water for a week in the upcountry hinterlands of Thailand where we entertained 10,000 Thai soldiers in a jet hangar; working forest clearings when stage-lights were jacked-up jeeps. The twenty-three of us went many nights without dinner, since restaurants weren't always open by the time we finished the show. And Joey & Co. gave out with their snappy songs 'n' fancy patter in a theater in Vietnam when all the while the bomb squad was casing it for mines.

"The biggest pain in your typewriter seems to be that nobody would know us over there. Well, in my personal interviews with Prime Minister Nehru, President Sukarno, the King and Queen of Thailand and the other leaders of the Asian world, y'know something??? They never heard of you!!! But the millions of little people whom the troupe entertained around the world and who accepted our hearts and outstretched hands know us. And they love us. And they'll never forget us for the warmth and love and joy our country has given them through Joey and his group . . . because they know, even if you don't, that a dose of joy is a spiritual cure. . . .

"While you were serving malice I was thrilled at the opportunity to serve my country even in a very small way. I love life. I love people. I love God and everything that stands for what's good and right and true. I don't have to try to hurt other people to get my satisfaction out of life. But just as David had to stand up to Goliath and hit him right between the eyes, I'm warning you not to stick your chin out any more. You can't spare it!"

Quite a few people said this open letter was a beaut. Miss Killjoy must have thought so, too, because six months later she slapped a one-million-dollar libel suit against my Cindy.

CHAPTER 20

Our Heart Belongs
to Mother India

From the halls of Madison Square Garden to the shores of Mahatma Gandhi, I've entertained every type of audience. But in Chembur, India, a little town just thirty minutes outside of Bombay, was the first time I was ever billed in a beggars' home.

Out of India's five hundred million people, four million seem to be professional beggars. In Bombay alone, there are fifteen thousand pros and another fifteen thousand apprentice beggars. The tools of their trade are wounds, disease, naked babies, borrowed children, and deformities. If you're in the business of begging, liabilities are your most valuable assets.

Children are for sale or rent by the hour, day or year. Babies are the biggest rupee-getters. It is not uncommon to see a little urchin of six carrying a hired infant in her arms. These beggars' helpers are cast carefully. Only sick, emaciated, and malformed children need apply. In this business there's no such formality as adoption. Often a mama beggar and a papa

237

beggar latch on to a baby, and he grows up with them until he becomes a full-sized adult beggar. Some parents even maim their children so they can bring more money in rentals.

The Indian Government has gone all out to kill begging. It is now prohibited to beg in the streets under penalty of one to three years in prison. The Government asks their people and all tourists not to give to the beggars. USIS does the same. This all sounds beautiful, but go tell it to the beggars.

They follow you down the streets. But not behind you. In front of you. They walk just a wee bit slower than you do so you have to actually trip over them to continue on your way. The bedraggled youngsters chant, "No Poppy. No Mommy." How can you avoid a child who is dragging an infant with one hand while her other one is extended right out in front of you and who paces you for blocks and blocks and blocks and blocks? You've got to break down.

The Indian Government has opened twenty beggars' homes as the first step in its campaign to keep the cities clean. In the Beggars' Home in Chembur where we entertained early one morning, there are nine hundred inmates—six hundred men, and three hundred women.

As we drove past the gate, the inmates were sitting on the ground in an open field enclosed by one-story wood and adobe buildings. Our stage was the porch of the Administration Building. During most of the show we actually went into the audience and worked among the people.

Men, women, and children all sat together. On the right side, sitting huddled together, was the leper colony—which comprised about one third of the Home. One building on the grounds is given over solely to them, so that at all times they remain isolated from the rest. Every one of our acts went out into the audience and did a special encore right in the center of the leper colony.

The women all wear saris. The men wear anything from Western-style shirts and trousers to the Indian dhotis (which are shirts with long tails that hang down to the knees), underneath which are pants that look like flowing diapers. Clothes are supplied by the Government.

We did the show in English, because within those gates alone fifteen major Indian languages were spoken and sixty major dialects, from Hindi and Tamil to Urdu and Punjabi.

At the Chembur Home the beggars are taught "work habits" which, the Superintendent explained, will break them from their "wandering habits" when they are released. The home teaches them the crafts of tailoring, weaving, broom-making, gardening, agriculture, spinning, knitting, and fancy work. In one room where their handicrafts were on view we were invited to buy whatever we liked. Among our group there was a big run on straw baskets.

According to their skill, the inmates are paid up to one rupee a day (about 20¢), which they save toward the time when they're on their own again. When they are released they are given a ticket for transportation and steered towards a small village rather than a big city. This way there is a greater chance to integrate and less opportunity or necessity for begging.

Ten per cent of those who leave the home are successful. They work like Alcoholics Anonymous. The one who makes it, tries to help the others—like the one ex-beggar who opened a carpentry shop in a small town; he has since employed only those who have a BA degree—Beggars Anonymous. Ten per cent of those released become repeaters at the home. Some of them start to beg the minute the gates shut behind them. According to the Superintendent, out of the five thousand who have been helped, not one has ever sent a contribution back to the Home.

Even an unsuccessful beggar drags down five tax-free rupees a day. And for a buck a day they can live pretty well. I mean, they don't put out anything for board and lodging. All they do is pull up a sidewalk and lie down.

The second biggest migraine for the authorities is trying to prevent the people from giving to the beggars in the first place. Buddhists and Hindus believe that to give alms to another is part of their religion. They believe that, in sharing what they have materially, they become purified and sanctified, and by helping another they are sure of a better after-life. According to Hindu belief, one who has received much in this life is honor bound to give something of it to others.

A big problem among the beggars is apathy. They're indifferent to their diseases and their plight. They figure they're of such low caste that it will make no difference whether or not they improve mentally or physically. They're not going to go anywhere in this lifetime anyway. Besides, their average span is only about forty-five years. Millions of people in India spend those years in the most abject misery.

With all its other problems India is extremely color conscious. A Berlin bombing or a new astronaut in space or the Eichmann hanging or even the Liz-Eddie-Burton bit would rate space on page 3; but a minor crisis in Little Rock would win a banner headline on every front page in India.

The day we arrived in Bombay, the *Bombay Free Press,* the English-language newspaper, welcomed us on their editorial page as follows: "Welcome Joey Adams. We like laughter. It is like sunshine. And also remember: there will not be a single restaurant all over the country which will refuse to serve you. When you go back to your country, you better tell about that to your stupid countrymen who insult our artistes visiting your country."

The *Bombay Free Press* was fighting mad because of the "Indrani Rehman Insult." It seems while we were traipsing through India on a six weeks' tour for our Government, the Indian star, Indrani Rehman, and her dance troupe were entertaining in our country in the true spirit of Cultural Exchange.

"How come," one reporter challenged at our press conference at the Indo-American Society, "your stupid countrymen wouldn't serve our famous Indian stars in a restaurant in Virginia?"

You could feel the hush permeate the hot, sticky room. Nobody moved. Everybody was sitting there, frozen. Staring at me. Waiting for my answer. I rose slowly. I didn't have to hurry. Nobody was exactly battling for this spot. Here I was, forced into the position of having to defend something that I've abhorred all my life.

"Today," I said quietly, "we entertained at the Beggars' Home in Chembur. Does that mean all the people of India are beggars? Last night I drove through one of the most famous red-light districts in the whole world. It's right here in Bombay. It's blocks and blocks and blocks of girls in cages. Wouldn't I be foolish to say this is a reflection on your entire Government? I know that a law has been passed in your country to abolish the caste system. But we all know that it still exists in some parts and the law is a little tough to enforce. And would I dare say your countrymen are stupid because they're unable to enforce the law all the time?

"We have laws in our country that guarantee everybody who comes to our shores life, liberty, and the pursuit of happiness. But every once in a while some one person or group sets out to challenge those civil rights and just like you are trying to clean up your beggars and your caste system, we are working just as hard to clean up those who are trying to tarnish our freedoms. But it can't be done in a day.

"I apologize for any embarrassment that was caused to Indrani and her troupe. But do you think that one incident in one community should besmirch a nation of one hundred eighty million Americans and cause headlines on two continents?

"We were treated ungraciously here in India, too, but we never mentioned it before or gave it to any newspaper reporter or complained to the Government or made any fuss about it or publicly labeled your countrymen 'stupid' as a result. You tell them what happened, Al."

Al Williams, one of the Step Brothers, stood up. He'd been straining at the leash ever since the conversation took this turn. "When we were in Bangalore," he began, "I went into a barber shop for a haircut and shave. The barber wasn't busy. There was nobody else there. But he wouldn't wait on me. He didn't even apologize. He just said, simply but definitely, 'We don't cut blacks' hair.' "

Maceo Anderson, the oldest of the Steps, stood up to be counted. "Did you know that you have a sign in front of your own race-track right here in Bombay that's a pretty good case of discrimination? It's right in front of the gate, before you even go inside. You can't miss it. And it says, 'No South Africans Allowed.' "

"Speaking of the South," said Prince, "how about what happened to me in Madras. A group of us went to the beach one morning. Everybody got beach chairs but me. It was pretty obvious that the fellow thought my color was a little too dark."

"Because we know," I said, "that isolated happenings like these could hardly be taken as a general rule, we did not intend to make a general nuisance of ourselves by complaining about this to the press or the Government. After all, we're here to plant harmony between our countries, not friction."

There were no further questions.

Every night after the show at the Bharatiya Vidya Bhavan Theatre in Bombay, my wife and I would spend hours prowling the city. We wanted to see the ordinary townspeople, and the only way to see a foreign port and meet its citizens is on foot.

Each night we'd start out in a different direction, but it didn't matter where we went. The story of India is not in the monuments or the buildings or the shrines. The true flavor of India is in the people. The streets are packed with people. They fill the sidewalks and the gutters. They're around you. They're on top of you. They're even underfoot.

When you're strolling along the streets, you have to step

over the bodies that are bedded down for the night. You have to side-step the professional beggars with their outstretched palms. You have to sidle through the teams of peddlers, aged eight to eighty, who try to sell everything from leis of flowers to necklaces of "genuine silver." You have to weasel by the black-market money-changers.

You see the manicurists, pedicurists, and barbers who are open for business on the street corners. The barber sets up shop under a tree. On the trunk he hangs a jagged hunk of mirror and he's ready for customers. He doesn't worry about unions, barber chairs, rent, electricity. Nothing. Not only doesn't a prospective client have to make an appointment in advance, but he doesn't even have to break his stride. If a passer-by decides he wants a haircut and shave, he and the owner-manager squat on their haunches for a few minutes, he gets his face and head scraped and continues on his way.

The store for the manicurists and pedicurists is on whatever curb they happen to grab you. They guarantee to remove corns, bunions, callouses, cuticles or your rupees cheerfully refunded. But suppose you want to complain two days later? Go find your operator. By then your Bombay street pedicurist has hung out his shingle in a gutter in Calcutta.

Al Williams decided he wanted his toes renovated. He's not a ballet dancer and nobody's ever seen his toes underneath the tap shoes, but Al's a type who will buy anything. He would buy the Taj Mahal if the price was right. Al shopped the whole city of Bombay and finally selected a surgeon. His corn specialist was in white puttees, barefoot, sitting cross-legged on the sidewalk in front of the famous Gateway to India and opposite the Taj Mahal Hotel.

When the surgeon saw this live one approaching, he dragged out his saws, blades, rusty nails, and scalpels. He made Al very comfortable on the cobblestones, removed his shoes and socks and started the operation. He cut, trimmed, and pared. And when he was all through, Al went direct to the hospital.

A good, rousing infection had set in; and Al was under

treatment for quite a while. "I don't want to say I told you so," I said, telling him so, "but at least if you find the guy he'll give you your money back."

"What money back," Al said. "I want my toe back."

When I saw Al six months later in Las Vegas he was still limping. The four Step Brothers are the only quartet in show business with thirty-nine toes.

Beside the overflowing crowds, you have to share the streets with the cows. These are sacred animals and they get a lot better treatment than some of the people. You can't push them, nudge them, milk them, or eat them. They wander around aimlessly, queens of all they survey. Which brings up another roadside business. The people who sell the hay to the pious who want the honor of feeding these sacred animals.

A street in India is like an obstacle course. If you're not mowed down by the people, the cars, or the cows, you've got to smash head on into a bicycle. Although cycles are the main mode of transportation, they are considered the lowest form of vehicle status. The right of way goes to the cow, then the car; this is followed by the camel; and last, and definitely least, is the lowly bicycle. And those camels are lousy drivers. Pedaling behind them is murder. They just refuse to signal when they're going to make a left.

Part of the scenery are the fakirs. Wherever one thinks he can draw a crowd, he pulls up a few inches of sidewalk and sets the stage. His partners are a cobra and a mongoose. He tootles the flute while his two chums go into a tango to the death.

After you've been in India awhile you can tell what part of the country a woman's from by the way she wraps her sari. As we walked along the streets, we used to play this game. If a lady pulled her sari through her legs and it looked like harem pants, we knew she was from the state of Maharashtra whose principal city is Bombay.

If the sari was over her head like a shawl, we guessed she hailed from Rajputana. If the border, called the *pillav,* was thrown over her left shoulder, she could be from anyplace in India but Gujrat. The province of Gujrat is the only place in the whole country where the women toss their *pillav* over the right shoulder.

The sari hides a multitude of sins. Whether you're constructed like Sophie Tucker or stacked like Gina Whatsername makes no nevermind. All the females bobble along looking the same. And that's gorgeous.

All over Asia, wherever the heat is intense, ankle-length clothing is the national dress for women. In Afghanistan, where it's very hot in summer, it's the floor-length chadari. In Nepal it's the sari. In Cambodia and Laos, it's the ankle-length sanpat. In Thailand, the national dress is a long sarong called the *pa yoke*. In Indonesia, the batik is wrapped sarong-style down to the shoe-tops. Saigon wears the long pants and the tunic. It was explained to us that the theory is it's much cooler when you wear full-length clothing in the heat. There are no constricting undergarments because the clothing is long and loose, and the full coverage protects you from the rays of the sun. (I must mention this to those tubby broads who waddle down to the beach at Rockaway oozing out of their bikinis.)

Once we set off in the direction of the silver bazaar. We were looking for a St. Christopher medal for Pellay, our driver. Pellay was one hundred per cent Hindu but from the other Americans he'd chauffeured since going to work for USIS, he'd heard about St. Christopher being the patron saint of travelers. And Pellay was a fella who wanted to say his prayers across the board.

Happens the silver bazaar was shut, but a nearby bookstore was open. Also happens—lo and behold—that there in the window was a copy of the book I scratched out in 1957, *Cindy and I*. What a thrill this was. And it was sitting in the window right next to John F. Kennedy. Even in America I never got such a position. I was so excited I bought all the

Cindy and I books they had in the store—only it turned out that this was the only copy. I brought it back to Pellay; he was thrilled.

"If I read this book," he asked, "do I get my St. Christopher medal?"

As you walk along the streets of India, you are constantly reminded that you are in the land of the occult. Besides fakirs, hypnotists, magicians, and seers, Mother India also spawns fortune-tellers. And Uncle Joey attracts them. Like the wizard who nailed me on Murzban Road. Ever since I lumbered onto a scale and the card said I was five pounds overweight, I haven't believed in fortunes. And the only fortune my wife believes in is the one her mother tells her I've got.

But this fellow who shuffled over to me was a professional card-carrying fortune-teller. He was interested in my fortune, all right. But not in telling it. In taking it. He wore a turquoise-greenish-bluish jacket with a belt in the back that must have been rejected by the Salvation Army. He wore shoes with holes and no socks. And when he smiled he had a beautiful set of gums. He weighed one hundred pounds soaking wet.

"You listen to me," he wheedled, "and I'll make you rich." I liked the idea, but his outfit did make me lose a little confidence in his powers. He grabbed my attention when he outlined my character as brilliant, intelligent, courageous, and modest. He lost my attention when he added "and generous!"

"You stick with me," he said. "I can tell the future. If you stay with me six months, I'll make you a millionaire."

"Shall we move in with him or is he going to move in with us?" Cindy asked.

He was the cutest man. We were standing on the street corner with him for an hour haggling over my future.

"You listen to me," he said, "and you'll have more money than you can ever spend."

"Maybe he ought to do a little homework," Cindy mumbled.

One of the first steps toward enhancing my fortune was to

give me a tip on a horse that was running at the Bombay race track that day. And one of the first steps toward enhancing his fortune was to tell me to put a few rupees on it for him, too.

But the one thing of which you are most aware in India is the teeming mass of never-ending humanity. In this country, which is about a third the size of the United States, they have nearly three times as many people. Their five hundred million citizens increase at the rate of about ten million per year. This flow was not helped by the eight million refugees who poured in from Pakistan in 1948.

According to Lady Dhanvanthi Rama Rau, there are several reasons for the population explosion in India. Lady Rama Rau's husband was Ambassador to the United States and to Japan and he was head of the Reserve Bank of India. Her daughter is Mrs. Santha Rama Rau Bowers, the writer whose adaptation of E. M. Forster's *Passage to India* was a successful Broadway play.

At lunch with Cindy and me at the Ritz Hotel, this handsome woman explained, "Indians think of children as financial assets. If an expectant mother is also a working mother, her pregnancy entitles her to three months' vacation with full pay, plus maternity benefits. So, the argument is, 'If you want me to stop having children, then pay me. Why should I stop having children and lose money?'

"Also, they claim that they need one child to watch after their cattle, one child to look after the children, and another to cook the meal for the family and so on. They say, 'If you want us to stop having children, then who will do the chores for our family?'"

Under the leadership of the dynamic Lady Rama Rau, who works full time, Family Planning Association is forging ahead. They have an army of health visitors who canvass from house to house in areas where the people have never known a midwife let alone a doctor. The health visitors help families plan for the arrival of new babies, and teach them to limit the number of children. Of the one million women in Bombay alone, 10,000 are today using contraceptive appliances. This work was begun in 1951 with five clinics. Today there are sixty clinics.

"So you see," explained Lady Rama Rau, "our beloved India is making great strides in solving these problems."

We did see her point. But if we had not seen the teeming millions of Indians, the entire discussion would have been mere statistics instead of dramatic reality.

CHAPTER 21

The Taj and Other Marvels

Bombay is a handsome city. It's hustling and bustling and international as are most port cities. Driving along the water front, it looks like the Riviera. It has fine restaurants, good shops, and comfortable hotels. It also has beautiful sights like the Hanging Gardens which is a botanical garden on top of the city. Nearby are the Towers of Silence where the Parsees expose their dead to be picked to the bone by vultures. By day there's the beautiful beach front and by night there's the string of lights—called the Queen's Necklace—which encircles the bay.

En route from New York to Kabul three months earlier, we'd stayed overnight at the Taj Mahal Hotel which looks like an old Mogul Palace. It is one of the better hotels in Bombay. But when we came back here for our eight-day stand, there were no rooms for us. So, USIS was forced to parcel us all out into smaller but pleasant hotels. USIS not only had to see that *we* were reasonably satisfied, but, since they were going to remain there way after we pulled out, they had to make sure that the hotel keepers were going to be reasonably satisfied and would not bill USIS for bookings that had not been taken up.

And did our little troupe of guys and dolls ever have specifications and needs! Since all of us were paying for everything ourselves, each one made his own special demands. One was on a budget. To another, price was no object. One wanted a single room. Another wanted to double up. The boys in the band kept switching from singles to doubles to triples and back to singles again depending upon their friendships at the moment. By the time we hit Bombay, the boys in the band were back to singles again; Jed Horner couldn't find a *Y,* so he took the last remaining single room, leaving Jerry Bell homeless.

This problem came right back to me as did every other problem in the troupe. What to do with a slightly used, slightly graying, slightly furious stage manager. USIS looked every place for a room for Jerry. So did we. So did Jerry. Nothing was available. The nearest room was in Pakistan. And that was a long walk to the Bharatiya Vidya Bhavan Theatre every night.

"C'mon, move in with us," Cindy said to Jerry, who was sulking in the lobby.

Jerry was reluctant. "Oh, I couldn't," he said. "How would it look to move in with a husband and wife?"

"How would it look to who?" Cindy said. "We're not going to be photographed for *House Beautiful.*"

"Sure," I said, "we have a two-room suite. You can sleep in the living room. Cindy and I will sleep in the bedroom and we'll meet in the bathroom." It was either that or put his bedroll on the sidewalk, and since most of the better sidewalks were taken, we won Jerry as a permanent house guest.

Jerry strung a washline in the living room and that became his closet. His socks, shirts, and valises were thrown across the couch which became his chifforobe. The hotel sent up a cot and Jerry's boudoir became an alley. His room was the only entrance or exit to our apartment. He couldn't get to the bathroom without passing our room and we couldn't get out without passing his room. So if he wanted to sleep late and we wanted to get up early or if he wanted to go to sleep early and we wanted to stay out late—forget it!

Indians are much like our Americans. They're an aggressive, friendly, forward people. They all have a song they want published or a kid they want to put into show business or they want to meet some of the troupe or they want to invite you to their house for dinner. Cindy's articles were appearing in the *Bombay Free Press* and the *Ambala Punjabi Tribune,* so she had her followers who wanted to be interviewed.

And since the Indians' day starts at daybreak, so did Jerry's. They came calling at 6:00 A.M., and at 7:00 A.M., and some of the insomniacs even banged on our door at 3:00 A.M. Jerry became the only doorman-butler in captivity whose uniform was a pair of pajamas. After three days, our haggard tenant broke his lease. "I'm better off sleeping in the street," he said. "At least in the street nobody will wake me up, knocking on the door. And it might be good public relations between our countries."

It was Thanksgiving. You've heard of June in January? You've heard of April in Paris? Well, we celebrated Thanksgiving in Bombay. Our Consul General, Robert M. Carr, and Mrs. Carr invited us to have turkey dinner with them. So, Cindy and I and 496 other Americans gathered together on the lawn of the Consulate to give thanks for all our blessings. The Embassy had flown in the turkeys and the cranberry sauce from the USA, and the Indian chefs had whipped us up the sweet potato pudding and the stuffing and all the Yankee-style trimmings that go with it. As our American family sat down to dinner, the Consul General read a Thanksgiving Day proclamation from the President of the United States.

In the center of our little colony of expatriates was a flag which flew all the way from the U.S. to Bombay. Overhead were the same stars that were winking down on our loved ones so many miles away. It will be a long time before any of us ever forget that small family of Americans that said their prayers at a Thanksgiving Day dinner on a lawn in Bombay, India.

We have a friend in India. His name is Dr. Hamid Ali. He's an attorney. In June of '61 he had been in the States and had met Cindy's father in Boston. They became very friendly. Naturally, my father-in-law bragged about his kids.

"Joey and Cindy," he said, "will be in India later this year."

"Well," said Dr. Ali, "if they ever happen to be passing by Guindy Road in Adyar, Madras, tell them to drop in." Just so happens that five months later we happened to be passing by Guindy Road in Adyar, Madras. So we dropped in. Dr. Ali is a very kind, gracious man of the old school. When he issued this open invitation to Harry Heller, my father-in-law, I'm sure he meant it. But it still must have been quite a jolt when he answered the knock at his door and opened it to find two grinning Americans with the message, "Harry sent us." Let's face it, how often does someone from Fifth Avenue in New York just happen to be passing by Guindy Road in Adyar, Madras?

For the week we were in Madras, Dr. Ali and his family were our devoted chums. They threw a sit-down dinner in our honor and in India when you have a sit-down dinner, you really sit down—on the floor, that is. It was a beautifully set floor, with damask and china and flowers.

When Hamid told us he was inviting all his friends and relatives, Cindy wanted to do him proud. She dragged out her slinkiest sheath with the tightest girdle and the highest heels. When we saw the dining room it became pretty obvious that we'd have to haul the food up to her because under no circumstances could she get down to it in that outfit. She couldn't even pleat herself down in sections. The only way she could join us on the floor was to lie down flat. And that would take up too much room at the table.

To keep the spirit of the evening and to get her hands on some of the food, Cindy had to get undressed, and our hostess bandaged her in the most expensive sari she had—a wedding sari—worn for special occasions. It was red Benares silk, heavily embroidered with gold thread. Everybody enjoyed the fact that she'd put on a sari, and Cindy was having fun showing it off, too. The only thing she was concerned about was crouching on the floor in it. It was just too beautiful. But when everybody cranked themselves down cross-legged onto their pillows, so did we.

One of the old traditions that still clings to Mother India is eating with your right hand. Now I've heard of wrestling chicken with your fingers. I've even held lamb chops in my fists. But rice? I was petrified. I didn't know what to do. The best I could hope for was to look like a pig. And here if you ask for a knife and fork you're considered gauche. Your hands are your own, and no one else has ever eaten with them, but to use utensils that had been used before by someone else! An unspeakably dirty Western habit.

I clawed at a mittful of rice, but only a few grains got to my mouth. The rest plopped right down on my suit and Cindy's voluminous borrowed sari. If you think that's tough, try their delicacy, which is yogurt poured on top of rice. It's delicious, but it has the consistency of chicken soup. Try getting that up with your fingers. With a little bit of luck some of it will stick to your thumbs like paste and you can lick it off. My governess in the candy store in Brooklyn, where we dined as kids, used to smack my hands for a lot less.

My poor wife was panicky altogether. She had a frantic look in her eyes. She loves this kind of food and she just couldn't get at it. By now the sauce had coagulated, gluing her fingers together, and she was ladling it up like a shovel. Cindy's beautiful borrowed sari acted as a bib, a napkin, and a net. She had more food in her lap than in her stomach. At the end of the evening, she unwrapped this greasy red and gold tablecloth she was wearing and sheepishly returned it to her hostess. I don't know whether we cemented Indian-American friendship with this meal, but it's for sure we congealed it an awful lot.

All over India we were sponsored by the Indo-American Society which is nonpolitical, nonprofitmaking and nonsectarian. Its aim is to promote understanding between the people of India and the people of the United States and to introduce each to the ways of life, culture and language of the other. By means of exhibits, lectures, and entertainment, the Society works to advance friendship and cooperation in all spheres of activity between the two countries.

The only city where we were not under the wing of the Indo-American Society was New Delhi. Here we were imported expressly to headline the American Pavilion at the Indian Industries Fair from December 3rd through the 11th.

When we arrived at the New Delhi airport we met V. K. Krishna Menon, India's former Minister for Defense and Chairman of the Indian Delegation to the United Nations. He stopped minding his country's business long enough to pass the time of day with me at the newsstand. I nearly didn't recognize him altogether, because the last time I'd seen him in New York he was wearing a regular businessman's suit. Here he was in his native garb: long flowing gown, sandals and all.

The diplomatic heavyweight has staged some quickie bouts with American newsmen who "bully me," he complained to us at the airport. But he was remarkably patient with Cindy and me. And though we didn't know it at the time, we were to find out later what an enormous decision the then Minister for Defense must have been faced with at that time.

"It is not true that I dislike Americans nor do I deliberately show contempt for your country as has been said," His Excellency told me. "Some people try to make themselves disliked. Others work hard at making themselves liked. Both are very stupid. I really don't care what my critics say of me. Perhaps I feel this because I was not born to be a diplomat. I would have been a lawyer but I never worked hard enough. If I had applied myself to the studies I would now be in law instead of politics."

"Do you really like the USA?" Cindy asked.

"I like a good deal about the United States. I have more friends there than you have. But not amongst the top echelon. Possibly it's because some of them haven't tried to make friends with me. However, I am very friendly with shopkeepers, cab-drivers, people at the bus stop—Negro and white. These people speak to me on the street, ask me questions. From them I get a good cross section."

He was asked if riding with a verbose hackie could alter a preconceived notion he might have had, and therefore turn the tables of history.

"I do not enter into an argument with my mind completely made up in advance. That is stupid. Nor do I turn to God for an answer. Why should I pray? How will that help? I listen to all sides, including opinions from taxi-drivers, then I decide what's best. I find cab-drivers very intelligent, more so than some of your commentators."

Throughout the conversation nobody bothered us. There were no police, no security guards, no secretary. Hundreds of people were streaming into the airport and hundreds were streaming out, but nobody even came near us. It was as though this handsome six-footer with the gray hair was not Krishna Menon, the strong man of India, but just any one of its millions of citizens.

Cindy, who never relaxes when she spies a possible interview, asked, "What do you do to relax?"

"My relaxation is subjective. I don't have to do anything to get it. I don't go to parties or such things, so my relaxation is while I'm working. Especially when I am at the UN listening to speeches." He permitted himself a small joke. "The only reason I don't fall asleep on the floor of the UN is that one of your photographers would probably print a picture of me."

Mr. Krishna Menon is a confirmed bachelor, and Cindy asked him if a wife would not be an asset to him in the social part of this work.

"How would I know?" he smiled blandly. "Besides, I was not aware that one married merely to have someone to accompany him to cocktail parties."

The ex-Minister is a spare man. He is spare of frame, spare of words, and some of our newspaper reporters have him down for being spare of patience. As he brushed a weary hand over his eyes, I asked him if he enjoyed his work.

"I don't enjoy it. I don't 'disenjoy' it. I don't enjoy anything. I am up at six in the morning. I am home every evening, usually working far into the night. I read what I have to read. I do what I have to do. I don't enjoy anything."

At which point the one-time Minister of Defense of five hundred million people bowed us good-bye, bought himself a twenty-five cent paperback mystery book, and pattered off.

Overcrowded India was particularly overcrowded during the ten days we were jazzing up New Delhi. They had the World Council of Churches, which brought clergy from all over the world. Parliament was in session, which brought the leaders from all over the world and the Industrial Fair, which was in full swing, brought visitors from all over the world. Besides that, Goa was exploding, which brought an influx of newspapermen. And José Ferrer, Horst Buchholz, Robert Morley, and a whole movie company were cluttering up the town filming *Nine Hours to Rama,* the story behind the assassination of Gandhi. This meant that for the poor, scraggly Joey Adams Troupe the nearest available hotel room was in Cincinnati. So, until the very second we landed in Delhi, we didn't know where we were going to lay our weary bones.

The Ashoka Hotel—which is probably the plushest in India —had turned down our reservations four months before. We'd tried making the reservations personally when we'd enjoyed a wonderful night's lodging there while passing through from

Kabul to Katmandu, or from Katmandu to Bangkok, or from somewhere to someplace else. They told us then that they were booked up for the month of December one year in advance.

"I guess they don't know who we are," Cindy had said at the time. "Tell them who we are."

"Do you know who we are?" I asked of the elegant gentleman in the black beard and white turban who was behind the registration desk.

"Yes, indeed, sir, we do," he said, looking at my passport. "And it's a pleasure to serve you, Mr. Amonds."

"Tell him," Cindy muttered. "Tell the gentleman that we *must* have a room for December 3rd."

"We must have a room for December 3rd," I told him.

"We would certainly appreciate your patronage, Mr. Arons," he said, "but we're all filled up."

"Tell him you're President of AGVA," Cindy mumbled. "He probably doesn't know you're President of AGVA. So tell him you're President of AGVA."

"I'm President of AGVA," I said.

"Congratulations, Mr. Allen," he said.

"Tell him we know a lot of important, influential people," she said.

"Yeah. We know a lot of important influential people," I said. Then I turned to Cindy. "Who do we know?"

"I don't know. Mention anybody. Try Mayor Wagner, Senator Keating, Congressman Halpern, Ralph Schneider . . ."

"Who's Ralph Schneider?" I asked.

"He's head of the Diners' Club," Cindy whispered.

"Oh, yeah," I said and turned to my friend behind the desk. "I know Mayor Wagner, Senator Keating, Congressman Halpern and Ralph Schneider."

"Ah, Ralph Schneider of the Diners' Club? That's nice, Mr. Alden, but I'm terribly sorry we have no rooms in December."

"Are you going to take 'no' for an answer?" Cindy asked, as

I slunk away. "Where would Marconi be if he had taken 'no' for an answer? Or where would Edison be if he had taken 'no' for an answer? Or where would Alexander Graham Bell be if he had taken 'no' for an answer?"

"I don't know where they would be, but I do know where they ain't gonna be. They ain't gonna be at the Ashoka Hotel in New Delhi in December. They are all booked up, Mrs. Amonds," I said.

By the time we reached New Delhi that December there wasn't a hotel room available. We had to go back to our old vaudeville days of boardinghouses. Our troupe was split up and stayed with Indian and American families all over town. Cindy and I were parcelled out to the home of Robert and Anna Goodman. Bob Goodman was PAO—Public Affairs Officer—of USIS, and is now stationed in Berlin. When we moved into the spare room at 24 Friends Colony West, New Delhi, the Goodmans gave me a key and told us to play house just like it was our own home. We raided the icebox, used the phone, borrowed their car, and even brought our stray chums back to dinner. We treated it so much like our own home, we did everything but sell it.

Connaught Circle, which is the main drag of Delhi, was like Hollywood & Vine the ten days we were there. We kept bumping into familiar faces from home. One afternoon we slammed head on into Larry Adler, who was in town on a concert tour. Naturally, we dragged him home to dinner. Another early morning from out of a crowd of beards and turbans came a familiar resonant baritone hollering, "Hey, Joey!" The voice belonged to José Ferrer. Naturally we dragged him home to dinner. Larry and José became permanent fixtures around 24 Friends Colony West.

After a few nights the club got larger. Paul Grimes, the *New York Times* correspondent, joined the membership. Larry invited a couple of his acquaintances, including his landlord. José rounded up the cast of *Nine Hours to Rama*. I brought back some of the strays from our troupe. And now and then even the Goodmans had the nerve to invite some of their own cronies.

It's the way of the United States Information Service officers to make friends with the local people. Any time you came home you were always bound to find a maharaja or two lying around or a spare maharani or an Indian newspaperman or a couple of Indian neighbors. Between their invitation list and ours, Chez Goodman was like a league of nations.

Never in a million years would we have spread ourselves out this way had not the Goodmans insisted on it. It was love at first sight. Cindy and I and Anna and Bob fell in love with one another from the very first night they met us at the chilly airport in New Delhi. We've corresponded ever since. We saw them when they came to the States on their way to Berlin. Bob Goodman is a perfect Public Affairs Officer. He loves people. Particularly show people. The one or two nights we didn't bring anyone home for dinner, he and Anna went out looking for last-minute replacements.

We not only had the run of the house, we had the run of the servants. In India everybody has a household staff. Even the unemployed have four in help. Wage standards are very low. The going rate is about $5 per week. And they and their families bunk in lean-tos in the back of the house. And what it takes one part-time girl to do here in the States, it takes four full-time sleep-in servants to do in India. This is not because one is incapable of doing all the work. Rather, it's because this makes for more employment in an overpopulated country.

So we had four servants which is three and a half more than we have at home. There was the dhobi; he comes bi-weekly to wash and iron. There was the bearer; he's the uniformed butler who serves the food, answers the phone, acts as major domo and looks down on the dhobi. Then there's the mali; he's the outside man; he takes care of the garden and occasionally doubles as sweeper. And there's the cook.

As Anna explained it to us, it doesn't work the way it does in the States. There the cook doesn't quit if the master of the house brings his boss home one dinnertime on short notice. In India the servants welcome extra work because they know that the more the guests the bigger the baksheesh (tips).

As my prophetic wife had been warning me for the past sixteen weeks, it was cold in Delhi. In fact, it was bloody cold. In fact, them as had it were wearing full-length fur coats. In our house, with the gas heaters and the fire going full blast, there was still a distinct chill. Cindy's disposition was sub-zero. It was freezing. She was ice cold. And I was the villain. After fourteen weeks of traveling in equatorial temperatures and dragging along the Persian lamb jacket, the red rabbit stole and that hot, heavy, woolly, warm, itchy, wintry, black-and-white checked coat, I had shipped the stuff home.

"But," I explained to Cindy, who wasn't talking to me at all, "we were overweight. We had to send something back."

"Yeah? Well, I know how we could have gotten rid of 170 pounds at one swell foop," shivered Cindy. "We could have shipped *you* home."

Bob offered Cindy a pullover sweater. Anna dug out an extra heavy coat. I even gave her my cashmere sport jacket with the white pearl buttons. She wrapped herself in all these secondhand clothes one night, but after a fast look in the mirror she complained, "I look like an ad that says, 'Send this child to camp.' "

"But," I said worried, "honey, you just can't go out in your little summer batiks. You'll freeze to death."

"Well, if I'm going to freeze to death anyway, I might as well freeze to death chic," she snapped and discarded the hand-me-downs.

And so she went to the theater in her stunning red batik and her lovely blue skin. Our theater was a fast slapped-together job, constructed only for the short duration of the fair. There was no heat backstage. The floor of the dressing room was the ground, and the door leading to the outside was makeshift, and the wind was coming in from all sides. After the opening, when my wife turned from blue to purple, she decided she'd had it—and me—and couldn't stand another minute of either.

I really felt horrible. I couldn't blame my little doll. The buck and a quarter I probably saved in overweight by shipping home her Persian lamb jacket, the red rabbit stole and that hot, heavy, woolly, warm, itchy, wintry, black-and-white checked coat wound up costing me over $200 and almost costing me my marriage. I was only able to save the marriage after I bought Cindy a whole load of woolen outfits.

It took Cindy three days to come out of the freezer. She finally thawed out when I promised to take her to see the Taj Mahal. Agra, the home of the Taj, is four hours by car from Delhi. The only way we could do it was to leave one night after the show, drive four hours through the night, go to sleep in a hotel in Agra, get up the next morning, feast our eyes, and drive back. Me, I was happy with the picture post cards I've seen of it, but my wife figured it was worth going without sleep one night to see it in person.

At this point, if Cindy wanted to roller skate to Poughkeepsie and back overnight, I'd have gone along. Early in the morning, we had a fast breakfast at the Imperial Hotel in Agra and aimed for the Taj Mahal. We went up one street, down another, past the antique shops and the venders, and then we executed a sudden left turn—and there it was. The blinding façade of beauty electrified us. It was as if a thousand violins were playing a symphony crying out for all the lovers of the world to rejoice.

We stood there breathlessly. Holding hands. After we had wandered past the fountains and the gardens, and had removed our shoes (as is the custom), to wander in stocking feet over the marble, and had gone downstairs to inspect the crypt and walked all around examining the precious stones inlaid on the walls, and it was time for us to go, Cindy said,

"Now there was a man with class. What he did for Mrs.

Mahal makes that creepy chinchilla you threw me last Christmas look pretty chintzy."

"So what," I said self-consciously. "So he built her a house. But he didn't build it for her till after she was dead. So? Didn't I offer to put you up a bungalow in Atlantic Beach last summer? A bungalow that you could enjoy while you were still alive?"

"Bungalow! You peasant! Bungalow! This little shack he nailed together happened to have set him back some twelve million clams in those days. Now that's what I call a husband!"

"Yeah, but she mothered thirteen children. Now that's what I call a wife!"

"Yeah, but he fathered thirteen children. Now that's what I call a man."

There was no doubt that this monument to love made me feel like a cheapskate. Obviously, however, I was not the only poor married bum who felt that way. I had plenty of company. That's why, I thought, it was more than mere coincidence that the road leading from the Taj was lined with dozens of jewelry shops. I'm no different from any other husband. I followed my wife into one of them. I figured if Mr. Mahal could buy his missus such a beautiful twelve-million-dollar keepsake, the least I could do was to fork up for a trinket or two.

So Mr. Singh of the Jewel House at Partap Pura, Agra and I made a trade. I handed him a half-inch of fifties and he handed me one genuine antique necklace set with pearls, diamonds, rubies, sapphires, and emeralds. For a few dollars extra he gave me a certificate which guaranteed that this genuine antique necklace set with pearls, diamonds, rubies, sapphires, and emeralds originally lay on the neck of a genuine antique maharani.

We almost missed the show that night, because the trip back from Agra to Delhi took twice as long as we expected. We were sharing the one-lane road with a caravan of Indian troops. The trucks and transports stretched for miles. Hour by hour we were chewing the dust ground up by the army trucks. Fortunately, we were armed with a jug of boiled water because the roads weren't exactly dotted with Howard Johnson watering holes.

Oh, we could pass a car or two. We could jump four or five bicycles at a clip. We could even cut off a camel, but go fool around with a couple of miles worth of Indian Army trucks.

As every headline in every newspaper all over the world proclaimed a few days later, these trucks were headed for Goa —the handiwork of my old airport chum, V. K. Krishna Menon.

With Red China nibbling away at India's border, Operation Goa, and Indian troops being killed in the Congo, India's Prime Minister Nehru stopped prime ministering long enough to receive two visiting Americans.

Dressed in contrast to Jawaharlal Nehru's private secretary, who wore a pullover sweater, guardsmen in turbans and yellow and red silk breeches ushered us into the Prime Minister's neat office in Parliament House.

"Please excuse me for being fifteen minutes late," apologized India's leader, "but I just finished speaking at the Asian History Congress; I'm addressing the Lok Sabha, our parliament, in a moment and since I've only just returned from America and leave tomorrow for the Taj Mahal with the King and Queen of Malaya, I've appointments every half hour through the evening."

The gracious statesman, who at that time was seventy-two years old, puffed a cigarette in a silver holder. "I'm kept going all day long. I'm up by seven every morning. I go to sleep around one. Occasionally I take a nap in the afternoon. Insomnia? Me? Never! No matter what the problems of state, I fall asleep immediately. I'm too tired at the finish of a day to have insomnia."

This was 5:30 P.M., the end of an exhausting afternoon. Wearily, he rubbed his eyes. "I usually try to take a nap during the day, but I think," said Mr. Nehru slowly, in a muted voice, "about my only relaxation nowadays is a long plane trip."

Cindy asked him what it was that maintained him during his darkest hours and whether he relied on faith.

"Panditji," India's pet name for him—*Pandit* meaning leader; *Ji,* denoting affection—retorted quickly, "I am not religious. That term is never applied to me. In fact, I am called irreligious. I don't believe in the dogma, creeds, and ritualism of religions. About looking to a Supreme Power to help relieve the load of personal responsibility, that is another matter altogether. But as for religion itself, I don't believe in it."

Sitting in front of a wall map of his country, facing a desk photograph and statue of Gandhi, he referred to the finale of our show, and his kindly face lit up. "My grandchildren adored the show, but somebody stole their balloons before they left."

I promised the Prime Minister that one hundred new balloons would be delivered to his Residence the next day. And they were. And when we arrived home there was a thank you note from him awaiting us.

We praised his capacity for enjoyment and the fact that all our newspapers had writen glowingly about his visit to Disneyland. Said "Panditji," his eyes twinkling merrily, "Your Ambassador Galbraith and the big guns in Washington did not approve of my enjoying myself like that. They thought it wasn't dignified."

"Maybe the big guns didn't appreciate your doing it, but the little guns in our country certainly did," I said.

"Did you have any inkling in your youth that some day you would be destined for greatness?" Cindy asked.

Mr. Nehru balked modestly at the word "greatness."

"I grew up in a political background. My father, whose original interest was law; my mother, two brothers, sister, wife and daughter were all imprisoned for their beliefs." He pulled on his lip thoughtfully. "As a youth, as a very young boy, I knew only that I must devote myself to freeing India."

A once-magnificent red rose drooped wearily out of his buttonhole.

"From a lady?" I asked.

"No," he sighed sadly, "from my gardener."

With that, one of the world's greatest diplomats put on his famous hat. It was a diplomatic way of cueing his guests that it was time to grab theirs.

When we met our brilliant Ambassador Kenneth Galbraith, who is a once-upon-a-time economics professor, a once-upon-a-time world-renowned economist and author and is, today, United States Ambassador to India, we related what Nehru had told us about him.

"The Prime Minister told us, Mr. Ambassador," I said, "that when he returned from America he regaled you with tales of the many joyful hours he spent at Disneyland, but he seems to be of the opinion that you clearly do not consider Disneyland among the seven wonders of the modern world."

"Why?" chuckled Ambassador Galbraith, "what did he say?"

"He said," I recounted, "that he told you that the trouble with you is you're too highbrow."

"Maybe I am," our Ambassador agreed. "I guess in my heart I'm still an old college professor who doesn't particularly like music or entertainment."

"In other words," I said, "sir, you are politely telling me I am a lowbrow."

With a twinkle in his eye, Galbraith said, "I guess I'm just a stuffy old economist at heart. Maybe they shouldn't make ambassadors out of college professors."

"Is that why you didn't come nor invite Prime Minister Nehru and all the other high Indian brass to our opening night?" I asked.

"Yes," he smiled as we lunched at the Residence one sunny day, "maybe Nehru is right. I guess I am a little too highbrow."

We found Kenneth Galbraith to be charming and delightful, with a wonderful sense of humor. But I must agree with Mr. Nehru and Mr. Galbraith that our Ambassador is a highbrow. In fact, he's the highest brow I ever met. He's 6 foot 8 inches tall.

After my six weeks in India—playing Bangalore, Madras, Bombay, New Delhi; visiting Calcutta, Agra and points East; seeing ruins of Mahabalipuram; and watching the dances of Bharatinatyam—I can truthfully say that I've faced more Indians than Custer. Fortunately, of course, these were the friendly kind. That is, most of them. There was, of course, that one night in New Delhi when I was making my big, patriotic, passionate end-of-the-show speech.

This was the commercial, this was the sponsor's voice coming in at the end of the program; this was where all the entertainers grouped themselves on stage behind me. I removed my straw hat and placed it over my chest. The music played softly behind me. The lights came up full. And this was where I made my usual pitch for everlasting brotherhood between our nations. It came right on the heels of our shooting the four hundred red, white and blue balloons into the audience for our finale. After the balloons settled, an expectant hush fell over the audience.

"I hope," I said, and I couldn't have been more sincere, "that the same friendship and love that is in this theater tonight will always be there between all of India and all of America."

Just as I finished this line, an Indian in the third row center pulled back and punched an American right smack in the mouth. "You stole my balloon," he yelled.

They dragged the exponents of "brotherhood between our nations" backstage to patch them up. And so, in the tiny, curtained dressing room, I finished my stirring speech of love and friendship to my busted-up, banged-up, bruised and bleeding audience of two.

CHAPTER 22

Making Iran
the Hard Way

W<small>E</small> ARRIVED in Teheran almost four and a half months after we started our tour. And after thousands and thousands of air miles we were right back where we started. We could practically yoo-hoo over to Afghanistan. Ask any travel agent and he'll tell you that the route we took must have been laid out by Wrong Way Corrigan. In our case the shortest distance between two points was a circle.

Even to somebody like me who gets lost in a walk-in closet, it would have sounded merely logical to go from Afghanistan to its next-door neighbor, Iran, or to its other near neighbor, India. And it would have seemed only slightly less than intelligent to have made the whole French Indochina route in one straight swing. We could really have done the Thailand-Laos-Cambodia-Vietnam circle all together. But the State Department was not running a Cook's Tour. They had reasons.

For instance, we had to be in Afghanistan the week of the Jeshyn Fair; that was August 23rd. We had to be in New

Delhi the week of the Industrial Fair; that was December 3rd. We had to be in Djakarta before the middle of October, because President Sukarno was scheduled to leave for Vienna for his kidney operation. And we couldn't be in Laos until the first of October, because that was when rainy season ended. So, here we were, sixteen weeks later, a hop, skip and a camel ride from Afghanistan, where it all began.

Now that we were in the home stretch, on our last week, some of the kids were beginning to fall apart. It was like we were wound up with just enough juice in us to last eighteen weeks. Two of the boys in the band, our pianist, Johnny Morris, and the vibraphone player, Mike Manieri, crawled right from the plane to their beds. Diagnosis: dysentery. Prince Spencer managed to inherit some kind of special ailment that was exclusive to him. Flash McDonald developed a galloping case of nerves and lonesomeness and we were beginning to lose him. And even our Iron Man, John Shirley, was starting to rust.

One of Celeste Evans' doves had the vapors. He'd lost weight, his feathers were all ruffled and the vet who checked him in Teheran told her the dove had better quit show business for a while. One of the twins—it was either Deanna or Deanda, I still don't know—ran a fever. We were like an eight-day clock on its eighth day. Everybody was slowly running down.

In this manner we limped into Teheran in the wee hours, after a night flight from Delhi. It was freezing cold. We got to our hotels, unpacked, undressed and fell into bed like a bunch of stretcher cases. We knew we couldn't even sleep late because we were scheduled for an early lunch date and briefing at the Iran-American Society.

About the last thing we needed or wanted in this world was to get another briefing or lunching. What we really needed and wanted was a little sleeping. Well, what the hell, it wasn't their fault. They couldn't be blamed because they happened to catch us on the tail end of a long, hard trek. To them it was all brand new.

After all, they figured, why should we be tired—we just got to Teheran! To them it was a whole new exciting round of luncheons, briefings, hand-shakings, picture takings, receptions, appearances, and benefits. But our consolation was that at least we didn't have any more traveling to do. We knew that now we were dug in for ten days in a big city like Teheran and that the next time we hoisted ourselves it would be to take the big bird to go home.

The Iran-American Society had planned a special smashing luncheon in our honor. This wasn't to be any ordinary sloughed-off, thrown-together ham-on-rye job. They were preparing a special treat. They'd planned this for weeks. They promised us we were going to have a taste sensation that we'd never had before. They told us they were serving a dish indigenous to their country and one for which Iranians are known the world over.

We sat down. And there it was. A big, steaming pot of the fluffiest, the whitest and the boiledest rice you ever saw. They were right. We hadn't had this kind of dish before. At least not that day. We hadn't had such a dish since two meals ago. Of course this rice was far different than anything we'd ever eaten. Over the Iranian rice you bust a raw egg. Naturally, this is far different from the Afghanistan rice which is eaten with pilau or the Laotian rice which is glutinous or the Indian rice which is drowned in curry or the rice in Chinese restaurants which is cold.

The only one who would have been happy had she been there was my whacked-up wife. She's just nuts about rice. In any form. I didn't know where she was. Something must have detained her. She told me to go ahead and that she'd meet me at the luncheon since I had to get there a little earlier. But it was getting pretty late and I didn't know where she was. Maybe she stopped off to get a bowl of rice.

We all admitted that the damn rice was delicious with the

raw egg in it. The only trouble was that at that moment I could not look another single solitary ri in the face.

Chaz Chase spoke for all of us when he said, "I have a wonderful daughter. She lives in California. She is the mother of my grandchildren. And my wife's favorite child. Of which we only have one. Whenever I visit her after a long trip, she eagerly cooks me all my favorite foods. She always tops off one of these meals with my favorite dish, which is rice pudding. Now, when I get home and I sit down to dinner and my dear, adorable, wonderful daughter who lives in California and is the mother of my grandchildren and my wife's favorite child of which we only have one and whom I love very dearly serves me rice pudding, I will dump it right on her head."

At this point the door burst open and in dashed my wife. She took one look at what was being served and said happily, "Ooooohh, wonderful. Rice!" It was too bad she wasn't getting married because we were all ready to throw it at her.

"What delayed you?" I said.

"I got lost!"

"How could you get lost?"

"What do you mean, how could I get lost? I wasn't exactly brought up here, y'know. I don't even spend my summers here. This will come as a shock to you, but I've never been here before. The only thing I know about Persia is they got wonderful melons. And I buy mine at the A & P. What do you mean, how could I get lost?"

"All you had to do was tell the taxi driver to take you to the Iran-American Society. Now that isn't too difficult, is it?"

"For me, no. For the driver, yes." Cindy's voice was reaching a crescendo.

"I asked him, 'Do you speak English?' He said, 'Yes.' So I said, 'Can you take me to the Iran-American Society? So he said, 'Yes.' And he drove me straight to the American Embassy. How was I to know that he has a short vocabulary and that the only English word he knows is 'yes'? I've been driving around like this for an hour."

"I don't know. I had no trouble. I got here okay."

"Who took you?"

"The head of the Iran-American Society."

As was my custom, I thanked our hosts publicly on behalf of all of us for their hospitality.

"Tired though we are, we're looking forward to our stay here," I said. "It will be a fine treat for all of us to be able to be in your beautiful city for ten whole days." As I sat down, Herbert Linneman, the USIS chief, stood up.

"Well," he said pleasantly, "we'd certainly love to have you here for ten whole days but you have to be on a plane in three hours for Abadan."

"Aba what?" somebody said.

"Get on a plane in three hours for where?" somebody else said. Even Cindy looked up from her rice. "We're leaving when for what?"

"You are leaving on a plane in three hours for Abadan, Iran, where you will be appearing for two nights at the Taj Theatre," said Linneman. "Abadan is a small town, but it is of big importance for us. It's the largest oil-refining plant in this part of the world and the second largest oil-refining plant in the whole world. Oil is the lifeblood of this country. It's very important to keep these people happy. When your show was announced," he said, "the tickets were all sold out in an hour."

There was no point in telling him that we'd been planning on spending ten days here as per the schedule. And since things were already "laid on," there was no point in telling him that half our cast was down sick. I also didn't know how we could ever make a plane in less than three hours since it was a half hour back to our hotels, and an hour's ride to the airport and we were all thoroughly unpacked and thoroughly unprepared.

When we'd checked in late the night before all of us had unpacked completely because we thought this was the last stop in our trip and because when you go back to the United States you have to pack differently. The laundry and junk is on the bottom, the gifts and customs declarations on the top.

Another thing. Teheran was freezing. Abadan, we were told, was hot. So now we had an additional problem. All of us had our wools front and center. Most of us had either shipped our cottons stateside or had them packed away for the trip home. Now we had to dig out the cottons and stash the woolens and repack.

Which presented another problem. We were returning here in four days but nobody wanted to pay two rents. On the other hand, we were going on such a small inter-country plane that there wasn't room enough for all the luggage. So in the hour allotted to us to get ourselves together, we had to pack twice. Once for the trip to Abadan and once for the storage room in Teheran.

I read somewhere that the show must go on. I'd like to meet the gent what coined this statement and ask him, "How?" I'm sure he must be out of the business by now. At any rate, we doctored each other up, threw ourselves together, paid our bills, arranged for our storage rooms, bundled ourselves into the cars and buses and zoomed to the airport just in time to be told that the plane for Abadan would be three hours late taking off.

I will not lie to you. There were a few minutes there when I entertained the thought of killing myself. And I would've, but I just didn't have the strength. And, anyway, who would introduce the acts in Abadan?

When we finally trudged into Abadan it was pretty late at night and we only had one aim in life. That was to lie down. But there was just one problem. The rooms. They had us set up at the Oil Club. Since they'd been reading all our ads, brochures, reviews, and advance publicity, they had the idea that we were just one great, big, happy, bear-hug of an American family. So they set us all up in a dormitory. Men, women, and doves—all together Army style.

I explained to the officials from the oil company who were our hosts. I told them that men, women, and doves just cannot get undressed in one room. Not even if they're show people. And one john between a couple of dozen people cannot under any circumstances be construed as House Beautiful. Not even by show people.

It worked out to our advantage. These gracious people moved us all to the Abadan Hotel, a brand new hostelry which is one of the most beautiful in that part of the world. Well, I always say it's worth it to sacrifice a little camaraderie and togetherness for a helluva lot of comfort and luxury.

Here we had a lovely room with adjoining caviar. The Iranian caviar is the greatest on this planet. I had it three times a day. Each cav was the size of an immy marble. I ate caviar and farina for breakfast, caviar and meat balls for lunch, caviar and rice for dinner, and my midnight snack was caviar and caviar. Even the bulletin that caviar has the same caloric value as cod-liver oil didn't deter me. I just couldn't help it. I was hooked. I had a sturgeon on my back. I soon found I couldn't even get out of bed in the morning without a quick belt of caviar.

Caviar is a big business in Iran. It's not just a cockomamie corner delicatessen item. In Iran it's an industry second only to the oil business. It's government-controlled and price-regulated. In fact the day we arrived in Iran there was a story on the front pages of the newspapers about how undercover agents had smashed a blackmarket caviar ring which included top government officials.

I found out that even the best "Russian" caviar comes from Iran but has a Russian label slapped on it. After ten days in Persia I can truthfully say I singlehandedly swelled the economy of the country and the blubber around my waistline.

Seen from your hotel window, Abadan looks like any Texas oil town, only the faces are different. It's flat desert land dominated by an enormous oil company within a town. There are one-room general stores which sell anything from radios to pajamas. These emporia are usually owned by the company. And there are company doctors and company dentists who serve the employees. The whole town is built around oil and the whole country is built around the town. This oil-refining plant is second only in size and output to the one at Baton Rouge, Louisiana, the largest in the world.

Like any Texas oil town it also has a multimillion-dollar, modern, expensive hotel hacked right out of the desert, complete with swimming pool, night club and all. On the other end of town it has the million-dollar, modern, smashing Taj Theater which is comparable to anything I've ever played. In between it's Galveston, Tyler or Amarillo.

Eighteen weeks and eleven countries after we left New York, we took our last bows in Teheran. We bowed the lowest to her Imperial Majesty, Farah Diba, the Empress of Iran. Opening night in the Mohammad Reza Shah Pahlavi gymnasium was for her favorite charity, the Iranian National Committee for the Protection of Children. When I brought my personal queen, Cindy, back to meet the Empress and Her Royal Highness, Princess Ashraf Pahlavi, the Shah's sister, Her Majesty and Her Royal Highness were most impressed with the fact that we threw around some instant Persian. What they didn't know was that we had learned it four and a half months ago in Afghanistan: Parsi is the language of both countries. Our USIS guys were amazed that Cindy spoke the language so well, especially since they hadn't arranged for an interpreter.

"Well," Cindy said with a straight face, "Joey and I always speak Parsi at home. I mean, doesn't everybody?"

Before the show, the Chief of Protocol made it a point to give me my royal *DO*'s and *DON'T*s. "The most important thing," he said, "is to address yourself only to Her Imperial Majesty and no one else. Under no circumstances are you to include the audience or the Ambassadors or anybody else in the greeting. There is to be no mention of the words 'Ladies and Gentlemen.'"

I explained respectfully to the Minister of Protocol that I

would be most pleased to greet Her Imperial Majesty in whatever manner protocol dictated. However, he would have to understand that this was a program sponsored by the American Government and that I could not, in all conscience, refuse to acknowledge the presence of our American Ambassador, Julius C. Holmes, who was sitting in the royal box with Her Majesty. I also explained that it's the American way to play to the entire audience and that as a professional performer I simply could not be made to ignore the thousands of people who were sitting out front and I had to include them in my greetings.

I still don't think the protocol man understands to this day, but came show time I trotted out onto the freezing cold stage of the unheated gymnasium, bowed low to the royal box which was heated with braziers, addressed the Queen in my broken Parsi, addressed the Ambassador in my broken English, and welcomed the ladies and gentlemen of Teheran. Then I braced myself a moment to see if anybody was going to handcuff me or pull me off the stage, but nothing happened. The show proceeded without any trouble. Nobody shot me. Nobody pulled the Persian rug out from under me. They didn't even punch a hole in my caviar ration-card.

Obviously Her Gorgeous Majesty wasn't the slightest whit perturbed that I'd included our Ambassador and her countrymen in my introduction. When we all came back single file after the show she couldn't have been more gracious.

The huge, barnlike, freezing-cold gymnasium was just the same as the one in which you and I used to take Physical Education, when we couldn't duck it in high school. Only this one had a slight difference. On one side of one wall, where the basketball backboard would ordinarily be, there was an overhanging shelf. This was the royal box. It seated about ten people comfortably, but it jammed about one hundred. Between her party, the guards, the police, the photographers, the interpreters, the USIS and Embassy personnel and our troupe it looked like a royal free-for-all.

Besides her grace and poise and fine command of the Queen's English, what surprises you most about Farah Diba is her extreme beauty. She wore a full-length blue tapestry-embroidered evening coat lined in honey-beige mink. She didn't remove it all evening. I cannot tell a lie. If I had a full-length blue tapestry-embroidered evening coat lined in honey-beige mink I probably wouldn't have removed it all evening either. On the top of her upsweep she'd perched a tiny blue hat about the size of a crown, which came complete with nose veil. Her flawless complexion, free of make-up, was as smooth as that of a Persian peach.

When I introduced her to my cast, she stood up, shook hands, and had a personal little compliment to make to each one of them. Cindy reminded her of her graciousness when they met again four months later at the Waldorf Astoria in New York City, when the Shah and his Empress were in the United States on their State visit.

My wife has really missed her calling. What she really should have been was a District Attorney. With a press card she now can ask any questions she likes and it comes under the heading of being a legitimate newspaper reporter. When she asked the same questions before, it came under the heading of being a busybody. They're exactly the same questions, only now she gets paid for it. What all the gossips in our troupe desperately wanted to know was what was Farah Diba's most difficult adjustment when she was transformed overnight from a commoner to the Empress of Iran. Cindy asked the Empress just this question.

"The most difficult adjustment I had to make was getting used to answering so many questions," smiled the twenty-three-year-old Queen of Iran. "Changing into a queen is not difficult. The proper way of walking, talking, and folding your legs when you sit, I learned as a child. Good manners aren't just for queens. Also, I am not artificial. I do not smile when I do not feel like smiling. My job is nothing compared to my husband's. I don't have to work every day. And official duties like visiting orphanages I find interesting."

"And did you feel kismet was at work in your youth and that someday this would happen to you?" Cindy asked.

"That is something very amusing," said the Empress who, at 10:30 A.M. when my wife came calling, sported an emerald and diamond pin the size of a license-plate, her early morning jewels. "I was the only Iranian girl in the School of Architecture in Paris. My friends always joked with me, saying, 'Some day the King of Iran will see you and he must marry you.' They said, 'You write the Shah a letter so he will know about you.' I answered, 'Okay. I do it.' But it was only a joke. I never thought it would happen."

Seated in the royal apartment flanked by two live statues— one man and one woman—Her Majesty announced that occasionally these old friends of hers still get invited over when she has a free afternoon.

When my wife mentioned that hers didn't exactly seem the kind of house where chums can just drop in for a cup of caviar, she answered:

"Yes, but if anyone with whom I had camaraderie is in Teheran, I see them. We are just like always. Only now, of course, they have to curtsy. They must first do the reverence. It is the protocol."

Brown-eyed Farah's lids were pencilled heavily into the Cleopatra look. Magnificently poised, her hands, tipped with silver nail polish, remained clasped throughout their conversation. Her dark curls were piled into an upsweep. ("I do it myself at home, but when we are on a State visit I must take a hairdresser because of our heavy program.") She keeps her beautiful figure by "doing a lot of sports." As usual the Empress was wearing the low heels which she orders from Paris to keep her the regulation inch shorter than His Majesty.

"Yes, before I give orders to the dressmaker I ask my husband, the Shah, for his opinion," she answered one question. "No, before I became Empress I did not wear Paris originals.

Of course not," she answered another. "I shopped in little stores, but now I must go to the *maisons*—the great fashion houses—in Paris. Iran has no ready-made clothiers. Nor designers. Just dressmakers who copy from magazines. No, they do not charge me more because I am an Empress. Yes, I wear the same clothes very often; I have to or I wouldn't have enough clothes. One of my favorite outfits is a two-year-old Dior suit. To be a slave to fashion you would have to buy new every six months. I couldn't afford it."

Cindy swears she wasn't sure, but she thinks at that point one of the statues—the male one—twitched an eyelid. Noticing that she and the Queen were both the same size, Cindy asked what does she do with her old, secondhand, used, beat-up two-and-a-half-year-old Diors.

"I give them to my maids," replied the Queen casually. And with that the male statue whispered a subtle hint in my wife's ear that Her Majesty was way behind schedule. By the time the interview came to a close Cindy was ready to swap her job as a reporter with one of Farah Diba's size-8 maids.

CHAPTER 23

Finale

in Teheran

For us, Teheran was the perfect jumping-off place between Asia and the United States. When we hit Teheran it was like being in the decompression chamber. It was cold, so you began to get the feeling of New York in January. Although the population is 98 per cent Moslem, Kris Kringle was showing up all over town in windows, stores, and bazaars. The same kind of nice, little Santa Claus that we have on any Main Street, USA, was decorating Takhte Jamshid Avenue, Abbas Abad Road, Shahpoor Alireza and the other main drags.

In Teheran, the water system is purified, so we were able to guzzle right out of the tap—which was a good rehearsal, because you'd feel kind of silly trundling into New York's classy Four Seasons restaurant and asking for a glass of ice cold boiled water.

Although there are still some women who wear chadari, the all-enveloping veil which was supposed to have been done away with in 1930, the average Teheranian female is very chic —but very. At every party, their basic black, pearls and furs could stamp them as being from New York, London, or Paris.

Cats, lambs, melons and rugs are not the only things Persia is known for. It is also known for the highest prices in Asia. New York and Paris are cut-rate compared to Teheran. That's due to the fact that they export oil, rugs and caviar, but they import almost everything else because—let's face it—how much oil, rugs and caviar can you use? About the only thing seventy-five rials (which is a hot buck) will entitle you to in this country is a sneer from the store clerk.

Almost all Western-type foodstuffs can be purchased with ease at the Iran Supermarket on Tahkte Jamshid Avenue, which is just a green stamp away from the American Embassy. The only problem is that with the high tariff on imports, the prices at the supermarket are a fortune.

The Teheran Galleries and adjacent shops on Nadiri are places to hit if you're itching to get rid of some hard-earned rials. Here one barters all one likes. It's expected. However, don't—and this we learned the hard way—don't allow your prowess to go to your head. No matter how fine a bargain you think you negotiated, the price you pay will not be a farthing less than that which the amiable merchant had in his mind all along.

Persia is the land of the magic carpet. After spending ten days there I now know why they invented the magic carpet. It's for sure you can't get around in a car. In Teheran there is no such animal as the right-of-way. They use the come-as-you-are method in driving. And not even Lloyds will write a policy on a pedestrian. Chiang Kai-Shek would be safer in Shanghai than a hiker in Teheran. The law says honking is disallowed, but it don't say nothing about hitting.

Teheran can satisfy almost everybody. If you go in for collecting brass, silverware, copper, turquoise or rugs, you'll find a great abundance here. If you like to browse through palaces, bazaars, archaeological museums and mosques—in which, in-

cidentally, you can't photograph—this is your town. If you're
strictly a gourmet or saloon man, you'll find restaurants and
clubs that will go later than you can. The Sho-Cuteh-Now runs
a four-hour show, the Miami has American talent. La Residence will cost you a Shah's ransom but the food is delicious.
The Coq d'Or has excellent French cuisine and excellent
Iranian prices. Teheran has food and entertainment for everyone. They even have a Hot Shoppe which is a strictly Yankee-
style Howard Johnson operation.

Me, I'm not the type who goes in for archaeology. Maybe
it's because I'm a little sensitive on account of my wife says
that when it comes to old ruins—I'm the biggest. And when
it comes to night clubs, I'm the president of all those we have
at home so I don't have to go find any more. Silver and turquoise altogether don't thrill me because my Cindy's favorite
hymn is "Diamonds Are a Girl's Best Friend" and when it
comes to mosques, I'm not exactly ready because I haven't even
been to a synagogue since two Jewish holidays ago. But I did
bring home some souvenirs from Teheran after all.

It happens that my favorite hobby is collecting jokes, some
of them so hoary that they could qualify for archaeological
items. And it so happens I discovered that the great-great-
great-great-great-grandfather of Joe Miller is a gent called
Mullah Nasir-ud-Din who lived in this neighborhood. He is
supposed to have roamed the earth some seven hundred years
ago, but his old jokes have withstood the years almost as well
as mine.

This Moslem Joe Miller had a sort of shaggy-camel-type
story. There are those who claim Mullah Nasir-ud-Din is a
legendary comic character. Others swear his rustic simplicity
and logic were for real. In any case, every Persian child is
familiar with his simple wit and the adults with the shrewd-
ness of his wisdom. In Islamic countries "Mullah" is a title. It
means "teacher" or "interpreter of the law of Islam." Mullah
Nasir-ud-Din was sort of a cross between a teacher, a priest,

and a judge. He had the wisdom of Solomon and the enchant-
ment of Omar Khayyám.

For instance, there's the one about Mullah attending the
funeral service of the richest man in the village. Since Mullah
was weeping bitterly, a man inquired sadly, "Was the deceased
one of your dear relatives?"

"No," said Mullah sorrowfully.

"Then why are you crying?" asked the stranger.

"Because I'm *not* one of the relatives," answered Mullah.

This was only one of the many jokes that had its origin
somewhere around the thirteenth century but is still going
strong in night clubs, on TV shows and house parties all over
the USA. So, although Nasir-ud-Din may be dead, his jokes
go on forever.

My stirring research has led me to believe that 'twas this
same jolly joker who originated the first mother-in-law gag.
Seems Nasir's mother-in-law was drowned while crossing a
river and, although all the villagers went downstream in search
of the body, Nasir-ud-Din insisted on going upstream. "If you
knew her as well as I did," he explained, "you would know
what a contrary woman she was." So the wit of Mullah Nasir-
ud-Din is eternal and will never grow stale. It is universal, too.
I had to go halfway around the world to discover that people
everywhere laugh at the same kind of jokes, and that they are
as fresh today as they were when they were first told centuries
ago. I should know because I'm still telling them.

Even hoarier than the jokes handed down from Nasir-ud-
Din are the ancient traditions of show business. Any kid old
enough to own his own scrapbook knows that on the closing
night of a show—anything goes! It's what a fraternity member
will do to a pledge on Hell Week. It's what Olsen did to
Johnson in *Hellzapoppin'*. It's the fighter giving the hotfoot to
his manager. In other words, kiddies, closing night of any show
is Louse-Up Time.

It makes no difference how long your show ran; when it
comes to closing night it's open season on practical jokes. For

instance, a few seasons ago I worked at the Latin Quarter night club in New York City for ten weeks. At the midnight show, which was the last performance of my run, I braced myself, although I still had no idea what tortures were in store for me. Meanwhile, my wife had been quietly getting her inspirations by studying the history of the Spanish Inquisition. She primed the whole ringside so that when I walked onstage, the entire audience got up and walked out on me.

It was eighteen weeks and hundreds of shows after our opening in Kabul that I clambered up the wooden stairs to our makeshift stage on the basketball court of the Mohammad Reza Shah Pahlavi Gymnasium for our final show. The spirit of our company was running high—just like it was when the Government wound us up and set us off. Everybody in the dressing room was full of love and hell.

Our last performance was a doozey. There are some people who feel that goofing up a final performance is unfair to those who paid their money to see you do your best. Maybe they're right, but I can only tell you that the audience in Teheran seemed to be having as good a time as we were. Our spirit was infectious. The audience was part of the fun and rolled right along with us. They screamed when Celeste's tricks didn't work. In one trick she cleverly pours a glass of colored water into a folded page from a magazine. Then she unfolds the magazine and *voilà!* No water. For eighteen weeks this trick had produced cheers and huzzahs. This night—thanks to some fiendishly ingenious musician—it produced a stage full of leaking colored water. Celeste, however, was prepared. She did a trick that she's never done before. She cracked raw eggs and threw them at the band. It was a helluva trick. And for the rest of the show we had scrambled band.

The audience always roared everytime Chaz liberally salted my straw hat as though he were going to eat it. This was a rehearsed piece of business. He'd been doing it straight along. But this night he actually ate great hunks of the hat—plaid band and all.

Poor old John Shirley had the worst trouble of all. His wife had punctured little holes in each of his balloons and nothing blew up—but John! He huffed and he puffed and he tore the house down. They just loved it. John had added trouble because ever since Afghanistan I had a hot bet going with him each show that he wouldn't be able to hit the apple off my head in our William Tell scene. If he shot if off my head I owed him a beer. If he missed he had to buy me two. By the time we reached our last appearance together he was still eight beers in the hole. I gave him a chance to get even. For his last try it was double or nothing.

Came the exciting moment. The drums rolled. The audience tensed. And John drew back on the bow with the one remaining balloon we'd let him have. But being true-blue, honorbright and honest-injun like I am, I'd arranged for a fan to go on just at that moment to knock the arrow off balance. And also by an odd coincidence it just so happened that I twitched at the psychological second. Even though I stacked the bet, John paid off. When I got back to the Park Hotel that night, there were sixteen glasses of beer lined up in front of my door.

The show was a whole chop suey. Somebody beheaded the rubber chicken that I used in my magic act; Jerry Bell put on an ugly mask and ran onstage to the excitement of absolutely no one; the Syltes blacked out their teeth. The band went into business for themselves. They were playing Yiddish music altogether. And the Step Brothers got into everybody's act. We were so spent from laughing and from tumulting that we barely had strength enough to beat one another over the head with the balloons at the finale.

And when I stepped out front to make my usual friendship speech, I had a convoy. Instead of going out alone, I was flanked by the girls of the show. With lipstick that they'd deliberately laid on two inches thick, each of them planted big, juicy smackers all over my face. The audience loved it. I wouldn't lie to ya; so did I.

Show people can be crying on the inside and laughing on

the outside. But it wasn't that way this particular night. This particular night we weren't wearing our professional smiles. We were genuinely happy that we'd made it. We were glad that we'd been able to hit the finish line together. We were all looking forward to going home but, looking backward, we were all grateful to have had this opportunity. A little bit we were feeling proud of ourselves. A little bit we were sorry for some of the things we had said and done. A little bit we were imbued with the Christmas spirit. A little bit we were moved by the sheer size of what we'd all just gone through.

It was the eve of Christmas Eve and we all of us had a little something extra in our mental stocking for each other. It was evident in the added bit of pressure in the handshake of Mike Manieri, our vibraphone player. It was evident when the three Syltes hugged me and whispered in my ear, "God bless you for letting us be part of this wonderful trip." It was apparent in Celeste's little friendship speech to Cindy. It showed up in the apple for the teacher which Al Williams gave me shyly and which turned out to be a gold and pearl tie pin. And the carved ivory cuff links Prince Spencer surreptitiously pressed into my hand. And the rushed little speech that Jerry Bell made in passing: "Boss, I'm ready. When do we go out again?"

There's something sad about undressing a Christmas tree after it has done its job, after the party's over. There's an empty feeling when you unwind its long string of brilliantly colored electric lights, and pluck off each piece of tinsel, and gather up the angel's hair that has covered your pretty tree, and unhook each striped candy cane, and you remove all the gay ornaments. Then, when you sweep away the snow and pack away the twinkling star that crowned the top, you see the tree for what it really is: a consumptive old bush with bits of garbage clinging to it.

I stood there in the empty gymnasium and watched them tear down our long string of brilliantly colored lights and lay away our shiny instruments and dismantle our glittery bandstand for the last time. I saw the comic's baggy pants lying on the trunk. These wonderful baggy pants that had made kids all over the world squeal with delight when he was inside them. But now they looked kind of pathetic as they lay there all crumpled up in a heap.

I saw the magician's magical table which rolls out onto the stage, bedecked in jewels and sequins. Thousands had fastened on it in wide-eyed wonderment as it produced gaily colored doves and cards and handkerchiefs and ropes and rubber balls and all kinds of treasures. But undressed and unhinged and lying on the floor ready for its long voyage home, it looked like a battered pile of junk.

Buddy Rich's drums, which were always front and center on our stage and had beat out that steady rhythm for our dancers and throbbingly accompanied our singers and swelled to a crashing crescendo for our finale, were sitting in a wooden crate. The cymbals were disconnected. The foot pedal was unscrewed. The wood block and the cow bell were detached. The drumsticks were scattered. It looked so forlorn.

There was somebody's glamorous sequin gown hanging inelegantly from a door hinge, garish under the naked light of the dressing room. There was somebody's book of music that carried the legend "first trumpet" on the cover. There was an old pair of scruffy tap shoes with one of the taps half off. And a chewed-up old straw hat which, in its heyday, had been doffed to kings and queens and was soon to be laid to rest.

I glanced at these bits of rags and tinsel and make-believe and realized the party was over. As I started towards the alley that led to the street, I took one last look over my shoulder. The huge barn was empty. The people were gone. My Cinderella music hall had already reverted to a plain gymnasium. In a dusty corner where the stage had been, partly hidden by a crumpled "Joey Adams" program, lay my little, headless, rubber chicken. The only tangible evidence of the twenty-five minstrels who had traveled around the world for their country.

Epilogue

OUR BIG Pan American jet purred softly through the night. I was alone with my thoughts. The whole world seemed to be asleep.

"Are you awake?" Cindy whispered.

"Yes," I said quietly.

"Joey . . ." she began.

"Yes?"

"Would you do it all over again?"

"Would I do it all over again? That's just what I was thinking. Yes, I guess I would. And you know why? Because I know the good that we did, that's why."

"But what good did we do, Joey? I was along with you. I know what we did and what we tried to do and what we went through. I went without sleep like the rest of the troupe did. I went without dinner, I washed the drip-drys, I visited the schools, I dodged the lizards and fought the dysentery and overlooked the fights. I was right along with everybody else. I know what we did. But what I want to know is, what actual, tangible good did we do?

"Let's face it," she continued, "there are plenty of critics of Cultural Exchange. Besides a couple of personal troublemakers we've managed to pick up along the way who maybe aren't too crazy about Joey and Cindy and Co. And don't forget those people who may think we were on a hell of a joy ride, seeing the world and having a ball at the taxpayers' expense.

"It's just possible that there's somebody in our country of 190 million who doesn't happen to think it was such a brilliant idea for our Government to send Joey and Cindy and a bunch of vaudevillians to save the world. After all, how do we tell the people at home about the good we did when just two days after we left New Delhi, relations between India and the United States got a little strained as a result of Nehru's take-over in Goa? And how about President Sukarno? You know and I know that he liked us all very much, but what the world knows is that soon after we left he began fighting with Dutch New Guinea despite protests of Adlai Stevenson and the UN.

"In Afghanistan they didn't even wait for us to get out of town before the Pak-Afghan rumble started and they closed the border altogether. It's history that Laos and Vietnam have gone steadily downhill after we passed through. They're in the headlines every day. Hong Kong has had nothing but tension over the refugee problem since our visit. Singapore is now locked in a power struggle. Since we brought our cheer to Cambodia, they've been fighting with Thailand and South Vietnam. I'm sure it's just a coincidence, but nevertheless the beautiful little kingdom of Nepal has had nothing but troubles since we were there."

"Well," I said cheerfully, "we haven't heard anything from Iran."

"Yeah, but maybe that's because we've only been out of there a couple of hours. Give them time."

What good did we do? I've thought about that a million times. How do you put your finger on love? How do you put friendship down in a diary of events? How do you chronicle joy? How do you weigh warmth? How do you put a little orphan's smile into a letter to a Congressman? How do you wrap up tears of gratitude from a wounded soldier and send it to the State Department?

"You want to know what good we did?" I said finally to Cindy. "I'll tell you what good we did. Remember the little baby whom I loved in the hospital in Singapore? Remember Lalida, aged four? Remember how she hugged me and clung to me with all her might? Well, someday she'll grow up. And maybe someday she'll be in a position to return the friendship of an American who cared.

"And there are thousands and thousands and thousands of Lalidas from four to twenty who, I'm sure, will always remember the bunch of Americans who went out of their way to bring them joy. And these children could be tomorrow's leaders, in business, in government. Perhaps in the coming generation, when these children will be making the decisions for their country, they'll think more kindly of Americans because of the Americans who thought kindly of them.

"Don't forget, we're all products of our environment and the influences around us. I remember when I was a kid. I lived in a rough, tough neighborhood in the East Harlem section of New York. We had gang fights every day. The Jews against the Italians or the Italians against the Irish or the Irish against the Jews.

"The first appearance I ever made in show business was at the Madison Theatre at an amateur show. The prize was five dollars. I was about twelve years old and filled with ambition. I charged out on stage like a tiger, shoving an old man who was standing in the wings. But I never even finished my first number. I slunk off like a whipped dog with the boos and cat-calls of a hostile audience ringing in my ears. And I found a dark corner where I sobbed my heart out. The little old, white haired stagehand, whom I'd brushed past on my way to the stage and glory, now put his arm around me. If ever a fresh, green kid needed a word of encouragement, this was it. 'Don't feel badly about this, sonny,' he said in a gentle brogue. 'I've seen 'em all. All you need is a chance. You're gonna be okay, kid.'

"This dear little old man who put the blood back in my veins and the very guts back in my body was the most lovable Irishman you ever saw. After that, how could I ever join in a fight against an Irishman again?

"I'm sure every human being has had an Irish stagehand in his life. Well, to all the Lalidas in all the countries we visited, we are that Irish stagehand. That's the good we did."

The big plane hummed on, hour after hour, bringing us closer to home. Cindy and I sat there in the darkness holding hands and talking softly on into the night.

"You want to know what good we did?" I said, "I'll tell you what good we did. Remember all those thousands of soldiers we worked to in the up-country jungles of Thailand? And the wounded veterans whom we visited, ward by ward, in the hospital in Saigon? And the Lao Army we entertained in Vientiane? And the thousands of young men who sat cross-legged on the ground in Afghanistan? And the fighting Nepali Gurkhas who filled our outdoor stadium in Katmandu that afternoon? And those blocks and blocks of refugees from Red China? Remember them?"

"Yes."

"Well, they'll remember us, too. And if the time ever comes that any of these men will be asked to point a gun in the direction of an American, maybe they'll think twice. Maybe they'll remember that they might be shooting at a little comic in baggy pants who made them laugh. Or at a thin, shy, little clarinet player with glasses, who held a jam session for them on the steps of a temple, or at the balloon man who fashioned toy animals for their children. Maybe they'll remember that we are their friends. That's the good we did.

"You want to know what good we did?" I said again. "I'll tell you what good we did. We showed these countries that Americans are human beings just like they are. That we laugh and fight and eat and cry just like they do. That we have problems just like they have. That we can share a rice bowl with them, that we're sensitive to their customs and can join in the Thai dancing of Thailand and can enjoy the Bharatanatyam dancing of India. We lived with them, walked with them, and talked with them. They saw one of us unhappy because we didn't get a letter from home, they saw one of us with a belly-ache, they saw another of us thrilled because we were getting the cloth their country was famous for or the stones their country was proud of and were able to send it home to a loved one.

"No more will we be just a faceless mass of wealth and power and atom bombs—or even numbers on a ledger to these people. Perhaps some of them know us now as flesh and blood people just like they are and not as the militaristic, imperialistic aggressors we're made out to be. Maybe America will be a singer with soft brown hair whom they heard in church one morning, or a comedian with a straw hat whose hand they shook one afternoon. Or a Negro dancer who showed them that we know the meaning of brotherhood. That's the good we did."

I sat back in the plane content with the good job we had done for our country. I looked at my twenty-five Yankee Doodle Dandies who had made patriotism so popular again. Little did we know that seven months later our tour would be target "A" in every newspaper in the country. The attacker was Brooklyn Congressman John Rooney who is chairman of the House Appropriations Subcommittee. It is this group that has the job of keeping a tight wallet on the State Department and its Operation Cultural Exchange. Congressman Rooney picked on us when he brought his sharp eye and ax to bear on the State Department's request for a $335 million appropriation for the coming year.

One of the things that upset Mr. Rooney was my wife's dastardly act of high treason when she called a prime minister

"Honey." Cindy read about it in the papers the following July.

"What's Congressman Rooney so excited about?" Cindy yawned. "What's he carrying on about? The Prime Minister didn't mind me calling him 'Honey.' In fact, he loved it."

I never did understand the problem. I mean, I'm her husband and I didn't care. And the Prime Minister was the Prime Minister and he didn't care. With Cindy everybody is "Honey" and with almost everybody Cindy is "Honey." That's how she is.

"What's the story?" I asked Cindy.

"Well, it happened on opening day of the Jeshyn Fair in Kabul. Our Ambassador Byroade had asked me to accompany him on a tour of the Fair grounds. That was the day the King officially opened Jeshyn and the diplomats from all the major pavilions who participated, plus friends and invited guests were to be present for the afternoon. You remember. That was the day we left at 9:00 A.M. and you were still asleep.

"Anyway, there was an enormous crush of people and somewhere Ambassador Byroade and I were separated. A very nice, dear, little man who had been in our party attached himself to me. He walked along with me with his arm linked in mine. Well, he was so friendly and everything and he kept calling me 'Dear.' I didn't know his name and I didn't want to be rude, so I called him 'Honey.' Later when I asked somebody who my friend was, they told me he was a prime minister.

"Well, when I found out I was terror-stricken. I apologized to the dear little man. I said to him, 'Oh, I'm so terribly sorry. I'd never have called you "Honey" if I'd known who you were.'

" 'It's all right, Dear,' he said, 'I loved it. It's fun to be liked like everybody else instead of receiving just stiff diplomatic courtesy all the time.' "

"Who was he?" I asked. "The Prime Minister of what?"

"How do I know?" she answered. "If I'd have known who he was I wouldn't have called him 'Honey' in the first place."

"Well, how did Congress find out about it?"

"Now, that's the ridiculous part of it. The Prime Minister never complained. His country never complained. Ambassador Byroade never complained. So, now, twelve thousand miles away and eleven months afterwards Congressman Rooney complains. I guess I leaked the story myself when I innocently wrote about it in my column. Just goes to prove that it's no sin if you call a friendly prime minister 'Honey.' The only sin is telling about it."

"The Congressman questions the propriety of your columns and whether or not your sassy reporting injured our country's relations."

Cindy looked up from her typewriter. "Listen, so injurious was I regarding Indonesia, for instance, that President Sukarno sent me a long, personal, handwritten thank you letter. And so frighteningly malicious were my Indian articles that Nehru sent me a thank you note after my NANA stories appeared in the *Ambala Punjabi Tribune*. And how's about Krishna Menon who has been known to go ten rounds with reporters at the airport, but invited me for tea and an exclusive interview when he was in this country. And that was *after* our visit to India. And so vicious was I to the country of Iran that when the Shah and Empress were here on their recent State visit, I was one of the few permitted to interview Their Majesties. And only this morning I received a warm thank you note from the Empress.

"Now, if it were true that I was the greatest scourge to the United States since Benedict Arnold, it's hardly likely that I'd be pen-pals with the leaders of these countries I was supposed to have murdered, right? And anyway what can Congress do to me? The worst that can happen is that they'll deport me to my native Bronx."

The other pain in Chairman Rooney's purse strings was that our show cost American taxpayers a "whopping" $256,000. What nobody bothered to mention was that $76,000 of it went for transportation. The remaining $180,000 was $10,000 per week for eighteen weeks. Now of this $10,000, 10 per cent came off the top right away for agent's commissions. This left $9,000. From this we had to pay welfare, insurance, manager's expenses, and what was left was divided between the twenty-five people involved in the tour. This averages out to about $300 per person per week. Out of this approximately $300 per person per week, we had to support ourselves on the road, plus taking care of our families at home and paying the rent.

A few years ago Cindy and I did GI shows in Germany, Turkey, North Africa, Greece, Crete, Italy and so on. We went for nothing. Gratis. Not a sou. My wife and I even refused the per diem offered us. But that was a shorter tour. It was six weeks. We could afford it. Nobody, however, can afford to live on nothing for eighteen weeks in places like Cambodia where tomato juice cost us $3.00 a serving. Nobody can afford to travel around without pay for 126 days while supporting families and paying two rents at one time.

The other item that bewitched, bothered and befuddled Congressman Rooney was our offstage feuding. "The Committee seems to be very upset that the United States Government would dare select twenty-five people who, after four and a half months of jungles and deserts and mosquitoes and dysentery and no sleep and no water, could end up having a few arguments," said Cindy.

"It *is* pretty surprising," I agreed. "By all rights we should never have had any arguments at all. We should have killed each other."

The simple truth of the matter is that we were sent to entertain the people of Asia, not one another. And if we had to kill each other a little bit to get the job done, that was all right too, because the job came first and our personal feelings came second.

Our big plane started to descend. We were coming in. "Fasten your seat belts," the stewardess said, "and observe the 'No Smoking' sign. We'll be landing at Idlewild Airport in New York in a few minutes."

At that moment I thought those were the nicest words I'd

ever heard in my life. I wonder if I would have been that happy had I known then that the Welcome Mat would be pulled out from under me so rudely seven months later by a Congressman from Brooklyn.

The plane ground to a halt. The steps were wheeled to the door. And the Joey Adams All-Star Variety Troupe—a little wearier, a little wiser and a lot thinner than when they had left a hundred years ago—made their last entrance as a team. A big brass band greeted us, a Boy Scout troop saluted us, flowers were given us, the cameramen photographed us, the newspapermen surrounded us, our families embraced us. It was "Hail to the Conquering Heroes" all the way.

As I was walking toward my car, an acrobat with whom I'd worked in Leon & Eddie's back in 1940 banged me on the back and hollered, "Well, if it ain't Joey Adams! What are ya doin' at the airport, pal? Where ya goin'?"

(Not printed at Government expense)

Congressional Record

United States
of America

PROCEEDINGS AND DEBATES OF THE 87th CONGRESS, SECOND SESSION

Joey Adams: A Great American and Ambassador of Good Will

SPEECH
OF
HON. SEYMOUR HALPERN
OF NEW YORK
IN THE HOUSE OF REPRESENTATIVES
Thursday, March 8, 1962

Mr. HALPERN. Mr. Speaker, it has been said that when man loses the ability to laugh, he has lost the world. There are parts of the world, however, where laughter is a luxury —where the harsh problems of everyday life would seem to preclude joy. Perhaps the greatest gift ever given to these people by our country was the chance to laugh—it was worth the equivalent of millions of dollars of foreign aid funds and, according to firsthand reports, those people will remember our Ambassador of Joy longer than they will remember our gifts of tools or arms.

That Ambassador was Joey Adams, an entertainer, author, and I should add, diplomat and psychologist—a man of rare ability and great warmth. He has recently returned from a 4½-month tour of the Middle and Far East during which time he visited 11 countries and left behind him the smiles and gratitude of countless thousands of people.

Joey Adams and his 24-member troupe, which included his exceptionally talented and charming wife, Cindy, are to be commended by this House and by the American people for the successful completion of their mission. It was a mission first suggested to President Kennedy by Mr.

Adams early last year. The President and our State Department agreed with the wisdom of this suggestion and their opinion has been justified by the unqualified success of the tour.

It has been my extreme pleasure to know and work with Joey Adams, both in his capacity as president of the American Guild of Variety Artists and in many charitable functions in New York and throughout the country. He is more than an entertainer. He is gifted with charm, dedication, and a seemingly endless storehouse of energy.

This good-will tour has brought accolades from news media throughout the world. The mission has been heralded by representatives of our Government and by officials and other representatives of the countries covered by our diplomat entertainers.

Typical of the American press comments are those expressed by Lee Mortimer, the noted, widely read correspondent for the New York Daily Mirror, and by Feature Writer Leonard Harris in his full-page story in the New York World-Telegram.

Mr. Speaker, I commend these two articles as excellent summaries of the Adams tour. They give a capsule wrap-up of the Adams mission:

[From the New York Sunday Mirror, Jan. 7, 1962]

COMEDIAN OR DIPLOMAT? BOTH—JOEY ADAMS WINS UNITED STATES FRIENDS OVERSEAS

(By Lee Mortimer)

A clown—in a diplomat's role? Yes, and there's nothing funny about it—except the quips comedian Joey Adams dropped before audiences roaring with laughter in far places of the world.

Joey, who graduated to the big-time from the borscht circuit after a boyhood on the Lower East Side, headed a troupe of 23 introducing American humor and cementing international relations with smiles in some Far Eastern trouble spots. The trip was part of President Kennedy's special international program for cultural relations.

The troupe won rounds of enthusiastic applause—and columns of favorable newspaper comment—in friendly countries such as Thailand, Vietnam, and Iran, and in neutralists such as India, Nepal, and Indonesia. The results in good will for America exceeded all expectations.

Joey returned on Christmas Day from the 5-month tour which covered 12 countries. Yesterday—his 51st birthday—he spent in his Fifth Avenue apartment reading the pile of congratulatory messages from the crowned heads and cabinet ministers he had entertained.

From the little people in the audiences, he had already heard—with the sound of their appreciative laughter.

One of the plaudits he treasures most was the comment of the Prime Minister of Indonesia to American Ambassador Howard Jones:

"If the price of rice goes up the people of Indonesia will revolt, but if the price of Joey Adams' show goes up the people will pay it gladly."

Actually, where admission prices were charged at all, they were in most cases turned over to local charities. The U.S. Government paid the troupe's expenses.

Another tribute was from American Ambassador Nolting, in Saigon, who wired the State Department that his office was "highly pleased with Joey Adams' contribution to Vietnamese-American relations * * * Adams' personal gifts in cementing U.S. Vietnamese relations most impressive."

Wherever the troupe appeared, Adams' pretty, witty wife Cindy introduced the acts in the native tongue—a gesture much appreciated by the people. The places visited included Afghanistan, Nepal, Thailand, Cambodia, Laos, Indonesia, Singapore, Hong Kong, South Vietnam, India, Pakistan, and Iran. The

Queen of Cambodia decorated Joey. The rulers of Thailand and Afghanistan pressed gifts on him. The Empress of Iran, the Nepalese royal family and a Lao prince all honored him.

But the impressive honors haven't turned the head of the funnyman who can also be serious, as president of the American Guild of Variety Artists. To all the praise and adulation for his accomplishment on the trip, he replies with a quip, "I'm very glad to have had this opportunity to serve my country—but I feel a bit self-conscious that the best way I can serve my country is to leave it."

[From the New York World-Telegram, Jan. 20, 1962]

STRIPED PANTS TROUPERS WIN RAVES FOR UNITED STATES

(By Leonard Harris)

Joey Adams can't count how many times he's stood in front of an audience and introduced a purely fictional joke with:

"This actually happened."

But, says the comic, who's just returned after heading a 4½-month, State Department-sponsored entertainment tour of the Middle and Far East, this actually happened:

"One morning in Saigon—at an orphanage—600 'kids' got up when our show was over and sang 'God Bless America' in English.

"People in hospitals—what did they have to be happy about?—beamed at us, laughed at us, reached out to us. Everywhere we put out a hand to people, they took it and shook it. There were no 'Yankee, Go Home,' signs, not one."

Joey first suggested the trip to President Kennedy about 8 months ago. The troupe played Afghanistan, India, Nepal, Thailand, Laos, Cambodia, South Vietnam, Hong Kong, Indonesia, Singapore, and Iran.

Joey and his pretty wife, Cindy, and others in the 24-member troupe took turns giving English lessons. But they hurdled the language barrier mainly by emphasizing visual things, broad comedy, music, dancing, magic.

Like any performers on tour, they

savor their memories of the things that "actually happened."

What they'll remember most is the faces—of the hospital patients in Thailand, the street full of Red Chinese refugees in Hong Kong, the lepers in a beggars' home in India. Especially the faces of the "kids" everywhere.

But like all performers, they'll remember the SRO audiences and the raves. Joey was proud to show some of the reviews, particularly the orchids from American officials who noted the effects on the local people. Here are a few:

"Comments from all sources regarding the show have been highly laudatory"— American Embassy in Katmandu, Nepal.

"Wonderful * * * Iranians feel most cordially towards the President and all Americans"—M. Ghaffari, Governor of Abadan.

"Your week's stay here has helped to bring cheer to a hard-pressed people and to give them a real feeling of America's sincerity and warmhearted support"— Frederick E. Nolting, Jr., U.S. Ambassador to South Vietnam.

"Joey Adams' Show Delights"; "90 minutes of sheer delight"—two papers in New Delhi, India.

"A packed house at Annamalai Manram last night roared with laughter witnessing the Joey Adams Variety Show" —the Madras (India) Mail.

Variety, writing under a Washington dateline, said: "State Department officials here point to a pile of reports from embassies and consulates throughout south Asia and proclaim that Uncle Sam's use of vaudeville as a good-will ambassador is a 'smash success.' The Joey Adams group * * * has drawn raves from American diplomats where they have performed."

Recently a veteran woman gossip columnist called the Adams tour a flop. This was contradicted by Heath Bowman, Chief of the State Department's Cultural Presentations Division.

"I must disagree with her," he said. "From reports from all our posts, from officials of the Asian countries, from numbers of people who saw it, we learned the tour was extremely good. It did a great deal for us.

"It played hospitals, orphanages, and charities. It played provincial cities. In Thailand, it went into the bushes; it played military camps and entertained wounded soldiers.

"We've never seen anything like this. In Kabul, Afghanistan, it played a fair. The Russians had a group at the fair, too. The Adams company completely eclipsed the Russians. We got a special wire from the Ambassador there thanking us."

Joey and Cindy Adams are proud that they worked a "24-hour day," giving shows at hospitals, orphanages, in the streets, in addition to scheduled performances. Mostly they entertained what Cindy called the plain "turban tops" of Asia.

"Many times we had no water, no electricity," she said. "We tramped through mud in evening gowns to get to our stages; we slept under mosquito netting with the temperature up to 110. We went 5 and 6 days at a time without baths— covered with layers and layers of gummy mosquito repellent. With five layers of that stuff on, we began to repel each other."

The mud and the mosquito repellent washed off, but the anecdotes came home with them—including a few awkward moments.

After a show in New Delhi, India, the troupe released hundreds of red, white, and blue peace and friendship balloons.

The peace balloons caused a brawl in the second row. An Indian belted the American next to him and shouted: "He took my balloon." Joey took them both backstage and gave each his own balloon.

The performers had been warned it was not good manners to touch royalty unless the royal person extended his hand first. In Afghanistan, a dancer was introduced to the crown prince. "It's a pleasure," said the hoofer. "I hope we get to play your country some day."

"This is his country," whispered Joey.

The dancer was effusively apologetic. He slapped the prince on the back vigorously—and repeatedly. "Aw, Princie boy, I'm sorry," he said. The prince, well, he was a prince about the whole thing.

This actually happened, too:

In Jakarta, Indonesia, the musicians' instruments arrived 4 hours late. Joey drew liberally from his years in show business for a challenge round of jokes which filled the time.

His comic opponent—who also chipped in by singing Negro spirituals—was Indonesian President Sukarno.

The Adams troupe included Buddy Rich and his Jazz Sextet, the Four Step Brothers, a dance team; fire-eater and clown Chaz Chase, magician Celeste Evans, John Shirley and Bonnie Dale, who make animals out of balloons; the Sylte Sisters, a singing trio; and Jerry Bell, stage manager.

Joey Adams calls them "entertainers in striped pants." He'd like to see many other teams of entertainers follow, and, as president of the American Guild of Variety Artists, he's going to work for it.

The trip might be compared to one of the many "industrials" that perform in this country. But here the sponsor was the United States, and the commercial: "Let's be friends." Joey thinks the customers in Asia went for it in a big way.

IT'S A GOING U.S. BUSINESS

The Joey Adams tour is just one example of the State Department's recognition that there's no business like show business for helping to thaw the cold war and representing this country overseas.

The Government's program of letting audiences on both sides of the Iron Curtain—and some in countries straddling it—see American dramatic, musical, variety, and athletic entertainment has been in operation for 8 years now.

Its budget runs to about $9 million a year and covers international trade fair exhibits and labor missions abroad, as well as artistic and athletic presentations. Last year about $3 million was allocated for the latter phase, consisting of 43 projects.

Despite this modest budget, the program of cultural presentations has run into some tough times at hearings from congressional critics.

Edward R. Murrow, Director of the U.S. Information Agency, thinks the program is important and should be expanded. While our presentation program has been constant, Mr. Murrow said, Communist countries in the past 2 years have stepped up theirs.

"We have the talent to match their achievements," said the head of the

USIA, "whether it be in the field of athletics, ballet, opera or acrobats. But we must send our talent abroad where it can be seen and heard."

Cultural exchange is even seen as valuable with our cold war opponents, the Soviets. Under the recently concluded agreement with the Russians, the Leningrad Philharmonic Orchestra will perform at the Lincoln Center in October, and then in many other cities, while the Robert Shaw Chorale and Orchestra will go to the Soviet Union.

Among others who will perform in the Soviet Union under the cultural exchange agreement are opera singer Dorothy Kirsten and pianist Grant Johannesen.

The 1962 worldwide trek of American entertainers has already started with four shows on the road and six more scheduled. The Baird Marionettes are in Southeast Asia; the Eastman Philharmonia is in Germany and will go to Poland and Russia; the Tapps Dance Co. is in Africa and soprano Camilla Williams is en route to the Far East.

Others set to go include the Ailey Dance Theater, a 17-member modern dance group, headed for the Far East and Australia; the Paul Winter Sextet, a jazz outfit, South and Central America; the Asten String Quartet, classical music, southern Europe and Iran; the University of Maine Theater Group, India and Pakistan; the Chad Mitchell Trio, Central America, and the Berea College Dancers, Latin America.

Mr. Speaker, other leading American newspapers gave wide coverage to the tour. Typical is the following article which appeared in the New York Times on September 8:

[From the New York Times, Sept. 8, 1961]

JOEY ADAMS TROUPE BRINGS JOY TO NEPAL ON A 3-DAY VISIT

KATMANDU, NEPAL, September 8.—The 3-day visit here of Joey Adams and his troupe as part of President Kennedy's special international program for Cultural relations has been a great success. Such was the demand for the tickets that an extra performance was arranged.

The party brought something new to Nepal, and the large audiences at the four scheduled shows reacted with full-throated approval.

But the show that touched the people's hearts was on the roadside, in the suburbs of Katmandu. Here crowds gathered and children gaped in wide-eyed joy.

They saw tap dancers, a woman magician who brought beauty and color to her show, a man and a woman with balloons and a comedian.

At schools where the troupe performed children laughed with glee and stampeded to catch hold of the balloons. Among the schools visited were St. Xavier's, run by the Reverend Marshall D. Moran, of Chicago and St. Mary's Convent.

In Bir Hospital here, members of the troupe went through the wards to entertain the patients.

Impressions of the show varied. "I liked the drumbeats," a taxi driver said.

"I bet I could do it," a schoolboy said after seeing the tap dancers.

"We also have magicians, but not such lovely ones," said a farmer.

This international experiment to create goodwill between nations can be considered a success. While the Nepalese were impressed, the troupe was no less impressed by the local people. "We had an intelligent audience. The children are cute," they said.

Representatives of our Government abroad hailed Adams and his company for their invaluable contribution to good will and the bettering of our international relations. Typical of the many complimentary letters Adams received are:

THE FOREIGN SERVICE OF THE
UNITED STATES OF AMERICA,
AMERICAN EMBASSY,
Kabul, Afghanistan, September 30, 1961.
Mr. JOEY ADAMS,
Joey Adams Variety Group, c/o U.S. Information Service, American Consulate General, Singapore, Malaya.

DEAR JOEY: Nearly a month has passed since you and your variety group were in Kabul, a month that has been filled for you with travel to several other countries far from home. I am sure that you must find these visits a rewarding experience, for you all give so generously of your talents and friendship that you must in return feel the warm appreciation that your audiences and hosts extend to you.

The visit of your group to Kabul was memorable, both for us in the American community and for the approximately 90,000 people of Afghanistan who came and came again to enjoy your show at the Jeshyn Fair. As you know, appearances of American artists and entertainers in Afghanistan are few and far between. Kabul is a long way from the Orpheum-Pantages circuit, and only a few Afghans have had any opportunity to see our really good American artists perform. That they like American entertainment is beyond question. That so many could see such fine and varied American entertainment here in Kabul will provide a topic of local conversation for a long time to come. There is no doubt that the Joey Adams Variety Show was the outstanding single attraction at the 1961 Jeshyn Fair.

Beyond entertaining your audiences in Kabul, you and the members of your group went out of your way to meet people on the streets and in the bazaars, generating good will by your gestures of friendliness. I particularly appreciated your willingness to perform, and perform often, under conditions that were unfamiliar and probably sometimes distracting.

The American community will not soon forget your group. During the nearly 2 weeks that you were here you literally changed our way of life, which was no small accomplishment in itself. That you also left many friends among your countrymen in Kabul, friends who will long remember you and what you did here, is equally apparent and more important.

On behalf of all of my staff as well as myself and Mrs. Byroade, I want to thank you all again for a job well done. I hope you will see that each member of your group knows of my feelings as expressed herein—for it applies to every member of the troupe.

With all good wishes for the remainder of your tour—and always.

Sincerely,
HENRY A. BYROADE,
Ambassador.

AMERICAN EMBASSY,
Vientiane, Laos, October 11, 1961.
Mr. JOEY ADAMS,
Hotel Settha Palace,
Vientiane.

DEAR JOEY ADAMS: I wish to thank you very warmly on behalf of all of us here for the fine work which you and your troupe have done in Laos.

We and the Lao have very much appreciated your willingness to give so many extra performances in addition to those regularly scheduled. Your visits to hospitals, schools, and other places have brought much pleasure and satisfaction. You have all certainly worked very hard here and deserve much credit for the good results.

You would be pleased to hear the nice things that have been said about you by the Lao, including the Prime Minister.

Please express my appreciation and thanks to all of your troupe.

Very sincerely yours,
WINTHROP G. BROWN,
American Ambassador.

[Telegram]
THE FOREIGN SERVICE OF THE UNITED STATES OF AMERICA
OCTOBER 16, 1961.

Joey Adams show breaking all records here with complete sellout sports hall for 4 nights: total attendance 40,000 people.

Near crisis developed night after arrival when instruments and equipment failed to arrive from Bangkok in time for scheduled show before President Sukarno at Bogor Palace to which entire cabinet, members diplomatic corps and other top-drawer guests had been invited. Group was kept waiting from 7 to 9 p.m. Plane with equipment touched down at Kemajoran airport at 7:30 p.m. where USIS had truck and driver waiting. With palace cooperation, truck was given motorcycle escort 40 miles to Bogor, certainly first time in history jazz orchestra has been so honored in Indonesia where rock and roll taboo.

Sukarno played the gracious host, displaying no impatience at delay and Adams skillfully exploited incident so that show was outstanding success.

Opening night at sports hall excited spectators began to arrive at 6 o'clock for 8 o'clock show. By the time I reached hall, shortly before 8, everyone was in his seat. First Minister Leimena, sitting next to me said, "If price of rice goes up, we're likely to have riots in Djakarta. But if the price of tickets to Joey Adams goes up, everybody would pay without complaint." Performers gave all they had and show was received with high enthusiasm.

HOWARD P. JONES,
Ambassador to Indonesia.

THE FOREIGN SERVICE OF THE UNITED STATES OF AMERICA,
November 13, 1961.

Mr. JOEY ADAMS,
Oceanic Hotel,
Madras.

DEAR JOEY AND CINDY: (I hope the billing is right.) I thought you might like to know that the "Joey Adams Show" was the biggest financial success we have had in Bangalore in my more than 4 years here. It was more than merely a financial success, however. Among the people we really wanted to reach it was also a thumping artistic success. Had we been able to get the hall for another night we could easily have filled it again.

You realize of course that while the show is the thing, there is also a total image which a group of prominent visiting Americans creates when traveling abroad. They are observed carefully, and their behavior is discussed over coffee for months afterward. In this department, too, your group scored very high, certainly higher than any large group I've had in Bangalore.

Bami called me a few minutes ago and remarked that "These are the kind of Americans we like to meet, warm and genuine." Having met her you understand why I have so high a regard for her opinion.

Elsie and I want to thank you for everything you've done for us. You will be remembered long and affectionately not only by us but by thousands of my fellow citizens of Bangalore.

Sincerely yours,
JOSEPH A. NORMA,
Public Affairs Officer.

P.S.—Enclosed are a couple of clippings: more later.

AMERICAN CONSULATE GENERAL
Singapore, October 25, 1961.
JOEY ADAMS, ESQ.,
Joey Adams All Star Show.

DEAR JOEY: On behalf of all members of the Consulate General may I express warm and heartfelt thanks to you and the members of your troupe for doing such a splendid job in promoting good will for our country in the State of Singapore. Moreover, I am sure that members of the American community share this view.

Your philosophy of love and laughter was exemplified by your activities and contacts here. It is difficult to imagine how any individual or any group of individuals could do more to carry out these qualities so much needed in the world today.

Please convey our grateful appreciation to all members of the Joey Adams All Star Show. May I also take this opportunity to say how much personally my wife and I enjoyed meeting and talking with all of you.

The very best of luck to you in your coming travels, and every good wish for continued success.

Sincerely yours,
ROBERT DOMBAUSER,
Counsel in Charge.

THE FOREIGN SERVICE OF THE
UNITED STATES OF AMERICA,
AMERICAN EMBASSY,
Saigon, Vietnam, November 8, 1961.
MR. JOEY ADAMS,
*Director, Joey Adams Variety Show,
Hotel Caravelle, Saigon.*

DEAR MR. ADAMS: Before your departure, I want to send you in writing what I have had the opportunity to say to you personally on several occasions —that I appreciate most sincerely the contribution which you and the members of the Variety Show have made, not only to the food relief fund, but even more importantly to the cause of United States-Vietnamese relations. From all reports I have, and from personal observation, your week's stay here has helped to bring cheer to a hard-pressed people and to give them a real feeling of America's sincerity and warmhearted support.

Frankly, as I told you, I was skeptical at first as to whether the variety show would fit the situation in Vietnam at the present time, which is one of national emergency bordering on wartime conditions. You were quick to appreciate this, and by your performances in hospitals, orphanages, and other informal appearances you created the right atmosphere and reactions.

I would like, through you, to extend both my personal and official thanks to all the members of your troupe, and to wish you all continued success in this good enterprise.

I shall send a copy of this letter to the Director of the President's Entertainment Fund in Washington.

My wife joins me in best regards to you and to Mrs. Adams—and thanks again for your book, which has already made us chuckle.

Sincerely yours,
FREDERICK E. NOLTING, JR.,
American Ambassador.

THE FOREIGN SERVICE OF THE
UNITED STATES OF AMERICA,
AMERICAN CONSULATE GENERAL,
Bombay, India, December 5, 1961.
MR. JOEY ADAMS,
*Care of U.S. Information Service,
New Delhi, India.*

DEAR JOEY: May I offer my congratulations to you and to the members of your troupe for the successful performances which were staged in Bombay. As we know, there was standing room only the last few days, attesting to the popularity of the show with the people of Bombay.

I was especially impressed by the performances which members of your group gave at hospitals, children's homes and at the beggars' home here. This was most commendable and greatly appreciated.

Both my wife and I were happy to have the opportunity of becoming acquainted with you and Cindy, as well as Jed Hornen, and of meeting the other members of your group.

Sincerely yours,
ROBERT M. CARR,
American Consul General.

GENERAL REACTIONS OF AMERICAN FOR-
EIGN SERVICE POSTS TO THE JOEY
ADAMS VARIETY SHOW

From Bombay, India: "Adams show still smash sellout and gone to standing room only. Charity performances, publicity going very well. Joey, Cindy and group quite cooperative."

From Djakarta, Indonesia: "Joey Adams breaking all records here with complete sellout sports hall for 4 nights: Total attendance, 40,000 people."

From Kabul, Afghanistan: "Embassy in Kabul reports that Jeshyn Fair formally opened morning of August 24. Variety show performed evening August 23. Americans tremendous success and stole show."

From Katmandu, Nepal: "Comments from all sources regarding Joey Adams show regard it highly laudatory, and there have been expressions of regret on part of Nepalis who were unable to purchase tickets."

From Saigon, Vietnam: "Embassy highly pleased with success of Joey Adams Variety show as contribution to Vietnamese-American relations. Show itself and Adams' personal gift of cementing United States-Vietnam relations most impressive. In addition to eight capacity performances for flood relief which widely publicized all media, Adams troupe generated widespread community goodwill by additional performances for war-wounded Vietnamese soldiers, orphans, Scout jamboree."

From Singapore: "Joey Adams show Singapore visit highly successful every angle. Adams, wife Cindy, Buddy Rich, cast, enthusiastically feted by sponsoring Jaycees, Singapore musicians, alumni group local citizens schooled in U.S. American community. Two public performances completely sold out 3 days before play date. Additional charity children's show packed. All appearances helpful promoting American friendship. Press, radio coverage outstanding, effective, from airport reception throughout stay. Joey, Cindy both did excellent radio programs, made hit on air, stage, using Malay appropriately. Shows received good notices: 'fun-loving, spirited, wholesome, nonstop laughter and cheering, America's salesmen had done a good job.' 'Joey, Shirleys, Chase visit to ortho-

pedic hospital hit front page southeast Asia's largest English language newspaper with five column human interest picture Joey, one of the children. Joey, singers visited School for Blind. Company cooperative with CG staff, Jaycees, appreciative efficient programing job. Management, crews tackled job intelligently, worked smoothly with sponsors. Adams earned kudos from Jaycees, public.'"

From Vientiane, Laos: "Joey Adams show extremely well-received Vientiane in four major performances plus special appearances hospitals, schools. Prime Minister invited troupe buffet supper with Lao entertainment."

Beyond this, Mr. Adams and his colleagues were hailed by official representatives of the countries in which his troupe entertained. They were extremely vocal in their praise and thanks. Just a few of these letters, Mr. Speaker, are offered here:

UDORNTHANI CHANGWAD HOSPITAL,
October 4, 1961.

Hon. Mr. KENNETH TODD YOUNG,
The American Ambassador,
Bangkok, Thailand.

SIR: As director of the Udorn Hospital and as a doctor, I want to express my appreciation for the good will which was brought to Udorn and the financial assistance given to the hospital as a result of the Joey Adams Variety Show's visit to Udornthani.

The first show given by the variety group on September 19, 1961, was a charity performance for the benefit of the hospital. The total proceeds were presented to the acting governor for the hospital that evening, amounting to $20,-354. This money will be used for the purchase of new operating equipment to be placed in the new wing of the hospital.

Mr. Adams, accompanied by Mrs. Murchie, wife of our USIS Director, personally visited the hospital and toured the various wards of adult and children patients. Mr. Adams stopped at each bed to give a smile and a "wai" to the patient. His personal touch was greatly appreciated by everyone. Although but few patients could understand Mr. Adams' words, they all could understand his entertaining personality and friendly smile.

It is my intention to place a metal plaque in the new wing of the hospital, when it is completed, which will carry the following inscription: "The Joey Adams Variety Show, as a sign of Thai-American friendship, donated to the Udorn Changwad Hospital $20,354, September 19, 1961."

Again let me thank Your Excellency, USIS Udorn and the Joey Adams Variety Show for aiding our Changwad Hospital and for displaying a spirit of Thai and American friendship which will long be remembered by the people of Udorn.

Sincerely yours,
KASEM CHIATAYASOTHORN,
Director.

——

REPUBLIC OF VIETNAM,
ARMY OF THE REPUBLIC OF VIETNAM,
CONG-HOA GENERAL HOSPITAL.
Mr. JOEY ADAMS,
Majestic Hotel,
Saigon, Vietnam.

DEAR MR. ADAMS: On November 3, 1961, you and your troop of entertainers performed a series of acts for the patients of this hospital. These acts were done so well and show the great amount of time, effort, and affection for the audience which all of you placed on this show.

You have brought into the hearts of these Vietnamese fighters for freedom, a measure of cheer and that they are remembered by the people of the free world.

The patients and staff of this hospital want to thank you and your troop for this fine show of humaneness.

We wish you and your troop will have always good success everywhere in the world.

LT. COL. VU NGOC HOAN, MC,
Cong-Hoa General Hospital Commander.

——

SINGAPORE JUNIOR
CHAMBER OF COMMERCE,
November 10, 1961.

DEAR MR. ADAMS: I would like to take this opportunity to thank you and all the members of your All-Star Variety Show for the tremendous success of your recent visit to Singapore. I can assure you that it has been by far the most successful of all the shows which we have had the pleasure of sponsoring.

Quite apart from the two public performances, which were completely sold out and enabled us to raise a considerable sum for our scholarship and welfare funds, we have had letters of appreciation from many of the groups of underprivileged children, who attended the special children's matinee, as well as letters of thanks from the Singapore School for the Blind and the St. Andrews Mission hospital for the visits by yourself and members of your troupe.

Last but not least, we would like to place on record our gratitude for your ready cooperation throughout your brief stay here and the very happy and cordial relationship which existed during that time between the members of your troupe and the members of our organization.

Your visit was a perfect example of international harmony and good will. We wish you every success for the remainder of your tour and we hope that many of you will visit Singapore again some day so that we can renew our friendship.

Please convey the very best wishes of all the members of the Singapore Junior Chamber of Commerce to Buddy Rich and his band, Celeste Evans, the Sylte Sisters, the Step Brothers, John Shirley and Bonnie, Chaz Chase, and to your charming wife Cindy and yourself.

Yours sincerely,
RONALD CHANG,
Acting President.

——

REMARKS OF THE HEAD OF NATIONAL
ORPHANAGE IN SAIGON

Ladies, gentlemen, how glad we have been in enjoying your very good performances. Coming from a distant country, you have kindness to get here, our national orphanage, in order to give us, the miserable orphan children, many minutes of entertainments.

We can say that you have brought a bright light of the culture of your country and a new movement of stimulating the desire of arts and sciences to the Vietnamese people and specially to the Vietnamese children.

Being compared to you, famous artists, famous actors and actresses, we are only the unexperienced players, making first steps in arts. But in order to answer to your benevolence, let us perform some national folk-dances. We hope they will be able to say you some Vietnamese characteristics and to offer you some ideas of Vietnamese culture.

REMARKS OF A YOUNG VIETNAMESE THANKING THE ADAMS TROUPE

Ladies, gentlemen, on the occasion of your friendship trip to Vietnam, you have reserved a nice show to our national orphanage, it is a great benefit, a precious gift that comforts us very much.

In this free world, the United States of America have given a good example on equality and friendship to many countries. Living in a distant country, you have had to cross ocean and pass thousands of miles to reach our country. After many difficulties, you have come to our dear country to share her joy as well as her sorrow. In this occasion, we think that you, the artists of "The Joey Adams Variety Show," have been able to accomplish an important task in strengthening the ties between the United States of America and Vietnam.

And today, you pay attention to these orphan children, visiting us and giving us a show to amuse us and make us joyful, to stimulate us and encourage us. How happy we are. We are now anxious to enjoy your performance.

What can we say to thank you of what you'll do for us today? We feel very happy in front of our dear benefactors. Let us have pleasure to present you our warmest feelings of thanks, and, please transfer our respectful gratitude to the Government and to the people of the United States of America. We wish the amity and cultural relations between the two peoples get more and more tied.

At last, we wish you good success in your friendship traveling in order to be able to develop arts, culture, and civilization of your fatherland to all countries in the whole world.

The press in these countries, too, noted the fine objectives of the tour and the tremendous good will it fostered. It lavished praise on the mission. I call just a few of these accounts to the attention of this House

and the American people, for they are positive proof of the inestimable value of such a tour and point up to the need for our Government to sponsor additional similar missions.

ADAMS TROUPE ENTERTAINS WOUNDED SOLDIERS

Vietnamese Republican Army soldiers recovering from wounds suffered in recent combat with the Viet Cong, including some who had participated in Wednesday's major battle in Phuoc Thanh Province, were enthusiastic in their reception of the Joey Adams Variety Show put on for their special benefit at the Cong Hoa General Hospital in Go Vap near Saigon on Friday afternoon.

The Adams troupe, on tour in Asia under sponsorship of the U.S. State Department's President's Fund, are currently presenting eight shows at the Hung Dao Theater in Saigon the proceeds of which will be donated to the relief of victims of the flood disaster in the Makong Delta.

The show opened Thursday night before an overflowing audience of some 1,700 who were delighted with the vibrant, fast moving show. A few tickets are still available at the Hung Dao Theater for the remaining performances.

Friday Joey Adams told the Vietnamese fighters for freedom that Americans have fought for years for the same great purpose to which the Vietnamese Republic Forces are dedicated—independence and human dignity.

"We are here," America's good-will entertainer told the soldiers and their families visting them, "to show the friendship and love of the American people for the people of Vietnam. Since you could not come to the theater to see the show, we have brought it to you." The smiles, laughter, and cheers which followed the performances in the wards and the hospital's theater by Adams and his group gave ample evidence of the soldiers' appreciation of the entertainers' efforts.

The Joey Adams troupe was virtually every minute of their spare time in Saigon booked for appearances in hospitals and orphanages. The show will leave Saigon next Wednesday for India.

[Article from New Delhi newspaper]
GOOD AMERICAN ENTERTAINMENT
(By Our Drama Critic)

It is difficult to beat the Americans in the show business. Mr. Joey Adams' all-star show, which opened on Monday night at the Industries Fair theater, is slick, entertaining, amusing, clever and charming. It gives 2 hours of very good variety, and never a dull moment.

Mr. Adams is the compere or master of ceremonies, and he keeps up a patter most of the time he is on the stage. Occasionally he joins in the dance to prove that he was the teacher of all his dancers.

The band is a lively lot of musicians, playing with obvious gusto, and their hot jazz is going to give heart throbs to the jazz crazy. One of their interesting items is a number played on a vibrophone, a pleasant sounding instrument of metal plates with resonance tubes suspended from the table. It is played somewhat like a gypsy cymbalom.

Probably the most outstanding in her own class is Miss Celeste Evans, a Canadian girl magician, whose tricks are excellent; handkerchiefs turn into pigeons at a flick of a finger, and cards pop up at her command. And there is a pretty finale to her act, when, against a dark stage, her kerchiefs and pigeons turn luminescent and fly about in weird colors. This number alone would make a visit to this show worth while.

Deanna, Deanda, and Joan, the Sylte Sisters, sing prettily and are clever at imitating other singing groups such as the Andrews Sisters.

The Four Step Brothers are tap dancers (their names are Williams, McDonald, Spencer and Anderson) and offer a great variety of tap dancing, in a large number of rhythms. Their agility is remarkable and in India, where rhythm is so important an element of music, their tapping will please many. They can also sing ("When saints go marchin' in") and crack jokes.

All this is great fun, but it is difficult to beat the dumb comedian, Mr. Chaz Chase, who never says a word and keeps you spellbound with his hilarious mime. He eats burning cigars, cigarettes, packets of flaming matches, his own shirt front, flowers and all, and is just about

to eat Mr. Adams well salted, when he is chased off the stage.

Mr. John Shirley and his wife, Bonnie, do wonders with balloons, hundreds of them. A delightful and original number, this would delight all children from 8 to 80.

Altogether, very good entertainment. Every night at 8:30 p.m. up to Sunday, December 10, at the Industries Fair theater.

[From the Times of Vietnam, Nov. 3, 1962]

JOEY ADAMS VARIETY SHOW OPENING NIGHT PERFORMANCE

SAIGON, November 3.—"Wonderful" was among the words of praise from spectators who attended the gala opening performance of Joey Adams' variety show at the Hung Dao theater here last night.

The show was the first of a series of 8 the 21-member troupe of American entertainers is scheduled to present for the benefit of Vietnamese flood victims. The troupe arrived Wednesday, under the sponsorship of the President's fund for cultural exchange.

Presiding at the first night gala was Mrs. Truong Vinh Le, wife of the National Assembly chairman.

The troupe opened before a large and enthusiastic audience with a program featuring American songs, jazz music and many variety numbers. Buddy Rich, world famous drummer, dominated the show with his skill, the equal of which has never been seen here before, as one spectator put it.

The singing Sylte Sisters, the four acrobatic-dancing Step Brothers, the balloon artists Mr. Shirley and Bonnie, the slender blonde magician Celeste Evans, and Chaz Chase, the clown, all brought repeated and deafening cheers from the audience.

To the obvious delight of everyone, noted Vietnamese crooner Tran Van Trach also appeared on the show, alone and with troupe leader Joey Adams. Adams added fun to the atmosphere and made it truly friendly with his jokes and, particularly his quickly learned Vietnamese—"toi la thay" (I am the teacher).

Mr. Adams and his wife, Cindy,

earlier introduced their troupe in Vietnamese.

———

[Article from New Delhi newspaper]
NINETY MINUTES OF SHEER FUN—
ALL-STAR SHOW OF JOEY ADAMS
(By Our Music Critic)

NEW DELHI, December 4.—Joey Adams' "All-Star Show" which opened this evening at the Industries Fair theater for a week-long run, is an hour and a half of rollicking entertainment—the best, perhaps, come this way since quite some time. Here are no pretensions to purpose and meanings; Adams with the others in his show have a go at the blues with hammer, tongs, pick and shovel, and by the time they are through, the hall is all in shambles, splitting and spilling over with laughter and gaiety.

Adams can surely count on the cheering and applause as long as he is here performing.

The bill of Adams' All-Star Show is made up of popular songs by one of America's top singing teams, the youthful Sylte Sisters trio; some absolutely fabulous tap dancing by the renowned Step Brothers; moving clowning by Chaz Chase; neat magic by the glamorous Celeste Evans; a balloon (hundreds of them) act by John Shirley and Bonnie in which the audience also join in. All this against a backdrop of delightful jazz by Mike Manieri and his band. Joey Adams himself acts as master of ceremonies, a role in which he not only joins with each of his stars in his or her act, but also has the audience splitting with laughter at his clever gags.

FUN FOR ALL

There is something for everyone in the show. For jazz fans there is both traditional dixieland as well as progressive jazz. The Step Brothers more than prove their virtuosity tapping and clicking their soles through half a dozen or so numbers. Celeste Evans is remarkably neat at her magic and clown (pantomimist, really). Chaz Chase manages to elicit more than just laughter.

There are some very moving undertones in his speechless act in which in feigned indifference he munches his way through the proverbial daisies to his own collar and another's hat. It is difficult to know whether Adams has intended it so, but his gags do strike one as being some sort of a mirror to a cliché ridden cliché tied way of life. One can even imagine Mr. Adams revolving around the all powerful cliché.

———

[From the Times of Vietnam, November 1961]

JOEY ADAMS PLEDGES SUPPORT FOR
FLOOD RELIEF

Joey Adams and his troupe of American entertainers arrived Tuesday at Tan Son Nhut Airport and expressed their sincere desire to contribute in any way they can as good will emissaries to Vietnam.

The group has already agreed to appear at hospitals and orphanages in their spare time.

Under sponsorship of the U.S. State Department's President's fund, Adams and his troupe of 21 artists will present 8 shows at the Hung Dao Theater. A gala formal opening took place last night.

Proceeds of all performances will be donated to disaster victims in the Mekong Delta.

"We are aware of President Diem's recent emergency declaration and want to express our eagerness to help in any way we can," said Adams upon his arrival from Honk Kong yesterday.

Fresh from successes in Djakarta, Bangkok, Singapore, Vientiane, Phnom, Penh, and other points in the Far East, Adams expressed enthusiasm over the warmth of Asian audiences everywhere.

Accompanying Adams was his comedienne wife, Cindy; the singing Sylte Sisters; the acrobatic-dancing Step Brothers; Celeste Evans, magician; Chaz Chase, pantomimist; and the balloon artists, Bonnie and Shirley.

Members of Vietnamese theater circles, including Star Comedian Tran Van Trach, who will appear on the show, made their acquaintance with Adams and his troupers Tuesday night at a reception held at the Vietnamese-American Association villa.

Tickets for all performances will be sold at the Hung Dao Theater.

The American Guild of Variety Artists is indeed fortunate to have Mr. Adams as their president. This organization's publication gave a full and detailed accounting of the tour. The following two articles graphically bear out that this is a man who literally carries out his words by his deeds.

A Study in Laughter

American Showman Joey Adams entered the St. Andrew's Orthopaedic Hospital in Bedok here today "all ready to jazz 'em up" with his wisecracks and tricks.

But before he could get started, the little boys and girls greeted him with a cheerful chorus of: "Good morning, Uncle Adams. Welcome to our home." They were all smiling too—despite their infirmities.

And for the next hour, there was nonstop laughter in the home for crippled children as Adams told his funny stories, and Chaz Chase swallowed matches, cigarettes, and anything he could lay his hands on, and John and Bonnie Shirley, the husband and wife team, gave a dazzling balloon show.

At the end of it all, Mr. Adams said: "I have been to a good many hospitals all over the world, but they all seemed to give me a depressed feeling, except this one. There they are all so full of joy. Before I could cheer them up, they had already cheered me up. These kids are physically handicapped, all of them. Yet they have found happiness. How many people in the world are plagued with unhappiness although they are physically fit."

Mr. Adams said his one regret was that he did not bring his whole troupe to the hospital today.

But he made this promise as he went from bed to bed: "We'll send you gifts when we return to America."

Later Mr. Adams and his entertainers visited the Home for the Blind in Thomson Road to cheer up the inmates there. The Joey Adams all-star variety show will give a matinee show for more than 800 underprivileged children at the Victoria Theater tomorrow.

Vaudeville Troupe Returns From State Department Asian Tour

The Joey Adams Variety Show has returned to the United States from a State Department tour of the Far East which showed that variety performers are among the best ambassadors of good will to people of other nations.

The troupe consisted of Joey and Cindy Adams, Chaz Chase, the Sylte Sisters, the Four Step Brothers, John Shirley and Bonnie, Celeste Evans, and the Buddy Rich Combo. They were received by heads of state in every country they visited, but more important were the shows given to the general public, many for local charities. In addition, members of the troupe visited hospitals and other institutions to bring happiness to children and to the sick.

Joey Adams Good Will Show Hailed in Southeast Asia

The Joey Adams Variety Show, under the sponsorship of the U.S. State Department, has been entertaining audiences throughout southern and southeast Asia to critical acclaim, and the gratitude of those who have seen American variety artists for the first time.

The troupe has played in such countries as Afghanistan, Nepal, Cambodia, Thailand, Laos, and the State of Hong Kong. Audiences have ranged from groups of youngsters in small, out-of-the-way villages, to command performances before royalty.

In addition to Joey Adams, and wife Cindy, the troupe consists of the well-known pantomimist Chaz Chase, the singing Sylte Sisters, the dancing Step Brothers, John Shirley and Bonnie's balloon act, and Magician Celeste Evans; together with Drummer Buddy Rich and his combo consisting of Mike Manieri, Rolf Erickson, Sam Most, Wyatt Ruther and John Morris.

In a letter quoted by Columnist Robert Coleman in the New York News, Joey writes: "Our stages are often put up in the forest or on steps of temples. We sometimes make up with insect repellent, and do without baths because the water and electricity are off. We have waded knee-high through morasses to get to impromptu stages, but our reward has been robust applause from those we have reached with such difficulty. And the enjoyment of our audiences seems to tell us that we are gaining friends for America and building a worldwide following for vaudeville."

Joey is quoted by columnist Nick Kenny in the same publication as saying, in part, "Down through the years, whenever there was tension, court jesters or the minstrels were called in to relieve the fever. I hope we've done that on this trip. We've played hospitals and schools, taught the children the crafts of show business, played for the armies, entertained the people and appeared at command performances for kings and queens of half-a-dozen countries. Every friend that we have won for our country has brought us nearer to peace and further away from the martial music and Khrushchev and his band. The password has been love. I've heard about the signs saying, 'Americans Go Home.' I can only tell you they have welcomed us with open arms and hearts."

Members of the troupe turned to teaching in Laos, to help in areas where the American wives, who had been teaching, were evacuated. Paul Johnson, Director of the Lao-American Association, wrote Joey, "Thanks from all of us for a fine all-round, and greatly appreciated show, the likes of which has never been seen here in Laos before. It had something for everybody, the Lao especially, and including the 'League of Nations' stationed here in the various embassy and government positions. Let's not forget the ICC too. The Lao Army, and public show that was extra was a big hit and Colonel Boonkhong is still talking of its success.

"For my part, please give special thanks to Cindy, your charming pedagogic wife, Mrs. Chase, and Mr. Prince Spencer for their fine, helpful teaching chores at the Lao-American Association. The local students greatly enjoyed their teaching and send their respectful and gracious regards. With the teaching situation being a bit tenuous, due to American wives not being available due to evacuation 14 months ago, their stints before the classes were much more valuable than ordinarily would be the case. Give them all our lasting thanks."

Howard P. Jones, U.S. Ambassador to Indonesia, writes: "This is to thank you both and the fine people who were with you for the contribution you made during your week's stay in Djakarta. Since your departure, I have heard many Indonesians say with real regret that you not only should have stayed longer but that people in other parts of the country should also have had an opportunity to see your show. This is the sincerest compliment an Indonesian can pay you —to want the rest of his people to enjoy the experience he himself had had.

"I hope you will pass on to the rest of your group too my appreciation for their patience and understanding, as well as for their superb performance. I know full well that they were not too comfortable at the hotel—I have stayed at hotels all over this country and know something about them—but I heard no word of complaint, even from the three lovely Sylte Sisters who I understand had to sleep in two single beds. Had there been a way to provide better accommodations for so large a group, you would have had them. I trust it will give all of your company satisfaction far exceeding the memory of any discomfort involved to know that they won the hearts of Indonesia and made a real contribution to American-Indonesian relations and to the understanding between our people that is so fundamental to progress in the right direction. I can only wish for you both and the rest of the troupe what I am certain is assured: continuation of the outstanding success that your show was here during the remainder of your travels."

Robert Donhauser, U.S. consul in Singapore, wrote: "On behalf of all members of the consulate general may I express warm and heartfelt thanks to you and the members of your troupe for doing such a splendid job in promoting good will for our country in the State of Singapore. Moreover, I am sure that members of the American community share this view.

"Your philosophy of love and laughter was exemplified by your activities and contacts here. It is difficult to imagine how any individual or any group of individuals could do more to carry out these qualities so much needed in the world today.

"Please convey our grateful appreciation to all members of the Joey Adams All Star Show. May I also take this opportunity to say how much personally my wife and I enjoyed meeting and talking with all of you.

"The very best of luck to you in your coming travels, and every good wish for continued success."

Mr. Speaker, I cite the above articles and documents as but typical of those written about and to Joey Adams and his good will mission. They clearly illustrate the success of the project and reflect due tribute to the man who made it possible.

Yes, Mr. Speaker, Joey Adams is a great American. His contribution to our foreign prestige is inimitable and invaluable. I know I speak for this Congress and the American people when I say "Hats off to Joey Adams and his Ambassadors of Good Will."

ABOUT THE AUTHOR

JOEY ADAMS is the energetic inhabitant of two worlds: one the laughing, brightly lit world of the show business comic, the other the serious domain of the civic and professional official. He is at home in both, because Joey's life has been a happy blending of earnest causes and a million laughs along the way.

As a nine-year-old, Joey stood on a Harlem street corner mimicking the campaign oratory of a young Congressional candidate to the amusement of assorted Jewish, Irish and Italian ragamuffins of the neighborhood. The candidate, a little man not much taller than the kids, was amused too. "Young man, I like your sentiments," said Fiorello La Guardia. From that night on, Joey was known as "La Guardia's boy," his protégé and unofficially adopted son.

La Guardia's civic-mindedness has been emulated by Joey ever since. He was appointed Commissioner of Youth for the City of New York by Mayor Robert F. Wagner. He holds a "Doctor of Comedy Degree" from three universities: Columbia, New York University and College of the City of New York (his alma mater). As president of the 20,000 members of AGVA (American Guild of Variety Artists), Chairman of the New York Boy Scouts Entertainment Committee and a popular toastmaster, television star and entertainer, Joey has a large and devoted following. This includes his beautiful and quick-witted wife Cindy, author and columnist, who has quite a following of her own.

On the Road for Uncle Sam is Joey's eighth book. His previous titles include *From Gags to Riches* and other best-selling books of humor and his warmly received marital autobiography, *Cindy and I.*

Date Due

4 Jan '67 WI			

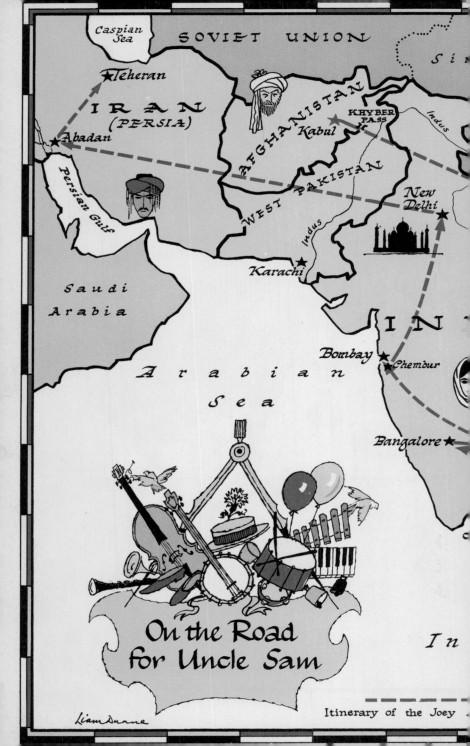

On the Road
for Uncle Sam

Itinerary of the Joey